PSYCHOANALYTIC PRACTICE AND STATE REGULATION

PSYCHOANALYTIC PRACTICE AND STATE REGULATION

Edited by

Ian Parker and Simona Revelli

Routledge
Taylor & Francis Group
LONDON AND NEW YORK

First published 2008 by Karnac Books Ltd.

Published 2018 by Routledge
2 Park Square, Milton Park, Abingdon, Oxon OX14 4RN
711 Third Avenue, New York, NY 10017, USA

Routledge is an imprint of the Taylor & Francis Group, an informa business

British Library Cataloguing in Publication Data

A C.I.P. for this book is available from the British Library

ISBN 9781855755338 (pbk)

Edited, designed and produced by The Studio Publishing Services Ltd
www.studiopublishingservicesuk.co.uk
e-mail: studio@publishingservicesuk.co.uk

CONTENTS

ABOUT THE EDITORS AND CONTRIBUTORS

Anna Barracco is a psychologist, psychotherapist and psychoanalyst with a Lacanian orientation. She has been a member of the European School of Psychoanalysis since 1990 and is an associate member of MoPi (Movimento Psicologi Indipendenti). She practises as a "free professional" in Milan, is involved with the politics of the profession, and has worked with multi-disciplinary teams in northern Italy as a consultant and supervisor within the fields of child-care, HIV and AIDS, psychiatry, and disability. She has taught clinical psychology at LUDeS University in Lugano and currently teaches at the School of Comparative Psychology in Pavia.

Jalil Bennani is a psychiatrist and psychoanalyst in Rabat, Morocco. He was co-founder and president of the Moroccan Association for Psychotherapy, and was a co-founder and past president of the Moroccan Psychoanalytic Society. He is a member of the international scientific committee for the review Santé Mentale au Quebec and the transcultural section of the World Psychiatric Association. He was the 2002 winner of the Sigmund Freud International Award of the city of Vienna. His publications include *Le*

Corps Suspect, Du Bilinguisme (collective work); *Parcours d' Enfants; La Psychanalyse au Pays des Saints*; and *Le Temps des Ados.*

Bernard Burgoyne is a practising psychoanalyst, a Professor of Psychoanalysis, and the Head of the Centre for Psychoanalysis at Middlesex University. He is a member of the World Association of Psychoanalysis, a founding member of the Centre for Freudian Analysis and Research, and was Karl Popper's Research Assistant during 1967–1968. His research interests include the theory and clinical practice of Freudian psychoanalysis. His publications include: "Response to Langs and Badalamenti by a Lacanian psychoanalyst", in *The British Journal of Psychotherapy*; "Interpretation", in *The Klein–Lacan Dialogues* (B. Burgoyne & M. Sullivan, Eds., 1997); and also "From the Letter to the Matheme: Lacan's scientific methods", in *The Cambridge Companion to Jacques Lacan.*

Vivien Burgoyne is a psychoanalyst practising privately in London. She is a member of the Centre for Freudian Analysis and Research, the Guild of Psychotherapists, a practising analyst of the World Association of Psychoanalysis and the New Lacanian School, and an associate of the Women's Therapy Centre.

Leslie Chapman practises privately as a psychoanalytic psychotherapist, and is an Associate Member of the Centre for Freudian Analysis and Research. His background is in sociology and mental health, which includes clinical experience within the National Health Service. He has also worked in senior management positions within the public sector, and has first-hand experience of the risk management and audit cultures in action. He has a particular interest in the application of psychoanalytic ideas to social and political issues.

Lorenzo Chiesa holds a doctorate in philosophy and is a Lecturer at SECL, University of Kent. He is the author of *Subjectivity and Otherness: A Philosophical Reading of Lacan* (MIT Press, 2007) and is completing a collection of papers on Lacan's Seminar VII (with Dany Nobus). Chiesa is a member of the Circle for Lacanian Ideology Critique (Maastricht, the Netherlands), an editor of the journal *S*, and serves as production editor for the *Journal for Lacanian Studies.*

Jacques China received his clinical training in psychoanalysis at The Guild of Psychotherapists, London. His background was in academic and research psychology at University College, London. He has a clinical PhD in psychology. He designed and ran, as course leader, an MA programme in clinical psychoanalysis at the University of Hertfordshire. His clinical work has been both within the National Health Service and in private practice. He has a keen interest in research and the scientific validation of psychoanalysis, particularly in relation to possible links with attachment theory. He has been trained to administer the Adult Attachment Interview (AAI). He was one of the founding members of The College of Psychoanalysts—UK and its first President.

Gillian Clayton is a psychoanalyst, member of the Centre for Freudian Analysis and Research (CFAR) and The College of Psychoanalysts—UK. She trained in Italy within a Lacanian orientation and practised there for several years. She now works in private practice in South London.

Jan De Vos is a psychology graduate of Ghent University where he also did a postgraduate course in psychoanalysis. He has worked as a psychologist in the field of special education, working with young people. His interests focus on how psychoanalysis relates to culture and society, and also, and more generally, on the position of the psy-sciences in relation to society as a whole. He has published various articles on the topic of psychologization.

Christian Ingo Lenz Dunker is from the University of São Paulo, is a practising psychoanalyst, a member of the Associação Universitária de Pesquisa em Psicopatologia Fundamental and Escola de Psicanálise dos Fóruns do Campo Lacaniano, and co-editor of *Žižek Critico: Política e psicanálise na era do multiculturalismo* (2004).

Richard House is Senior Lecturer in the Research Centre for Therapeutic Education, Roehampton University. An IPN founder–participant, he has published numerous challenges to the institutional professionalization of the therapy field, including *Therapy Beyond Modernity* (Karnac, 2003), *Implausible Professions* (co-edited with Nick Totton, 1997) and *Ethically Challenged Professions* (co-edited with Yvonne Bates, 2003).

Darian Leader is a psychoanalyst practising in London and a member of the Centre for Freudian Analysis and Research. His books include *Why Do Women Write More Letters Than They Post?*; *Freud's Footnotes*; *Stealing the Mona Lisa: What Art Stops Us from Seeing*; and *Why Do People Get Ill?* (with David Corfield). *The New Black: Mourning, Melancholia and Depression* was published in February 2008.

Robert Lévy holds a doctorate in clinical psychology and is a professor of psychology, a psychoanalyst, and a founding member of The Association Analyse Freudienne, where he is responsible for training. He was a member of the École freudienne de Paris. He was one of the organizers of the conference "Joyce Lacan in Dublin" in June 2005.

Roger Litten is the current Chair of the Association for Lacanian Psychoanalysis in the UK and a member of the London Society of the New Lacanian School.

Del Loewenthal is Professor of Psychotherapy and Counselling at Roehampton University. He is an analytic psychotherapist, editor of the *European Journal of Psychotherapy and Counselling*, and a member of the Universities Psychotherapy and Counselling Association and Philadelphia Association.

René Major is a psychoanalyst practising in Paris. He is President of the Institute of Advanced Psychoanalytic Studies (Institut des Hautes Études en Psychanalyse). As well as being one of France's best known analysts, he has been actively engaged in the debates about psychoanalysis and state regulation in France.

John Miller has a background in education, first as a teacher and then as psychological consultant for Special Needs to both state and independent schools. His initial psychoanalytical training was with The Association of Jungian Analysts. Subsequently, he developed a strong post-Kleinian focus as a result of close association with the late Donald Meltzer. He has a full-time analytical practice in Oxford.

Chris Oakley is a member of the Site for Contemporary Psychoanalysis. His latest publication is *Football Delirium* (Karnac, 2007).

Haya Oakley has been practising and teaching psychoanalysis in London for over thirty years. She is a member of the College of Psychoanalysis (CPA), The College of Psychoanalysts—UK, The Guild of Psychotherapists, and The Site for Contemporary Psychoanalysis.

Ian Parker is Professor of Psychology at Manchester Metropolitan University and secretary of Manchester Psychoanalytic Matrix. He is a practising psychoanalyst, member of the Centre for Freudian Analysis and Research, the London Society of the New Lacanian School, and the College of Psychoanalysts—UK.

Denis Postle is a psychotherapist in independent practice. A founder participant of The Independent Practitioners Network (IPN), his research interests include co-operative inquiry and action research. Over the past sixteen years he has been active in confronting the professionalization of UK psychopractice through journal articles and the ipnosis website: http://ipnosis.postle.net/

Simona Revelli is a practising analyst in London. She works privately and in the NHS and is the translator of a number of psychoanalytic texts. She is a member of the College of Psychoanalysts—UK, and an affiliate member of CFAR.

Mauro Santacatterina is a psychoanalyst with a Lacanian orientation. He was a member of the European School of Psychoanalysis between 1990 and 1995, but resigned from it as a result of the state regulation of psychotherapy. He practises psychoanalysis as a "free professional" in Vicenza, and has worked as a psychologist and psychotherapist in several health institutions where he is a supervisor. He was the secretary of the Italian Movement for Lay Psychoanalysis and is currently a member of MoPI (Movimento Psicologi Indipendenti) and the Accademia Platonica delle Arti.

Kazushige Shingu is based at the University of Kyoto, and is Japanese secretary of the Groupe franco-japonais in the Champ freudien, author of the Japanese introduction to Lacan's work, *Rakan no seishin-bunseki,* recently translated into English as *Being Irrational: Lacan, the Objet a, and the Golden Mean* (Gakuju Shoin, 2004).

FOREWORD

Jacques China

This book arises out of an important international conference held in March 2006 to discuss how regulation by the state has affected psychoanalysis as a clinical discipline in many different parts of the world. There were participants and papers from Europe and beyond: from Africa; from both North and South America; from Asia; and, of course, from the UK, where an important debate is now being conducted about current government proposals to regulate practitioners of all the mainstream modalities of psychological therapies, including psychoanalysis. This conference was the first international event held by The College of Psychoanalysts—UK and hosted by the London School of Economics and Political Science.

The papers given at that conference, with reflections from across the world, comprise the contents of this book. However, in this foreword, I shall concentrate on the issues that are now urgently faced by practitioners of psychoanalysis in the UK.

There can be no point in regulating, purely for the sake of regulation, a body of professional people, if the result is that the profession concerned becomes a pale shadow of what has been, historically, an effective and vibrant discipline that has, by and large, successfully met the needs of members of the public. Arguably, the interests of the discipline concerned and of the public are most likely to be served adequately if there is sound administration and regulation of a clearly identifiable profession, which is able to promote effectively the discipline concerned and to register and regulate its practitioners in a manner that accommodates the interests of both members of the public and members of the profession. Whether this is done voluntarily or compulsorily is secondary to the need for this to be achieved effectively. Better, surely, for this to be achieved voluntarily but successfully than to be achieved compulsorily but ineffectively or even destructively.

The two principal voluntary regulatory bodies, in the UK, for the registration and regulation of psychoanalytic practitioners, are the United Kingdom Council for Psychotherapy (UKCP) and the British Psychoanalytic Council (BPC). However, the newly combined PP and AP Sections of UKCP comprise a group of psychoanalytic practitioners within UKCP—the Council for Psychoanalysis and Jugian Analysis—that is greater in numbers than that of BPC, and is, therefore, arguably, more representative of the discipline of psychoanalysis.

It is important here to highlight a significant distinction that exists between UKCP and BPC in regard to the discipline of psychoanalysis. BPC registers psychoanalysts, as such, only when their training is recognized by the International Psychoanalytical Association (IPA) and refuses to recognize or register any other psychoanalysts. UKCP, despite representations from various interested parties, for many years refused to register any psychoanalysts, as such, whether IPA affiliated or otherwise, although it does register psychoanalytic practitioners using other professional titles related to psychoanalysis. It was this situation that, *inter alia,* led to the formation of The College of Psychoanalysts—UK. However, The College is not a regulatory body. It is a professional body that exists primarily to advance the interests of psychoanalytic practitioners from all schools of psychoanalysis in the UK, as well as to promote the right of all such practitioners, all of whom have undergone a recognized training in psychoanalysis, to use the professional title *psychoanalyst,* whether or not that training is recognized by the IPA. The College is also a learned society for the promotion and recognition of psychoanalysis as a pluralistic discipline, without privileging any one or more of the many different schools of psychoanalysis that exist in the world today.

It is against this background that it is necessary to think about attempts to regulate psychoanalysis in the UK.

The origin of the stimulus for regulation of psychoanalysis and the other psychological therapies can be traced back to two rather different and, in some respects, conflicting drives: from practitioners themselves and from the state.

Many practitioners, from across the whole spectrum of the psychological therapies, have yearned for a long time for some form of regulation, backed by statutory powers. It was thought that such regulation would provide due recognition of a profession in the eyes of members of the public, from the public services, and from other related professionals with whom psychoanalytic practitioners have a close working relationship. The goal has been for a clearly discernible profession in its own right and with a standing comparable to that of the medical and legal professions. Of course, all of this has always been justified on the basis of an ostensible need to protect members of the public from incompetent or unscrupulous practitioners.

The government, however, has resisted all attempts by the current voluntary regulatory bodies of the psychological therapies for any form of regulation that remains largely in the hands of the professions concerned. The latest British government proposals, set out in the White Paper *Trust, Assurance and Safety—The Regulation of Health Professionals in the 21st Century* (February 2007) make it clear that the registration and associated disciplinary powers will be vested instead, if they are adopted, in the already existing Health Professions Council (HPC). This is a public body, administered entirely by public servants and, ultimately, controlled by the government pursuant to government-promoted Orders of the Privy Council, under legislation intended to govern professions related to medicine, rather than pursuant to a specific statute relating solely to any single profession.

Historically, the state has never been very interested in the compulsory registration and regulation of practitioners of the psychological therapies. This is presumably because, from the point of view of whichever government has been in power, there seemed no very good reason for setting aside time for legislation in an area that has, by and large, been effectively self-governed and where, in those very occasional cases where members of the public have suffered real harm as a result of the behaviour of practitioners, they could always have recourse to the courts of the land, which still remains and will always be the case. However, that situation began to change when, some years ago, there was a substantial public demand for legislation to curb the activities of the Church of Scientology, which, it was claimed, used psychological measures in the recruitment and control of its members.

Without doubt, the principal stimulus for any change of policy by the government lies within the much more recent Shipman Enquiry (focusing on the murder by a medical practitioner, Harold Shipman, of a number of his patients) and the poor light this shed on the control and discipline of the medical profession by its own members via the General Medical Council. As a result of this, statutory regulation of medical practitioners will now be largely removed from the control of members of that profession.

HPC was set up to operate entirely around the principle of establishing protected professional titles; that is, it concerns itself with who is entitled to use a specified professional title, which is related to professional work within the realms of physiological or psychological health, other than that carried out by medical doctors. By no stretch of the imagination can HPC be compared with a professional body. Its functions are purely regulatory, in relation to the use of protected professional titles and the registration of professionals entitled to the exclusive use of such titles, together with the continued regulation of such professionals as a condition of their remaining on the statutory register of HPC.

Although HPC may not be compared with a professional body, it does encourage entirely voluntary links with any established professional bodies of the professions it regulates. There is, however, no such representation on the disciplinary bodies set up to administer its complaints procedures, although there is provision for lay representation on such bodies.

What few practitioners appear to appreciate, in relation to the form of state registration and regulation envisaged by HPC, is that, once registered with HPC, there will be no obligation on those registered to retain their membership of any other organization, whether a professional body or a voluntary regulatory body. Indeed, it is difficult to see what need, if any, there would be for the continued existence of an organization such as UKCP, which, currently at least, has no function other than regulation that is in the interests of members of the public. It is, maybe, for this reason that UKCP is contemplating substantial reorganization of its structures, which may lead to individual registrants becoming members of that organization in their own right and its various modality sections becoming separate organizations or "colleges" of UKCP. Maybe it hopes thereby to become a professional, rather than a regulatory, body. This would require, in effect, the setting up of a completely new and different organization, membership of which, within the profession concerned, would nevertheless remain entirely voluntary on the part of individual practitioners. It is, at present, very difficult to see what advantage there might be for practitioners to pay for the privilege of voluntary membership of such a body when all they need, in order to practise, is registration with HPC and for a fee that would almost certainly be considerably less than any subscription payable to any voluntary regulatory body.

A great deal of time, effort, and expense has gone into the pursuit of the goal of statutory regulation of the psychological therapies by a generation or more of well-meaning practitioners. It is now clear that their goal will never be achieved. At a time when the long-established learned professions of medicine and law are themselves slipping out of statutory regulation into a process that closely resembles state regulation, it has become quite clear that all that will be achieved for the psychological therapies, at least in the foreseeable future, is a form of regulation by the state and its agencies.

It is regrettable that a wonderful opportunity for the setting up of a newly-recognized profession for psychoanalysis and the other psychological therapies, existing for the benefit of both practitioners and members of the public and centred around principles of mutual respect, understanding, and co-operation, has been allowed to slip away in pursuit of regulation, purely for the sake of regulation, and without giving adequate thought as to how that might best be achieved in the interests of everyone.

If those who lead were to pursue a more constructive course of action, they would have nothing to lose and possibly everything to gain on behalf of us all. Once the present momentum for state regulation had been stopped, they could concentrate their efforts on promoting a properly recognized discipline and recognized profession governed, at least for the time being, entirely by the voluntary means by which its practitioners are currently governed and which has, for some years now, served the public interest extremely well.

Members of the public are already protected, and effectively so. It is becoming increasingly common for members of the public to enquire whether practitioners are on one of the recognized voluntary professional registers, such as that of UKCP. This is what forms the basis of their protection. No form of registration or degree of regulation, of any form, will entirely eliminate professional conduct that is unsatisfactory and unacceptable. It should, nevertheless, remain the goal of any reputable profession to minimize the possibility of such conduct occurring. However, it remains to be seen whether regulation by the state will achieve that goal any more satisfactorily than the various forms of voluntary regulation that have preceded this new drive for regulation by the state. It is by no means impossible that such a form of regulation, through misguided enthusiasm, could diminish or even destroy the effectiveness of psychoanalysis and the other professions concerned and thereby deprive the public of a hitherto valuable and unique resource for their well-being.

By encouraging government interest, and without realizing what they are doing, practitioners of psychoanalysis in the UK may well be dragged along by the enthusiasm of the current voluntary regulatory bodies, albeit with the most honourable of intentions, into selling their professional birthright for a mess of regulatory pottage.

Introduction: psychoanalytic practice and state regulation

Ian Parker and Simona Revelli

Psychoanalytic practice is under threat. This book explores that threat and draws together arguments against it. Our point of focus is the attempt by government agencies in Britain to register psychotherapists, but you will see from the contributions gathered in the book from around the world that there are wider lessons. We can learn from the regulatory process in other countries about the particular dangers for psychoanalytic practitioners here, and the strategies we develop will have repercussions for our colleagues abroad. Psychoanalysis historically has operated as an international phenomenon, and debates over theory and therapy have transcended national state boundaries. Our responsibility now is not only to our analysands and colleagues in this little part of the world, but also to all those keeping alive an impossible profession that values and attends to unconscious conflict and political division.

Contexts

The setting for these debates was an initiative by the College of Psychoanalysts—UK to bring together speakers from a range of different analytic traditions, and to turn that diversity of perspectives from being weakness into strength. The British government, following on the heels of other nation states, has signalled its intention to "regulate" psychotherapy. What this would mean specifically for psychoanalysts is not clear, and some psychoanalytic organizations responded to the many different proposals inside and outside parliament with studied indifference. This magnificent defence, so tempting in the short-term but potentially fatal in the long run, rested on an assumption, in the "British tradition", that psychoanalysis was above such petty provincial dealings. It did seem prudent to avoid what was happening, and to hope that because psychoanalysts have had close ties with the Royal College of Psychiatrists and the ruling class, new administrative procedures would simply not apply to them.

The squabbles in the forerunner to the United Kingdom Council for Psychotherapy (UKCP), which led to the departure of representatives of the British Psychoanalytical Society (BPAS), who founded their own registration body—now called the British Psychoanalytic Council (BPC)—are indicative. (One of the features of the manoeuvres to shepherd the therapists into one registration body and their intense antipathy to each other when they are brought together, it should be said, is that hosts of acronyms have proliferated and often succeeded in protecting the "insiders" to these sometimes arcane debates.) The UKCP, which had, in different guises, for many years been the front-runner in negotiations with the government (and we will try to spare you more acronyms now in this complicated history of changes of name), worked on the principle that if it could anticipate how the government would police psychotherapy, it would be able to implement the procedures itself. Then it would be chosen as a loyal serious contender to manage state regulation when it was eventually legislated for. That principle has guided the UKCP to this day.

However, it first had to contend with the more patrician psychoanalysts who really did imagine that they could keep their hands clean, and who argued inside that first "voluntary" registration body that there should be an upper tier, equivalent they said, to the security council of the United Nations, and that as that upper tier (which should, it goes without saying, be composed of the psychoanalysts), they would be able to govern and correct the rest of the therapists. Would anything else, they argued during the bitter internal debates that followed, not be like letting students mark their own examination papers? They failed, and left, and so a first deep scar is visible in British psychotherapy, between the UKCP (in which some psychoanalysts remained to maintain some united front with psychoanalytic psychotherapists) and what is now the BPC (which managed to cluster together some other organizations on the basis that there would be a clear status hierarchy with psychoanalysts at the top).

Now, we need to be clear that this process by which social divisions are crystallized in rival organizations does not solve the problem for either side. One needs only the barest understanding of psychoanalytic theory to know that splitting as a mode of defence simply re-energizes the forces that led to that defence in the first place. So, on the side of the UKCP, we have not at all seen a democratic egalitarian community of like-minded souls emerge from this mess that is now willing to struggle together against the state. Rather, many in the UKCP have been keen to continue operating on the principle that they should demonstrate how sensible they are to government representatives, and they have sought to differentiate themselves from those who are lower down in the pecking order. This means that they have been very reluctant to make common cause with mere psychodynamic counsellors, or still less any other counsellors, registered with the third big acronym group, the British Association for Counselling and Psychotherapy (BACP). The 'P' word was added quite recently in a jostling for status with the UKCP that has been met with scorn and annoyance (and by the formation of a "psychotherapeutic counsellor" group inside the UKCP). The split that saw the "security council" depart has, then, left behind an organization that has reproduced an orientation for status and recognition that sabotages joint activity with those that will also be badly affected by state regulation.

And, on the side of the BPC, the hope that it would at least be free of the sordid business of registration and regulation has quickly come to grief. That organization had to recognize that it could not escape, that the dispensation of power in Britain has changed such that the drive for accountability and administration on the part of the state will draw in all the old privileged professional layers. This has meant that the BPC has had to move fast to refashion itself as another, equally loyal partner in any proposed registration process, and representatives of the BPC have also been avidly attending meetings with government agencies, even sitting at the same table as their erstwhile enemies in the UKCP and even, god forbid, the hoi polloi in the shape of the BACP.

It is in that context of deep division—of open wounds running between the three major representative organizations in psychoanalysis, psychotherapy and counselling—that the College of Psychoanalysts—UK was formed. The College has provided a safe haven for psychoanalytic practitioners who may still be members of the UKCP, BPC, or even, formally speaking, the BACP, and a site for thinking through strategic questions. These questions have been posed all the more sharply in recent years by the intensification of the threat of state regulation with new proposals to bring "psychotherapists" (and that professional category will include psychoanalysts and counsellors of all stripes) under the auspices of the Health Professions Council (HPC—one last and most worrying acronym for now). This would seem to have lain to rest a distinction that the College has often made in its representations to government, between "statutory" and "state" regulation. That distinction is an important one and some form of statutory regulation is a principle of self-organization and responsibility that psychoanalysts have always adhered to. Beyond clarity concerning training and qualifications and accountability to the public so that they have some recourse to representative organizations, of course, there is already ample legal protection against abuse, coercion, and fraudulence.

The attempt to regulate the practice of psychotherapy by the state with specific bodies and procedures does not only go well beyond that, but it introduces quite another dimension into clinical work, a dimension of surveillance and control that will destroy anything remotely psychoanalytic. That is the context for the current debates spelt out in detail in the first part of this book. Psychoanalytic practitioners are being drawn into a mode of working and reporting that is antithetical to psychoanalysis, but quite compatible with the cheaper, shallower "cognitive behavioural therapies" the government favours, as Bernard Burgoyne points out in Chapter One. In Chapter Two, Roger Litten demonstrates how a drive to "evaluation" and "audit" underpins such apparently innocuous record-keeping that is being introduced into national health services and that will be demanded of every practitioner in the private sector.

The new generation of psychoanalytic practitioners must then be schooled so that moral rules come to stand in the place of an ethical engagement with the difficulties of living that psychoanalysis tackles. In Chapter Three, Haya Oakley shows how this kind of "education" of psychoanalysts may come to fit all too neatly with some presuppositions about morality that the British tradition of psychoanalysis has concerned itself with. The ethical edge of psychoanalytic thinking around such questions is clearly at work in a contribution by John Miller (Chapter Four), a Jungian, whose participation in this edited volume exemplifies the need to keep open the grounds of the debate so that all those who will be affected are now included in opposition to the state. In Chapter Five, we can see clearly from Chris Oakley's scathing assessment of how psychotherapists have abased themselves in their attempt to be thought well-behaved that a degree of anger at the machinations of the HPC and its friends must be mobilized now if we are to stave off this latest, most insidious demand that we show ourselves good for those who would like to define what "health" is and what a "health professional" should do to make people healthy in its own image.

Responses

It is one thing to make a diagnosis of what the problem is—encroaching state control and the erosion of space in which an analysand might at least attempt to follow the fundamental technical rule of free association—and quite another to begin the process of mobilizing conceptual resources to address that problem. The contributors to this book are well aware that the drive to state regulation is not at all something that comes as a sudden strange assault from outside psychoanalysis, as if such things have never happened before and as if psychoanalysis was not itself deeply implicated in the problem. So, now we need to elaborate a deeper and more wide-ranging analysis of the conditions in which "regulation" by the state comes to threaten psychoanalysis. And that means tackling two key questions.

The first concerns the way in which psychoanalysts are implicated in those very regulative procedures they now complain about. There is an important respect in which psychoanalysis is as much part of the problem as it is, potentially, part of the solution. Psychoanalysis is not a programmatic series of procedures that can simply be implemented to make things better, which is a claim that cognitive behavioural therapists might make about their own practice. The recognition and working through of the problem in psychoanalysis is, rather, essential if any step forward with respect to these questions is to be taken at all. In the very process of producing the "problem" as symptom, the curative action also takes place.

It is necessary to acknowledge, then, that the state has always been involved in psychoanalysis. This has been the case through the attempt to define it as a medical speciality, which is a self-definition that many psychoanalysts in the English-speaking world (at least, but not only so) colluded with in their mistaken attempt to keep a distance from the "charlatans" practising lay analysis. And it has been the case when the state has attempted to render it into something coeval with standard legal definitions of good heterosexuality and moral health (which, once again, called upon the good offices of many psychoanalysts eager to show that they could tell the difference between normality and abnormality).

Now there is a deeper, more intense sense in which psychoanalysis is part of the problem in so far as it would already like to see itself as a "health profession" and already buys into the idea that it can promote "well-being" and adjustment of individuals to existing norms of good "healthy" behaviour. In days past, psychoanalysis often allied itself with psychiatry as one of the most powerful and prestigious of the normalizing disciplines, and it is here that "lay analysis" was sidelined, against the express wishes of Freud. Nowadays, the alliance that psychoanalysis would like to make is more likely to be psychology, and to understand why that hitherto poor cousin of psychiatry has assumed centre stage (even to the point where the British Psychological Society thought it could step in and take the reins of power to head a registration body as an alternative to the HPC for a brief heady moment in 2006), we need to understand how psychoanalysis has always operated, and all the more so now operates as part of a dense network of theories and practices, the "psy-complex".

In contemporary globalizing neo-liberal culture, psychology promises to reach the parts that other disciplines do not reach. While psychiatry reduced itself to a medical administrative apparatus that would make diagnoses and eventually operate as little more than a hand-maiden to the pharmaceutical industry, psychology has keyed into the now even more pernicious sense that each individual has that each social problem can be addressed by them looking inwards, at themselves, at their own psychology. At the same time, psychology historically has been ahead of the game in terms of assessment and measurement, and is now making a bid to define what counts as "evidence" in the evaluation of therapy. It does this on its own terms, of course, but what we have to notice is that psychoanalysts have often found this irresistible, and they have hoped that if they can come up to those standards of evidence they will be thought of as reliable and trustworthy, and then perhaps they will be allowed to carry on doing their own form of therapy on the basis that it reaches deepest down into the kind of "mind" that psychology specifies as lying inside the individual.

There are crucial methodological issues here that have profound consequences for therapeutic practice, for if a methodology that has been developed as part of the psy-complex comes to define therapeutic work, then that methodology will also define the assessment, and, logically, the training of therapists. Any tactical advantage that psychoanalysts might gain in making themselves part of this problem will evaporate as they then become unable to disentangle themselves from it.

The second key question concerns the way state regulation comes to be so alluring to those psychoanalytic practitioners who should by rights be totally opposed to it. The pathetic squabbles between different "wannabe" regulatory organizations do reveal the depth at which neo-liberal government and the psy-complex has taken hold at the level of the individual. And what is at stake here is not only the kind of individual who comes into therapy, but also the kind of individual who trains to be a psychotherapist. It has been difficult to keep critical perspectives on the agenda in the debates over state regulation in recent years, not only because psychoanalytic practitioners are either afraid to speak out against what looms ahead or have cynically adapted themselves to a state of affairs they hope they can profit from (whether as those who keep their heads down, or those who aim to take charge of the regulatory bodies), but also because the administrative apparatus is, at some level, enjoyable. The drawing up of competencies by which psychotherapy is delivered and taught to others has turned into something that produces no end of fascinating puzzles, and there is much pleasure to be gained from devising complicated flow diagrams by which others can be led around conceptual mazes and warned of what will befall them if they do not participate, and want to participate.

So, in Chapter Six, Leslie Chapman traces how the new procedures to "govern the soul" are now embedded in an atmosphere of risk assessment in which it seems unreasonable for anyone not to want to participate. This operates as the wider cultural setting in which the "culture of competencies" described by Vivien Burgoyne in Chapter Seven comes to function to the detriment of psychoanalysis. The question of state regulation is intermeshed with the way psychoanalytic training is now increasingly expected to take place in the context of academic institutions. However, it is not so much the physical space of the university that poses a problem for psychoanalysis as the discourse of the university, a discourse that becomes ever-present in the context of state regulation, and present in the way psychoanalysis is transmitted. Thus, in Chapter Eight, Lorenzo Chiesa traces a key analytic study of the "discourse of the university". The conceptual resources to begin building upon critiques of state regulation to offer alternatives include, of course, an attention to ethics, as is outlined by Del Loewenthal in Chapter Nine.

International contexts and responses

A momentous and necessary step in the formation of psychoanalysis was the founding of the International Psychoanalytic Association (IPA) in Nuremberg in 1910, with Carl Jung as first president. From that moment, psychoanalytic practice has been implicated not only in the endeavours of various state apparatuses that would like it to operate as an instrument of adaptation, but also in a countermovement as a diasporic tradition that refuses any allegiance to any particular state or to any ideal to which individuals might be expected to adapt.

During the rise of fascism in Europe, the centre of gravity of the IPA shifted to the USA, and it is there where, in recent years, some of the harshest attempts to bring psychoanalysts into local state regulation frameworks have taken place. The rise of cheaper and quicker cognitive behavioural therapy combined with health service regimes of "managed care", in which the cost of therapy is also assessed against what can be provided by the drug companies, has put immense pressure on USA psychoanalytic organizations to adapt their work. The recent drive to registration and regulation has actually occurred first in the USA, and then has provided a model for the bureaucratic initiatives in Europe. However, unlike Britain, in which the local franchise of the IPA (the BPAS) managed to avoid a split after bitter internal disputes during the Second World War, the American psychoanalytic training bodies did separate into distinct organizations. This has actually made more open the debates over proposals for state regulation and the strategies to keep regulation at bay, so that now we can engage with healthy contradictions alive between psychoanalytic practitioners.

Outside the English-speaking world, the development of psychoanalysis has been much more diverse, and it is accepted by many practitioners that the diversity of theoretical orientation will be reflected in the existence of separate organizations. This is also the context for a much livelier and combative response to attempts to monitor and administer analytic work.

In France, for example, there is a good deal of diversity over training requirements even between different groups affiliated to the IPA, including over the thorny question of the number of times a week an analysand should come to the clinic for the work to count as being properly psychoanalytic. This is in contrast with some of the more ridiculous tidy solutions discussed in the pro-registration bodies in Britain—in which, at one point, the idea took hold that the clinical world could be segmented into psychoanalysis at five times a week, psychoanalytic psychotherapy at four times a week, non-analytic psychotherapy at three times a week, psychodynamic counselling at twice a week, and basic counselling at a rate of once a week. The vast number of IPA and non-IPA psychoanalytic organizations in France turned out to be an advantage when mobilizations took place against parliamentary proposals to register psychotherapists, including psychoanalysts. In other parts of Europe, in contrast, the situation has been much grimmer, and the spectre of centralized EU directives has gone hand-in-glove with local state intentions to bring the analysts to heel.

We have included reflections on these mobilizations of psychoanalysts in France, and have representation of some different assessments that have been made of the outcome of those events. In Chapter Ten, Robert Lévy elaborates some reasons why psychoanalysts should refuse to engage in any kind of concordat with the French state. In Chapter Eleven, the role of psychology and the insidious psychologisation of social phenomena is highlighted by Jan De Vos's detailed commentary on the events. The account offered by René Major, in Chapter Twelve, concludes with a more optimistic appraisal of the situation and with the hope that now, at last, the government might have accepted the psychoanalysts' arguments that they can be trusted to adhere to agreed codes of ethical conduct. In Chapter Thirteen, the contribution by Jalil Bennani, we also see repercussions of these broader issues in Morocco, where, so far, French-speaking psychoanalysis has been able to develop outside the gaze of the state. Each particular cultural context calls into play distinctive state procedures and psychoanalytic responses, as can be seen in Chapter Fourteen from Kazushige Shingu's conceptual analysis of the role of Buddhism in Japan.

The role of neighbouring disciplines in the formation and survival of psychoanalysis is a key issue in the process of state regulation in Italy, in particular the role of psychology. In Chapter Fifteen, Gillian Clayton provides a detailed account of the history of Italian psychoanalysis and the lessons we can draw from recent attempts to tame the analysts. The place of psychoanalysis among the other "psy" professions is also emphasized by Anna Barracco in her account in Chapter Sixteen. Mauro Santacatterina (Chapter Seventeen) concludes this little trio with an impassioned call to resist the lure of "recognition" and with the hope that the debates currently focused on psychoanalytic practice in Britain might re-energize analysts in other parts of the world.

Lessons and directions

One overriding lesson that emerges from these discussions is that while we have some quite specific ethical objections to state regulation (standard procedures for diagnosing and treating categories of disorder, accountability to a third party outside the analytic relationship, and monitoring of what goes on inside the clinic by external agencies are anathema to psychoanalysis), we cannot fight this battle on our own. Or, it may be that if we lose this battle fighting it on our own, we will not be able even to maintain the conditions in which it will still be possible to keep some form of psychoanalytic practice alive.

The three concluding chapters, then, are from three quite different places. In Chapter Eighteen, Christian Ingo Lenz Dunker shows how the drive to state regulation in Brazil has been taken up by some bizarre religious organizations, and draws upon the resistance to this process to formulate some general principles that psychoanalysts in Europe could take up. As he points out, while regulation of psychotherapy is being implemented in a piecemeal way in different countries, the logic of state regulation is to bring about conformity to standards of training that their proponents hope will be inter-governmental, and will thus have a global character. In Chapter Nineteen, Richard House and Denis Postle come at this question of the homogenization of psychotherapy from another direction, and they make some specific proposals that could bring together psychoanalytic practitioners with a number of other professions that are also being hit by the recent attempt to impose regulation upon those deemed to be "health professions". Finally, in Chapter Twenty, Darian Leader reviews some of the gloomy prognoses that could be made for the survival of psychoanalysis in the light of convergence of interest between the state and "scientific" evaluation of therapy being developed from some working from within the British tradition of psychoanalysis. He points out that if psychoanalysis becomes a "health profession", then a concern with "mental hygiene" will follow shortly after.

Additional resources

The chapters in this book include specific references to academic and therapeutic literature. Here, we focus on those resources that are publicly available on the internet. These include discussions of the issues with which this book is concerned as well as organizational forums that have set themselves against state regulation.

At www.psychoanalysis-cpuk.org/professional%20forum.html, Paola Mieli reviews the situation in the USA, and at www.psychoanalysis-cpuk.org/italian%20connection%201.html there is a wide-ranging exchange about law and ethics between two Italian analysts, Ettore Perrella and Antonello Sciacchitano.

On the website of the *Journal of European Psychoanalysis* (www.psychomedia.it/jep), there are fascinating discussions by Italian psychoanalysts—debates which trace the ethics of psychoanalysis in relation to state regulation without prescribing one correct course of action. These are particularly developed in the roundtable discussion at www.psychomedia.it/jep/number18/roundtable.htm .

The Association of Psychoanalysis Users (at www.psychoanalysisuser.com/) has been formed as an organization that refuses to play patsy to the government in its pretence to administer psychotherapists in order to "protect" the public. The organization has already made representations to the government over the importance of keeping the field of psychoanalysis free from intervention.

Psychotherapists who, from the first murmurings about regulation driven by the European Union, have refused to buy into the idea that they should be registered by the state, have a useful web resource with detailed commentary on all the latest shenanigans at ipnosis.postle.net/.

The College of Psychoanalysts—UK has a website at www.psychoanalysis-cpuk.org). In this, there are records of recent responses to demands by government agencies, debates over the context of state regulation, and information about cognate debates.

PART I
CONTEXTS

CHAPTER ONE

Psychoanalysis and state regulation

Bernard Burgoyne

Where are we now with the professions put forward by the state to be able to govern psychoanalysis and related fields? The days when the state took itself to be an arbitrator, acting on the margins of civil society, are no longer here. Instead there is a more intrusive governance—one that aims to decide on questions of competence, on questions of appropriate training, on questions of personal ability, even on questions of reason. But what are the *bona fides* of such claims? What are the competencies offered by the agencies of the state?

Self-harming is more prevalent in the young here in the UK than in any other European country. The young people affected need help—more extended and more accessible help than is currently available. What are these young people offered now? They are offered insufficient and inadequately structured services that have not been well enough thought through in terms of what problem they are addressing and attempting to resolve. It is as though the state were averse to thinking; as though there were something in the nature of knowledge that gave it cause for alarm.

Some problems are complex, and best formulated and resolved by professionals, whose training enables them to deal with this complexity. Compared to this, national government is often in a state of relative and often absolute ignorance. Yet still, there is a regular initiative that comes from the state to intervene in such areas, and to replace the proficiency of professionals with rules of the state's own devising.

Examinations for schoolchildren are being changed: the present system has introduced too much stress, too much worry, too much strain. After subjecting children to this—not before, as you might expect—the state is deciding to replace its own system with another one, a system that, in all likelihood, it will withdraw in similar circumstances in five years' time. Such changes have been tormenting the working lives of children for many years now. And there has been a further effect. Each such change has also introduced an immense lowering of standards.

Many children in Britain are obese—and the government takes it as its responsibility to intervene. The government here is well into the schedule of the programme that it has devised; it is, in fact, within two years of having to achieve its first round of targets. But it has not yet decided even how to measure obesity, let alone start the implementation of any policy based on this decision. Meanwhile, British children are still waiting for an agency that is capable of adequate response.

Teaching standards are determined by government administrators, nowadays. What this means is that where in the past teachers used to govern a subject, government departments now set indices of quality. Immense amounts of time are now spent by teachers at all levels of education completing paperwork that demonstrates the attainment of targets set by people ignorant of their field. A government quality index is therefore an indicator of the reverse of quality: it is an index of how much time—and we are talking very large amounts of time—has been wasted by professionals who would in other circumstances have been getting on with their work. The government claims that it needs to demonstrate that its interventions have led to increases in quality: but "demonstration" in this context is also something of a joke. The imposed language of outcomes and targets is itself regulated so as to be "unambiguous and clear", and this means that a wooden language is introduced into the targets so that they can be trivially achieved. You may wonder what kind of target I am talking about: after much deliberation, the

Department of Health decided that among the indices in the first round of quality attributes proposed for the ability to work as a psychotherapist was "the ability to sit still for fifty minutes".

All of these moves towards State regulation and control lead to an enormous decrease in the power and effectiveness of professionals. Rather, the authority to govern a field is given to administrators: junior and senior officials in the civil service, junior ministers, senior ministers, and Secretaries of State.

And what about the achievement of the targets set by the wooden language? Trivialized perhaps, therefore easy? No: you start off with targets, cascaded targets, and quality indices. You then find that you have to write reports on good practice, and on the achievement of targets, cascaded targets, and quality indices. You then have to have training on writing reports on good practice, and so on; and then training on how to do peer reviewing of reports on good practice, and cascaded targets, and so on. And then there is the checking of outcomes and feedback—little boxes and ticks to be added to the reports about wooden language. And then there follow more reviews and assessments, and reorganization, and reformulation of targets, and changed systems, and the need to retrain people concerning the difficulties of the attainment of quality. There is little time left for the real work of professionals; and, in all of this, "quality" means the opposite of quality. And dissent about such things almost always results in loss of government income, and in loss of resource. The government is likely to lower resourcing anyway. And some of these targets are insisted on by government for reasons of political expediency; it is for this reason that hospitals in Britain are losing thousands of staff.

Adult learning and evening classes are currently being cut; the number of classes is being reduced massively, fees doubled: why? Because taxpayer's money would be better spent improving the skills of others. This is the reply of the government. Who are these others? They are the people that the government has already failed to educate at school. Who is to lose access? The loss will be borne by those who have already demonstrated a real interest in knowledge and learning. Here, as elsewhere, the Government allows guilt about the real standards built into its provision to allow it to destroy achieved standards elsewhere. The Association of Colleges estimates that one million places will be lost in this way. The government claims that this is an appropriate outcome, because it has a "new economic mission": it wants increasingly specialized tuition in skills that will support courses "valued by employers". So it compounds its motivation by guilt with an assumption that markets, rather than knowledge, will provide the solution: the government claims that there is a lack in this country of skills necessary for "productive employment".

It may be worthwhile remembering at this point that what used to be called the Department of Education is now called the Department for Innovation, Universities and Skills. It is clear which of these two terms—education and skills—the government takes as a quality indicator. And what is the result of this? At the moment we achieve rank twenty-four out of twenty-nine developed countries in terms of the proportion of sixteen-year-olds who are in education or training. So, a state whose regulations have produced this dire result now wants to reorganize, in order to put more emphasis on attainable and measurable criteria of its own devising. Colleges that fail to meet these new requirements will be closed—taken over by private companies who will be hired to meet targets and to redress "any failure to meet standards". What standards represent in such a context is fairly clear: a destruction of national general culture; the removal of a critical climate of opinion; the destruction of a search for knowledge; the destruction of the valuing of knowledge; and the replacement of knowledge by skills.

There used to be a series of ideas—fairly well received in this country—concerning the Socratic functioning of the state. Civil society would best be served, it was claimed, by formulating as the duty of the state the support of a critical climate of opinion, and the support and inducement of shifts to better theories within the body of publicly available knowledge. Last year the two hundredth anniversary of the birth of John Stuart Mill was celebrated by an International Congress in University College London. Mill, together with his friend George Grote—later to be Vice-Chancellor of London University—struggled to give a real Parliamentary voice to such a theory of knowledge. This notion of a Socratic change of opinion was very influential on Freud: the detail of how this gave form to many of his notions of psychoanalytical technique was one of the themes investigated at this bicentennial congress. Questions like this—of opinions and how they can shift—are at the centre of psychoanalysis; so also are questions of the relation between interpretation and transference; the phasing of beginning, middle, and end moments of analysis, the nature of unconscious phantasy, all of which are related to this central question of what effects are brought into being when a person changes some basic elements in their view of the world. How many of these central themes will the government include as markers of quality in the fields of psychoanalysis and psychotherapy? The government's advisers are unlikely to spend much time on this Mill–Freud question. You can see their preference for unambiguous wooden language, for the trivialization of problems, for published lists of targets, for the permanent reorganization of professionals, and the proliferation of employer-generated skills.

You may think perhaps that this destructive drive to reorganize and master professionals is something new. I have a quote here taken from a Mediterranean country, and from some while ago. It is often attributed to Caius Petronius, Roman Consul in 66 AD:

> We trained hard, but it seemed that every time we were beginning to form up in teams, we would be reorganized. I was to learn in later life that we tend to meet any new situation by reorganizing—and a wonderful method it can be for creating illusion of progress, while producing confusion, inefficiency and demoralization.

So, then, we are faced with the current situation—a proposal in the UK that the government decide on the proper content of a psychotherapy training, and decide also on what it means for a psychotherapist to be of good character. Previous proposals for legislation in this field had been put forward; the government decided that they were not to their taste, and they abolished them. But these previous proposals were at least being introduced by parliamentary means. The Bill put forward by Lord Alderdice was blocked by government intervention in the House of Lords: the government was in the process of writing its election manifesto, and wanting to include in it details and quality aims other than those found in the Bill. During the progress of this Bill through the Lords, there had been constructive and insightful critical proposals put by a number of Members of the Lords who took these issues affecting the human condition seriously. Here are some of the interventions made by Lord Wedderburn of Charlton:

> The Bill cannot succeed except on some basis of professional consensus . . . there is no point in regulating for the sake of regulation, nor indeed of choosing a form of regulation which loses something which has been built up in the recent past . . .
>
> Historically, problems which range across the field of psychotherapy have arisen because of various orientations, or modalities, as they have come to be called, which find their interpretation either in different analytical fields . . . or in more recent analysts than the masters such as Klein, Lacan, or Winnicott . . .
> We must be careful not to lose what is a precious historical oddity; namely the freedom of groups to find new ways to practise and to introduce new concepts in the field . . . I have always thought that when Sigmund Freud was convinced that he had to leave Vienna, he came to the right place where freedom of enquiry is something which regulation must respect.

But this discussion was stopped. And now what is proposed to replace it is the authority of the Health Professions Council—an Agency of State determined by the government to be an appropriate regulator in this field. The Health Professions Council advertised—a year or so ago—on the tube trains. You may have seen their advert. It was to do with a range of therapies—including, I think, art therapy—taking up their membership of the HPC. Drawings on the tube posters showed alarming creatures meant to represent the unregulated professionals. "There is no need to fear any longer such monsters and charlatans", said the advertisement, hoping to calm anxieties in the public. Needless to say, until this advertisement appeared, no one had categorized these practitioners as monsters and wolves. But the government was simply trying to establish and implement standards in the field.

Cognitive behavioural therapy is given high-quality rating by the government: it is cheap, and it is quick, and is approved of by government for both financial reasons and for reasons to do with what kind of therapy best keeps people in the workforce. That is, able to work in the sense of "those who have skills to operate in private companies": skills and finance are usually found at the centre of the government's programme of regulation. The question of whether or nor China is buying euros or dollars has more to do with the government's motivation in such matters than have professional concerns in the psychotherapeutic field.

Listen again to the words of Petronius: confusion, inefficiency, demoralization. To them we could add incapacity, ignorance, and hostility to knowledge. This is what the state has laid up in store for a profession to which it seeks to give rules. The state is not a good listener, and does not provide an environment for the good of psychotherapy. The state does not support knowledge—in fact it barely tolerates it. Not itself possessing the knowledge held by professionals, the state seeks to replace it with something of its own devising. The result is the pauperization of the universities, the emiseration of the Health Service, the subordination of professionals to regulation, and the continuation and augmentation of the suffering of ordinary people. Psychotherapy will not benefit from being further subjected to such administrative bureaucracies. As in the case of psychotherapy generally, the natural environment for the governance of psychoanalysis is that of the critical culture of professionals in its field.

CHAPTER TWO

Responsibility and accountability in psychoanalysis

Roger Litten

We are faced with a move towards the state regulation of what are called the talking therapies in this country. The most obvious difficulty for opponents of this move is the apparent self-evidence of the need for regulation—the demand for enforceable standards of practice to counter the risk to the public posed by unqualified or incompetent practitioners.

This makes it difficult even to raise the question of whether in fact we need regulation of these forms of therapy, especially when the call for regulation is supported by the majority of professional bodies themselves. The debate in this country seems already to have moved beyond the question of whether regulation is necessary to a discussion of the pragmatic details of how to be regulated, losing sight of any basis for attempts to oppose the principle of regulation itself.

In order to find ways to oppose regulation, we thus need in the first instance to bring the apparent self-evidence of the demand for regulation back into question. I want to suggest that the most effective way of doing this is to examine the relation between the why and the how of regulation in an attempt to make visible the logic at stake in the current move towards regulation. I hope in this way to be able to identify a possible basis for effective opposition.

I would like to start with a distinction between what we might call the rationale and the logic of regulation. I propose to examine the rationale of the demand for regulation in an attempt to expose an alternative logic at stake.

This approach turns on the articulation between the discourse of regulation and a more complex and insidious discourse of evaluation, accountability, and audit. I would like to suggest that it is this discourse of evaluation and audit that lies behind the government's push towards state regulation of the talking therapies, and must thus be exposed as the hidden stake of the discourse of regulation.

The rationale for regulation is summed up in the common refrain of the need for public protection and the maintenance of standards of practice. Already here in the two elements of this refrain, which has become so familiar that we no longer question the self-evidence of the association between public protection and maintenance of standards, I suggest we can make out the nuclear articulation between the discourse of regulation and that of evaluation.

I would like to follow through the rationale of this discourse to the point where regulation articulates with the question of evaluation in order to expose the logic at stake and the contradictions entailed. In this way I hope to arrive at the point where not only does regulation not achieve what it claims to set out to achieve—that is, does not do what it says on the tin—but also entails consequences and effects that just happen to be the very opposite of what we start out with.

In other words, we set out from a rationale for regulation elaborated on the basis of a discourse of public protection only to stumble into a system of audit and accountability that at certain points can be seen to provide no protection at all to the very people it claims to serve. By following this trajectory I hope to elaborate a symptomatic and diagnostic reading of the discourse of regulation that will provide the basis for effective opposition to that discourse by elaborating a psychoanalytic critique of the logic at stake.

I have suggested that it is the apparent self-evidence of the rationale for regulation that makes it so difficult to challenge. The difficulty in getting a hearing for the question of why we need regulation does not in the first instance prevent us from introducing questions such as: well, why now, and why like this? The prospect of regulation of the psychotherapies has been on the horizon for decades, yet it is only now that the government seems to have built up a head of steam to push it through.

We will thus start with the question "why now?" in order to return to the question "why at all?". There are at least two possible answers to the question "why now?", one extremely localized and the other more complex and diffuse. I will trace a relation between the two in order to provide a framework for discussion of the apparatus of regulation outlined in the current proposals for the regulation of the talking therapies by the Health Professionals Council.

I think it would be a mistake to lose sight of the fact that this programme of regulation is not aimed at psychoanalysis in particular, nor even necessarily at the talking therapies in general. It is rather part of a broader programme of governmental regulation being unrolled on various fronts in education and health and that is only now being extended into the sphere of the talking therapies, which will, by implication, include psychoanalysis at one level or another.

It is the scale of this programme of regulation that makes it all the more difficult for us to find a point of purchase to challenge it when it encroaches on our domain. But, at the same time, it is even more imperative for us to do so, because if psychoanalysis is not able to mount a critique of these proposals, then who can we expect to do so on our behalf?

I have suggested that there are two possible answers to the question why now. I will start with the most localized answer, which can go under the name of Dr Harold Shipman, the doctor who murdered a number of his patients for no apparent reason apart from the fact that he seemed to have a taste for it, was addicted to killing.

We can use this singular instance of the flagrant betrayal of everything the figure of the doctor is supposed to stand for to mark a point of breakdown in the traditional relation between patient and doctor—the loss of public trust in the figure of medical authority accompanied by a loss of confidence in the profession as a whole.

The impact of the Shipman case must, of course, be situated in relation to other contemporary medical scandals, such as Alder Hey and the Bristol Royal Infirmary, cases of medical negligence and incompetence that appear to have continued undetected for years.

These have raised justified questions about the ability of the General Medical Council, the body representing medical authority and professional self-regulation, to safeguard the public from malpractice by its own members.

These scandals thus mark a point of erosion of the autonomy of medical self-regulation. The failure of the professional body responsible for ensuring public protection and the maintenance of standards of practice within the medical profession leaves the door open to a demand for government intervention, for a system of external monitoring that would be independent, transparent, and accountable to the state.

I am using this example of the position of one of the most influential professional bodies in this country as the quickest way to sketch the shift away from a culture of professional self-regulation towards a culture of accountability and state regulation. I am aware that this is a very rapid sketch, taking a number of shortcuts, in what is itself a highly complex problematic. I am attempting only to situate the most general framework of this shift in order to go on to identify pressure points in the argument for regulation, hoping to demonstrate that we can use a common logic of analysis at each point.

The perceived failure of the system of self-regulation by professional organizations, their failure to safeguard their position of responsibility and medical authority, coincides with a breakdown in the relation of trust between patient and doctor and, ultimately, with a loss of confidence in the profession as a whole. This opens the door of the clinic to the intervention of an independent third party that assumes an external point of arbitration in the name of transparency and accountability, able to hear complaints from patients, respond to them, and, ultimately, to judge on the adequacy of professional practice.

The shift in the external legal and statutory framework of professional practice entails profound modifications, some of which have already been outlined in Christopher Bollas and Mark Sundelson's (1996) work on confidentiality, for the internal dynamics of a psychoanalytic clinic founded on the privileging of the transferential relation between patient and analyst.

The notion of a shift from a discourse of responsibility to one of accountability is one way to bring into focus the more profound shift that we see taking place in the discursive framework surrounding psychoanalytic practice in contemporary society. It is this framework that provides the context for the emergence of the Health Professionals Council, the new regulatory body for the health professions supplementary to medicine.

In the first instance, the Health Professionals Council, or HPC, appears to be no more than a glorified complaints body with a remit to hear complaints laid by members of the public against practitioners and to provide independent judgement of the legitimacy of those complaints.

It is, of course, possible to trace in detail the subtle and progressive extension of this remit on a number of fronts: from hearing complaints to judging fitness to practice, from the setting of standards to the issuing or with-holding of licence to practice, from the vetting of qualifications and accreditation of training courses to having a say not just in the curricula of those training courses, but also in the criteria according to which trainees are selected.

Here I wish to highlight just one aspect of the HPC's work: its responsibility for drawing up a standard template of codes of ethics and practice that will be binding for each profession under its remit. It is clear that for an external body to hear complaints against practitioners from a wide range of professions it will need objective standards against which competence and deviance can be judged. This is one way of understanding the increased emphasis now being placed on codes of professional practice.

These codes lay out the objective standards of conduct and practice to which members of a profession must adhere. They are to be made available to potential users of a service so that they are fully informed in advance about the rights and obligations of the parties concerned. These codes of practice then form the basis for deciding whether there are valid grounds for complaint, on the grounds that there has been an identified failure to meet the standards of practice laid out in that code.

The legitimacy of a complaint against a practitioner thus comes to be judged on the basis of the question of whether or not the stated codes of practice have been breached. Within this environment the judgement of the competence or adequacy of professional practice in general, in a field as complex and multi-faceted as interpersonal therapy, quickly becomes reduced to the question of whether the practitioner has adhered to the standards laid out in the relevant code of practice.

We find codes of professional ethics and practice thus effectively reduced to a customer charter. A psychoanalyst or psychotherapist provides a service no different from a plumber or a mechanic, one that requires protection of customer rights with a service guarantee, complaints procedures, and refunds if not fully satisfied, with the possibility of recourse to an independent regulatory body if something goes wrong.

Without wishing to diminish the importance of what is undoubtedly a complex and serious issue, I suggest that the role being played by contemporary codes of ethics and practice needs to be considered within the framework of the shift from a discourse of responsibility to one of accountability.

This is not simply a question of the subtle slippage involved in the distinction between a code of ethics and a code of conduct. What we are experiencing is a transformation of the external statutory framework of psychoanalytic practice. This is a transformation that entails a shift from a conception of ethics and responsibility internal to the relation between patient and practitioner to a notion of accountability based on the introduction of an independent court of appeal made possible by the objective standards contained in professional codes of practice.

It would be interesting to consider the changes in the vocabulary, content, and role of these codes that accompany this shift. We see a proliferation of codes of practice within the profession of psychotherapy, codes that are ever more comprehensive, designed to cover the full range of all possible incidents and situations, that attempt to provide for every possible ethical dilemma or scenario, fill the gaps of every possible source of risk with a guarantee.

We need to be able to question what is at stake in this rationale. At root, all these codes are designed to safeguard the relation between patient and practitioner. Yet, we could suggest that the very proliferation of these codes can be read as a sign of the difficulties being encountered in conceptualizing the nature and grounds of that relation itself. The reduction of the relation between practitioner and patient to a commercial contract between service provider and consumer can only involve a profound misrecognition of the ethical basis of the transferential relationship on which all psychotherapeutic practice is founded.

The current attempts to give a contractual form to that relationship, together with the effects of objectification and commodification involved, would require far more detailed consideration than is possible here. I merely wanted to highlight this zone as one of the most obvious areas where changes in the external statutory framework have a direct impact on the internal dynamics of the psychoanalytic clinic. It is also the point at which it becomes possible to see that the shift in that framework has the effect of disrupting the ethical basis of the very relation it seeks to safeguard, leading us into a terrain that will ultimately provide no protection or safeguard at all.

I am aware that this is a somewhat hasty approach to a fundamental question that would need to be approached in detail via the psychoanalytic theory of transference. We would have to examine the rise of the notion of the "therapeutic alliance" in contemporary psychoanalysis as laying the ground for a notion of the therapeutic relationship as a contract between equal partners, a contract entered into at the start of a treatment leading towards agreed ends.

This is the point at which the customer charter notion of the therapeutic contract, as filtered through the contemporary discourse of codes of practice, not only involves a complete misunderstanding of the subjective ethics of the transferential relation but also entails a subtle but profound abdication of responsibility for the psychoanalytic position in favour of an external guarantee of false accountability.

A betrayal of the subjective ethics of the psychoanalytic relation, the only true source of analytic responsibility, can, however, only be accompanied by the loss of the source of any possible therapeutic efficacy of psychoanalytic work in general.

The point at which we find ourselves subscribing to a culture of accountability that attempts to safeguard the empty shell of the psychoanalytic relation with an external apparatus of contract and guarantee is also the point at which we would have to question whether it is not the psychoanalytic organizations themselves that have lost sight of this question. This would explain not only their vulnerability to demands for regulation and their silence in the face of these developments, but also their eagerness to comply with the state's wishes, precisely in order to mask their own difficulties at this point.

References

Bollas, C., & Sundelson, M. (1996). *The New Informants: Betrayal of Confidentiality in Psychoanalysis and Psychotherapy*. London: Karnac.

CHAPTER THREE

Morals and psychoanalytic education

Haya Oakley

East Grinstead is hardly a location that is likely to feature in psychoanalytic history books, but it was there, in 1960, that an event took place which would alter the future of psychotherapy in the UK forever. The headmistress of the local primary school was undergoing a course in Scientology. Inspired by what she experienced, she was, according to the 1971 Foster Report, "reported to be taking pupils of hers aged between seven and eleven through an exercise in which they were asked to imagine they were dead and turning to dust, as a result of which one small boy was said to have fainted". The English press had a field day. Some psychotherapy organizations began to make representations to the Department of Health (DoH) demanding something be done to restrict the practice of Scientology. The question was first raised in Parliament in 1966, when the Minister of Health was asked (again, the words of the Foster Report) "[w]hether he will initiate an Inquiry into the scope and practice in this country of so-called Scientology, *and the practice of psychology for fee or reward by persons who have no medical or psychological qualifications*" [my italics].

After much resistance, the government eventually commissioned the Foster Report into Scientology. The report (available on

Her Majesty's Government website) makes fascinating reading. Foster concluded: "Even if the Scientology leadership were quacks, I doubt whether they would be committing any offences under English law as it stands", that the law does provide a civil remedy "for patients who have been abused", that Scientology is without a doubt a psychotherapy, and, therefore, "The question which I have to consider is whether there is a case for legislation in the United Kingdom to control the practice of psychological medicine".

Relying heavily on selected quotes from Freud, Foster made the case to Parliament that such legislation is essential and he congratulated Scientology for highlighting this need. It is, he explains, the phenomenon of the transference that makes our patients vulnerable to abuse. A therapy session may look like an innocent scene in which "two people" are simply "talking to each other",

> Yet the danger in anything other than the most skilled hands is great and, what is worst, the possibilities of abuse by the unscrupulous are immense . . . It is fatally easy for the unscrupulous therapist, who knows enough to create the dependency in the first place, to exploit it for years on end to his own advantage in the form of steady income, to say nothing of the opportunities for sexual gratification.

Foster proposed setting up a "Psychotherapy Council", with powers to regulate the profession. Once such a Council existed, he argued, Scientology could apply to be recognized by it as a form of a legitimate therapy and would be welcomed with open arms by the profession, providing they could

> satisfy the proposed professional body that they are qualified to do so, that their techniques are sound, that their practitioners receive adequate training and operate under a stringent ethical code, and that there is no hint of exploitation.

To strengthen his arguments, Foster returns to Freud and quotes from "The question of lay analysis", in which Freud argues that

> The analyst should possess personal qualities that make him *trustworthy*, and should have acquired the knowledge and understanding as well as the experience which alone can make it possible for him to fulfil his task. [Freud, 1926c, p. 187]

It is open to analytic interpretation as to why Foster ends his report with a note on "The privileged position of religious bodies". The analogy with our own institutions, who peddle articles of faith as if they were scientific truths, is only too tempting.

The Foster review was followed in 1978 by the Sighart Report, which recommended "indicative registration" for psychotherapists, and by the first Psychotherapy Bill, which fell at the second reading. Although the government seemed to have lost interest, that Bill caught the imagination of the psychotherapists, who clubbed together to form a voluntary register. Practitioners and organizations of all modalities rose to the call and lined up to be regulated, controlled, and policed, initially by way of voluntary registers but always with the hope of achieving their ultimate goal: some form of recognition by the state that would take the form of an act of Parliament through a psychotherapy Bill or, if need be, proper statutory regulation. Even when the government lost all interest in the process, we kept going at it, telling ourselves that if we did not do it, someone else would in a more draconian way. We urged "the authorities" to keep an eye on us and in the meantime, we started to practise on ourselves what we hoped would be done to us once we were "legit".

It is a well-documented fact that the vast majority of the delegates who represented the psychotherapy organizations at the time shared a profound innocence, often blatant ignorance, of anything to do with statutory legislation, state regulation, or the implications of professionalization. Even the Principle Case Manager of the short-lived Independent Complaints Organization (ICO, set up by the UKCP), in the Spring 2007 edition of the UKCP official publication *The Psychotherapist*, wrote that such an organization would be necessary "until statutory regulation comes into force"; and this even when the government has made it clear that it does not and will not consider statutory regulation (that is, a psychotherapy Bill) and that it is intent on proceeding with state regulation via the DoH and the Health Professions Council (HPC).

It could be said that a naïve belief was enthusiastically shared by most, if not all, delegates to UKCP: that we were doing something that would improve the standards of existing trainings, make psychotherapy more available, and, most of all, protect the vulnerable public from unscrupulous practitioners. We also shared the fantasy that, once we all agreed amongst ourselves as to what constituted a basic training and drew up the outer parameter of who was in and who should be excluded, the government would look at our documents and adopt them as the law of the land. In fact, it would not be incorrect to say that most changes that have occurred within the UKCP were driven by the notion that if we did it to ourselves first—through drafting "codes of ethics", "complaints procedures", "training standards" and "outcome-based competencies"—the government would then be bound to go along with what we had "cooked up".

I would even go as far as to hazard a guess that it is only when actually dealing with the HPC that erstwhile champions of state regulation have suffered a rude awakening to what is involved. In other words, now they can see the detrimental effect such a move might have on our ability to practise anything remotely resembling psychoanalysis as we know it if we were to become a "health profession". Following Lacan's comment that "[t]o make oneself the guarantor of the possibility that a subject will in some way be able to find happiness even in analysis is a form of fraud" (Lacan, 1992, p. 303), would claiming that psychoanalysis is a "mental health profession", in itself, not be unethical? Did Freud not consider health benefits a possible and only occasional by-product of analysis?

I will not write more about what, by now, is a familiar tale of trying to reach agreement on what could possibly be a generic, standardized basis of our knowledge and experience, the sound technique and adequate training Foster envisages as the basis for recognizing psychotherapy as capable of fulfilling the task as a unified profession. One thing is clear: so far, as a community, we have failed to disabuse the powers to be—to which we are proposing to hand over control of the profession—of the notion that psychoanalysis can be transmitted through a set of generic, or even modality-specific, competencies designed for the "service of goods" (*ibid.*). Instead, I would like to say something about the remaining crucial ingredient that Foster, following Freud, sees as the cornerstone of the making of a professional therapist; that is, what Freud calls the "personal qualities" that make one trustworthy (what Foster would call the ability to adhere to a stringent code of ethics). How may we train and launch the practitioner in such a way that he or she does not have to carry a health warning?

For example, the current set of competencies, prepared in 2001 as an "outcomes grid" for psychoanalytic trainings within UKCP, states that before qualifying a psychoanalytic trainee must be able to demonstrate. among other things,

> An awareness of the duties and responsibilities of a psychotherapist towards patients and the general public, an appreciation of ethical concerns, a knowledge of ethical codes and structures and a basic awareness of legal issues.

If we believe that this is remotely possible and/or desirable, how do we think we can bring it about? Do we practise ethically and competently because we adhere to a "code of ethics", or because we have an understanding of the psychoanalytic project? Many psychoanalytic organizations knew nothing of codes of ethics for most of their existence. Why are we not content to make do with a basic code, the principles of which no one seems to object to; one that upholds fundamental notions such as not having a sexual relationship with our patients, not attacking them physically, not exploiting them financially, not making false claims about our qualifications, and respecting confidentiality? Instead, we have driven ourselves to the bleakest limits of "fitness to practise", in which anything and everything could be complained about, from record keeping to the nature of an interpretation, not to mention the fabric used to decorate our consulting rooms and the proximity of the latter to the toilet. If you think this list is simply poetic licence on my part to make the point, do check out the requirements of the Health Care Commission (not to be confused with HPC), which is already in operation.

Why are we about to entrust such scrutiny of our daily practice and the judging of psychoanalysts to a body specializing in the hearing of complaints by standards applicable to professions supplementary to medicine, like chiropody and radiography? Can we not see that shifting complaints from a clearly defined area of specific codes of ethics to an all encompassing framework that stipulates "fitness to practise" might pose a serious risk for working with the transference? It could even become

> a licence for acting out and destroy[ing] the therapeutic alliance; to discourage the flowering of a therapeutic and mutative transference;

> and to encourage the development of a malign and destructive transference that will, in effect, become policed by those who know nothing of such matters. [Jacques China, unpublished paper]

And, above all, why do so many of us seem happy, or at least very apathetic, about this?

A holocaust survivor, who dedicated her life to telling the story of the war, said in a filmed interview that there has never been a single day in her life in which she did not think or talk about what had happened. The interviewer asked her, "And how did you feel on the day that you gave birth to your son?" The woman did not hesitate for a second when she replied,

> When they put my son in my arms for the first time, I looked at him and the first thought which crossed my mind was: the soldiers who carried out the atrocities, they too where once someone's new born baby, they were loved, cherished and cared for, how did they become moral monsters, how did they turn from lovely little babies into murderers?

Forgive me for using such an extreme and dramatic example to formulate a question that human beings have been struggling with since Cain and Abel and that, in a less dramatic way, yet with potentially grave implications for the future of psychoanalysis, we are faced with today. It is the question of the formation of what Freud calls a "trustworthy" person, or what we now call an ethical practitioner.

In a little known paper, written in 1963 and titled "Morals and education", Winnicott (1965) offers his view of the way the human infant acquires morals. Understanding the capacity for morality and ethics as primarily "the evolution of a personal superego", Winnicott sets out a binary opposition between what he calls the moral educationalist and the "good enough" parent. The former, the moral educationalist, he says, has "stolen the good from the developing individual child, and has then set up an artificial scheme for injecting this that has been stolen back into the child, and has called it 'moral education'". He goes on to say that "[i]t is the ideas bound up with the organisation of moral education that deplete the individual of individual creativity" (p.94).

Such an education will not succeed unless the child has managed to develop what he calls a "belief in". The child acquires "the capacity to 'believe in', for having a moral sense, for experiencing a sense of guilt and for setting up an ideal" (p. 93) in what Winnicott calls the "facilitating environment", the provision of which is firmly placed in the mother's real and metaphorical lap. In short, the formation of the would-be scrupulous adult is a function of the individual superego, which, in turn, is seen as a product of the good enough and reliable care by the primary carer:

> To a child who has started life in this way, the idea of goodness and of a reliable and personal parent or God can follow naturally . . . This is the first principle of moral education, that moral education is no substitute for love. [*ibid.*, p. 97]

The whole process, claims Winnicott, takes place in a "pre-verbal" time when love is conveyed through the mother's physical care-taking actions. Rules, Gods, ideals, and the like will be introduced at a later stage when the child has acquired the capacity for "believing in", and will be left around in the facilitating environment to be picked up, adopted, and adhered to. It is not a joke, Winnicott claims, to say that man created God in his own image. God, he says, is

> a place [for man] to put that which is good in himself, and which he might spoil if he kept it in himself with all the hate and destructiveness which is also to be found there. [*ibid.*, p. 94]

Well, if God is a projection of goodness, then, surely, the rules governing the "fitness to practise" must be a reflection of our collective self-hatred.

This is possibly Winnicott at his worst. The paper is full of theoretical black holes, such as the notion that a parent is free of moral judgement and that the infant only comes up against parental approval or disapproval when it acquires language. It is also predicated on the notion that the basic template of human relations is that of a need conjoined to an object of satisfaction and that there is such a thing as a pre-verbal environment. Nevertheless, if you have a moment to spare, you might like to read the paper. If you do, try to replace the word "infant" with "trainee". A picture then emerges of a familiar misguided and concrete reading of the British object-relations theoretical tradition, in which what was meant to be a description of unconscious infantile fantasies is too often taken to be a commentary on "real relationships".

Close observation of the field would reveal that psychoanalytic schools that believe trainees are infants and the school is there to love, nurture, and protect them (rather than to educate them in a mature, mutually respectful, adult manner) will find it difficult to exercise authority as well as foster it in its graduates. Convinced that the institution's role is to be a "good enough mother", it will find that discipline, erudition, and a search for clinical and ethical excellence become very awkward tasks. Psychotherapy schools are notoriously bad at expelling poor trainees and useless trainers. Furthermore, if the trainee fails, it is often experienced as the failure of the "mother school" for not being good enough and for not providing a facilitating enough environment. Fear of the infant trainees, and an overwhelming sense of responsibility for them and their baby patients, can drive an organization to seek discipline elsewhere, to farm it out to outside "baddies", as well as to wish to make up for all the gaps in the provisions of care by offering supervision for life and more and more complex and intrusive control. Electric socket blockers, drawer stoppers, stair gates and buggy harnesses come to mind; but while these might be inevitable in a modern world, children do grow out of them and, normally, do not require supervision for life. One result of this is that instead of fearing EU directives, the Health Commission, Fitness to Practise rules, and third party complaints, we become afraid of our students and our patients and, very soon, of one another.

Another possible reading of the insatiability of the demand for more control is offered by Freud in *Civilization and its Discontents* (1930a), where he points out that the economy by which the superego operates is one where "the more one sacrifices to it, the more it demands" (p. 302). In the days of the great debates within the British Psychoanalytical Society, the inability to resolve theoretical and clinical differences resulted in cutting a deal about the technical rules of engagement. Maybe now we see the return of the repressed of this deal, in which the less there is of our ability to articulate what we are about, the more absurd the rules we seek to fix and define us; rules that put an edifice of a solid existence where fluidity, flexibility, and freedom should be. This is to turn the mystery tour of the unconscious into a medically-stated destination, transparent and well-designed in advance, with all possible dangers and unexpected surprises removed.

Freud attributes the rational inscription of the moral agency in man to the castrating father rather than to the failings of the providing mother. Lacan expands this argument:

> It is this imaginary father and not the real one which is the basis of the providential image of God. And the function of the superego, in the end, from its final point of view, is hatred for God, the reproach that God has handled things so badly. [Lacan, 1992, p. 308]

Reading Lacan's "moral goals of psychoanalysis" is a painful reminder of that which drives us to protect the public from our own omnipotence and what we wrongly believe psychoanalysis is capable of doing. The end of a training analysis is not a moral cleansing; but is where a "subject should reach and should know the domain and the level of the experience of absolute disarray" (*ibid.*, p. 304).

Cultural differences have shaped much of the history of the psychoanalytic movement. Traditionally, countries where trainings are delivered for the most part by universities and controlled by private medical insurance companies—and which, then, are dependent on medical approval—have found it easier to legislate using psychology and psychiatry as the foundation for the licence to practise. In France, where psychoanalysis has been more closely associated with literature and philosophy, the resistance to state intervention is shared by all parts of the profession. In the UK, a long tradition of organized deregulation worked in our favour for many productive generations, but a combination of empty-handedness in the face of the lack of a "standard edition", unresolved rivalries between the different psychoanalytic schools, a deeply-embedded class system, and the fantasy that we are Her Majesty's subjects and not citizens of Europe, has driven us to hand over power to the Department of Health and HPC. Could it be our collective unconscious wish that *it* would finally be able to distinguish the legitimate inheritors of the mantle from the impostors?

Nowadays, when the House of Lords concerns itself with our personal happiness, it might be apt to give the final word to the one who, by his excommunication from a "civilized" psychoanalytic society, attempted, with all the problematics that come with it, to reopen the creative and imaginative gap:

> A little more rigor and firmness are required in our confrontation with the human condition. . . . The services of goods or the shift of the demand for happiness onto the political stage has its consequences. The movement that the world we live in is caught up in, of wanting to establish the universal spread of the service of goods as far as conceivably possible, implies an amputation, sacrifice, indeed a kind of Puritanism in the relationship to desire that has occurred historically. The establishment of the service of goods at a universal level does not in itself resolve the problem of the present relationship of each individual man to his desire in the short period of time between his birth and his death. [*ibid.*, p. 303]

References

China, J. unpublished paper.

Freud, S. (1926e). The question of lay analysis: conversations with an impartial person. *S.E., 20,* London: Hogarth.

Freud, S. (1930a). *Civilization and its Discontents. S.E., 21*. London: Hogarth.

Lacan, J. (1992). *The Ethics of Psychoanalysis 1959–1960: The Seminar of Jacques Lacan Book VII*. D. Porter (Trans.). London: Routledge.

Winnicott, D. W. (1965). Morals and education. In: *The Maturational Processes and the Facilitating Environment* (pp. 93–105). London: Hogarth.

CHAPTER FOUR

Why is psychoanalysis not in trouble?

John Miller

The invention of psychoanalysis is usually attributed to Freud, but its spiritual father could be said to be Socrates. It was he, in the Western tradition, who was the first person to dedicate his life to encouraging people to try to think clearly and examine their true motivation. He foreshadowed Bion in his recognition of the way people tend to make assumptions that they do not examine. In fact, it was his insistence on questioning the assumptions his fellow Athenians made about the need for war that led to his own death sentence. It was in his defence speech at his trial that he made the comment "the unexamined life is a life not worth living" (Plato,1908), a good motto for psychoanalysis. On the same lines, any person or agency that is dedicated to a genuine struggle against ignorance, prejudice, mindlessness, and so on can be expected to be met with unpopularity, and attempts to silence them. Like Socrates, they can be expected to be in trouble.

My thesis in this chapter is that psychoanalysis, if it is really being true to itself and its task, ought to be in trouble with important sectors of society. We would expect that in its concern for "Truth", it would be coming into conflict with any groups and lobbies in society which have a vested interest in distorting the truth: the advertising industry, which wants consumers to see themselves as heroic and admirable instead of impressionable and childish; politicians, who rely on "spin"; religious bodies trying to get obedience to dogma, etc. The fact that, as far as I can see, there is very little sign of it being in trouble in this way suggests to me that it is in deep trouble in a more serious sense—that of being in terminal decline.

The application of psychoanalysis to group and organizational behaviour has led to the realization that states of mind that are highly pathological in an individual are a normal part of group or organizational behaviour. Selvini Palazzoli (1990) describes how The Milan Institute for Family Therapy found that the work that they did with psychotic families was directly applicable to any business or institutions.

This raises the question as to whether training organizations and institutions, even without state regulation, are a contradiction in terms when applied to psychoanalysis. As analysts should know better than anyone else, meeting the requirements of membership of an institution and submitting to its rules is inevitably depersonalizing and infantilizing. This is diametrically opposed to the aims of analysis to cultivate adult functioning, a sense of personal identity, and the capacity to think for oneself. That is all very well in theory, the objection might be made, but surely there have to be some sort of external controls? Let us examine this question very carefully. What is it exactly that needs to be controlled and how is this expected to happen?

The main basic assumption that needs to be flushed out of the undergrowth here is that psychoanalysis—and indeed all forms of psychotherapy—are analogous to medical practice. The patient presenting for analysis, like the doctor's patient, has to trust the integrity and expertise of the person he or she is consulting. It is, therefore, necessary to take steps to guarantee the competence and probity of the analyst as it is with the doctor. Few people would disagree with the intention here. The question, however, is to what extent psychoanalysis and analytical therapy are comparable. There are several major discrepancies.

First, medicine is concerned with an agreed-upon body of knowledge and practice. Human anatomy, surgical procedures, and medication for particular conditions are matters of fact: all human beings have the same organs, which develop the same conditions and are treatable by the same surgery, medication, or procedures the world over. Psychoanalysis, on the other hand, is by no means an agreed-upon body of knowledge, as witness the preponderance of drug and behavioural therapy in the world at large, and the massive, sectarian conflicts that rage between the various analytical schools of thought. Any doubts about the latter can be removed by reviewing the saga of the United Kingdom Council for Psychotherapy (UKCP), which was able to do no more than require that each therapy group establish the norms and acceptable practices in its own domain. It is perfectly possible (and not uncommon) to find professional practice and attitudes that are anathema to one therapy group being seen as desirable, or even a requirement, in another one. Although UKCP covered the whole range of therapies, exactly the same situation arises within psychoanalysis. Needless to say, each group firmly believes that they, and only they, have the analytical Holy Grail. A particularly important consideration that emerges from this is that psychoanalysis and psychotherapy in any form is not, and can never be a profession, since a profession, by definition, has to involve an agreed-upon body of knowledge and practice. Strictly speaking, even teaching was not a profession in Britain until the advent of the National Curriculum, since, up to that time, there were no legal requirements about what had to be taught in school except, ironically, for religion! The reason for this latter anomaly was because the origin of the school system in the nineteenth century was Sunday schools, the original purpose of which was not to educate children, but to provide mass child-minding to free parents for the workforce.

Consequently, any idea of competence or correct practice as a justification for regulated institutions is completely untenable. By the same token, it is equally impossible for state regulation to be applicable to incompetence or malpractice. Moreover, complaints and claims of malpractice are just as likely to be compounded by state regulation, by encouraging interest groups to form kangaroo courts.

The simple fact of the matter is that no system or piece of legislation can, in itself, be a guarantee of security, and the belief that it can usually leads to things getting worse rather than better.

Perhaps the best illustration of another basic assumption is that of the Age of Consent. Surveys over the last three decades have suggested that as much as 60% of the population has its first sexual experience under the age of consent. Not only that, but there are indications that the most alarming trends—pregnancy in girls of thirteen and under, for example, are increasing exponentially. This is not to suggest that there should not be an age of consent—the legislation may be a useful tool in certain circumstances—but it is clearly preposterous to imagine that the existence of legislation, in itself, in some way controls the sexual behaviour of young people. Yet, there is clearly a widespread unspoken assumption that legislation and codes of practice somehow do control behaviour, perhaps summed up in the apocryphal remark, "He cannot be lying—he is a Boy Scout!"

From senior colleagues on committees of various psychoanalytical organizations, I get the impression that scandals of sexual impropriety in psychoanalytic practice have shown no sign whatsoever of decreasing in the face of "ethics committees" and registration.

So, if regulation cannot make things better, the question has to be asked as to whether it can actually make them worse.

First, there is the general consideration that the moment something becomes embodied in rules, regulations, and legislation, all sorts of problems and deficiencies can flourish more easily because it is no longer good judgement and commonsense that is applied to them, but technicalities and points of order. There is no point in having a register of people known to have been involved in child pornography if the Education Secretary does not see that as a reason for preventing some of them from working with children. Gun licences are of limited value if the authorities issuing them do not see paedophile tendencies as a reason for withholding them—as in the case of Thomas Hamilton, who massacred sixteen children and their teacher in Dunblane.

If psychoanalysis is a vocation, and not a profession, it can only be practised by people who have sufficient experience, capacity for concern, and adult functioning to be able to do so. Whether a particular person meets these requirements sufficiently is something that can only be decided by good judgement, not bureaucratic procedures. If, on the other hand, it is a profession or occupation, anyone has a right to do it, only provided that they satisfy all the official requirements. These, however, are likely to have precious little to do with the person's character and maturity, and a great deal to do with their persona. Is there, then, no role for institutions? The only one I can see is that of feeding back to society the collective experience and professional response of the members of the institution. While it is true that real changes take place in people's lives through individual learning, there is still a part to be played by influencing public opinion. We are familiar with motoring organizations commenting and advising on transport, the Police Federation making observations about public order and safety, the British Medical Association on matters of health, and so on. Yet I have never once heard reference in a news bulletin to comments on the mental health or emotional welfare of the population by any analytical group, much less the psychoanalytical community as a whole.

What sort of things might one have expected analytical institutions to comment on? In January 2003 the *British Medical Journal* published an article describing the blatant and unashamed efforts of a number of pharmaceutical companies to sponsor the invention of a new condition for which they could then manufacture and market the medication (Moynihan, 2003). Why is there not a squeak of collective protest from analysts who must surely spend more time than anyone else trying to sort out genuine sexual problems? This is just a rather breathtaking individual example. In more general terms, it would be no exaggeration to say that our society is in crisis. Drug addiction—whether via the prescription pad or the local dealer—is ubiquitous. All the lessons learned in the 1960s about the crucial role of attachment and good, early mothering have been forgotten or ignored, as toddlers and even babies are farmed out to nurseries and child-minders like so many unwanted pets. Partly as a result, the capacity for long-term relationships is so eroded that a significant proportion of the housing shortage is caused not by increased population but the increasing number of sad singles, which some estimates suggest may be the majority in the not too distant future.

It must be acknowledged that a great deal of good work is done both by organizations and individual analysts in trying to address these problems with the thinking public. My point is that the only constructive justification for analytical organizations is to provide a mouthpiece to challenge the emotionally unhealthy and anti-developmental trends in society, and of this there is no sign.

Bion (1961) distinguishes between the Basic Assumption Group in organizations, which is concerned with image, status, and so on, and the Work Group, which gets on with the task. So, outside of sessions with patients, what is the task of the Work Group in psychoanalysis? Something on the lines of the continuing quest for deeper understanding of emotional development and psychic life. What are the requirements for this? Good personal analysis, good supervision, and, perhaps, teachers and colleagues with whom one can discuss the literature. None of this requires an institution, although an informal, interest group could help. What, in practice, do members of psychoanalytical organizations devote their work time and energy to, outside of sessions? What is the purpose of the endless committees, sub-committees, quorums, rules, regulations, bylaws, etc? None of this has any direct bearing on the task, but everything to do with hierarchy, image, and status—in other words the Basic Assumption Group. The same thing applies to membership fees: an analytical organization is not a kind of club—like a sports centre, where you pay for use of the facilities—or a service like a bank. All you buy with your annual fee is a licence to practise legally. In fact, it is effectively "protection money".

But it is through the anomaly of "continuing professional development" (CPD) that Big Brother (in the original Orwellian sense) is marching steadily into the consulting room. Since, as we have already observed, psychoanalysis cannot be a profession, it makes nonsense to talk about professional development. The misconception that it is a profession provides a pretext for the institution not only to decide the conditions of membership that are necessary for someone to practise legally, but to insist on a continuing right to intrude and interfere in their work on a permanent basis. Anyway, what would a good analytical CPD plan feature? Membership of committees? Attendance at conferences? Number of sessions clocked up? Books have been written about analysts who eat, drink, and sleep therapy and treat their family members as patients. They would undoubtedly have most impressive CPD plans; but is not that almost the opposite of the kind of person required? What do I honestly believe has been contributing most to my development as an analyst? The greater ease with which I can avoid coming to blows with my teenage daughters? My recent experience of rereading *Pride and Prejudice*? The victory over my obsessionality represented by now being able to cook dinner without looking at the recipe book? Who is in a position to evaluate any of this apart from my wife or my best friend (assuming I have either) or my analyst (assuming he or she is still alive)? But wait a minute! This is not professional development but personal development; and it is nobody's damn business except mine! We have been overlooking something fundamental about psychoanalysis: it is not a treatment or a problem-solving device, but a uniquely educational project focused on the central role of meaning in emotional—and even physical—health. The Founding Fathers (and Mothers) of psychoanalysis all came to the same conclusion: that at the heart of mental health there is always a moral issue. Essentially, this concerns how far the individual has the courage and honesty to struggle against the destructive and perverse parts of the personality. Even in psychosis (whatever factors may be involved in its aetiology) how far the patient is at the mercy of their illness depends on how far, in the words of the poet Milton, they decide they would rather "rule in Hell than serve in Heaven". This, of course, is completely at loggerheads with the current *Zeitgeist*, which views society as composed of innocent victims of mysterious inanimate forces it is the job of some kind of invisible, cosmic Mummy to fix. The Nanny State is only too happy to reinforce and even cultivate this attitude of infantile dependency, which invites ever-increasing state interference in private life in a way that is striking more and more at the heart of democracy and civil liberties.

Central to all analytical work is the issue of freedom, not just from external tyranny, but, more importantly, from the internal infantile fantasies of control. This comes about through emotional growth, which can only come about through experiencing love and concern in a personal, parental relationship. This is psychoanalysis in a nutshell. External, impersonal systems can not only never promote this, but actually encourage the abrogation of personal responsibility and the equating of obedience and conformity with morality. (We may remind ourselves here of the defence put forward at the trial of Adolph Eichmann that he was "only obeying orders".) Psychoanalysis is not about observable behaviour, but inner experience. It is about emotional development, not information and programming. Above all, it is about the all-important fact that emotional growth and development can only come about through a spontaneous response to nurture. It is impossible to force it. The philanthropist Thomas Coram founded the first hospital for abandoned babies in the eighteenth century in London. To begin with, almost all the babies rescued and brought to his hospital died. The reason? Simply, that the worthy philanthropists in charge of the hospital (all of them, needless to say, men) had somehow failed to register the fact that small babies cannot be fed on solids (Wagner, 2004). In the 1950s, in New York foundling hospitals, the mortality rate was still almost 100% (Montague, 1970). By this time, the patriarchal society had woken up to the fact that small babies need milk, but they had overlooked something equally important: a baby may have warmth, milk, and hygiene, but without the possibility of a personal relationship to a mother figure it cannot thrive. The cause of death on the babies' death certificates was invariably *Marasmus*, a Greek word, which just means that they wasted away. Institutionalized, state-regulated analysis is just as well-meaning, misguided, and, ultimately, lethal.

Freud's defined psychoanalysis as "a cure of the soul through love" (Bettelheim, 1986). Love is the polar opposite of power and control. Power and control pave the way to tyranny and depersonalization.

Psychoanalysis long ago lost the plot through its willingness to have Institutions of any sort. This has further been compounded by the lamentable proliferation of academic degree courses in psychoanalytical psychotherapy, implicitly reinforcing the misconception that analysis is some kind of intellectual activity.

The biggest issue, however, is the growing menace of state interference in private life. Where psychoanalysis ought to be most in trouble is in championing freedom of thought and belief, both inside and outside the consulting room, which it cannot do unless it refuses to submit itself to state control. To the extent that it is failing to address, in this way, the threat to everything it stands for, psychoanalysis invalidates itself and is fast becoming irrelevant to modern life.

The government has recently declared its firm intention to regulate psychotherapy, counselling, and psychoanalysis through the Health Professions Council. This means treating all forms of therapy as if they were medical procedures, and treating all practitioners as if the NHS employed them. A set of crude "competences" will be drawn up, against which all practice and training will be measured. Although signatures are apparently being collected for a petition, many therapy organizations seem to be quite unaware of either the petition or the problem it addresses.

In general, the psychoanalytical community can still be likened to a householder in Pompeii in AD 79, who, on 24 August, can think of nothing more important than home improvements and redecoration.

References

Bettelheim, B. (1986). *Freud and Man's Soul*. Harmondsworth: Pelican.

Bion, W. (1961). *Experiences in Groups, and Other Papers*. London: Tavistock.

Montague, A. (1970). *Touching: The Human Significance of the Skin*. New York: Harper Row.

Moynihan, R. (2003). The making of a disease: female sexual dysfunction. *British Medical Journal, 326*: 45–47.

Plato (1908). *Apology* (38a). in *The Trial and Death of Socrates*. F. J. Church (Trans.). London: Macmillan and Co.

Selvini Palazzoli, M. (1990). *The Hidden Games of Organisations*. London: Taylor & Francis.

Wagner, G. (2004). *Thomas Coram*. Gent: Boydell.

CHAPTER FIVE

Psychoanalysis and its self-mutilation

Chris Oakley

We have all become the same kind of people who think the same kind of things, and who, for the most part, partake of the same kind of knowledge. It would appear that the vast majority all seem to share the same belief, perhaps just the other side of the same despair, that all must submit to a particular conviction that psychoanalysis, psychotherapy, call it what you will, it is all the same to me, would be best served in all of its three forms: as discourse, as community, as a therapy through increased regulation, increased surveillance, and increased work ethic. And this has been going on for years. We have all become somnambulists in an occupied territory, a territory preoccupied with a subliminal ideology. Or, on closer inspection, not so subliminal at all. The model is one that is so familiar to "New Labour" and the Blair legacy of "market management", although the beginnings were always prompted by the witch from Grantham and her "enterprise culture".

The novelist Iain Sinclair was recently on television airing his prophesies regarding the effect that the Olympics will have on his beloved East End. What he suggested will happen is that an area that once one could feely roam and wander around within, discovering aspects of its history in one's own time and at one's own pace (the modality of drift so close to the heart of the psychoanalytic enterprise) will be taken over by blue plaque heritage trails, where all will be dragooned into following a set of pre-ordained paths (the modality of consumer choice). This is Marilyn Strathern's thesis in her article "The tyranny of transparency" (2000), in which one kind of reality is eclipsed by another. And, as with all occupied territories, violence is never far away. The weapons that operate are the vocabulary used. Or, perhaps more appropriately put, the word is not so much violence as a virulence, for it is a virus that has infected the communities of psychoanalysis. This has spawned a contagion, a grotesque chain reaction that congeals around a particular symptom: registers and registration. All immunity or any power to resist has been destroyed. A contagion of collaboration unfolds. All appear cowed and timorous in the face of an avalanche of undigested proposals for a safer, more secured existence. It is Winnicott that I associate with the idea that when we are caught up in an anxiety that the dreadful is about to happen (now posited as state or statutory regulation), the catastrophe has always already occurred. We all must situate ourselves in so-called "centres of excellence", and we all so obediently line up to be anointed by these violations. Recently, my own organization engaged in the familiar self-preening when the word was enthusiastically disseminated that "the inspectors had passed the organization's training, claiming it of be a 'beacon of excellence'". So that's all right then.

Let us begin by examining the genealogy of registration and explore the relation between the universal and the singular. Psychoanalysis is always on the side of the singular, as there is no repeatability in play. Philosophers of Science will argue that the status of a particular discourse as science does not inevitably require repeatability, but for the rest of us it starts to make things look pretty difficult. But, back to the issue of registration and the proliferation of lists, of regulatory bodies, one example of which would be the comparatively newly formed College of Psychoanalysts. What you will witness is a weakening, a flight into the lowest common denominator, all driven by a desire for expansion corresponding to the weakest definition.

But why pick on the poor College? After all, this proliferation of lists has been going on for some considerable time, and this seemingly unstaunchable diffusion of registration over anything and everything has increasingly taken on pornographic proportions; an interactive copulation so in our faces, so obscenely magnified in importance as all obediently march in step to sign on for the post Cartesian imperative "I register, therefore I am". And, inevitably, this swirls, this circulates like oil or capital, all is marinated in these concerns, and akin to the universality of globalization all appears irreversible. From the disassociated margins one can marvel at the faultless mastery of this almost invisible operation. Invisible because it blinds us all, particularly to the excess of surveillance that was always already there, and to the unrelenting extrusion of singularity, the latter barely an accidental consequence, for it merely follows the very logic of registration. It is hardly controversial to point to the compulsive homogenization, the undifferentiated universality that saturates the terrain, a regime of safety in numbers as all huddle to avoid the overarching panoptic searchlight of suspicion that engulfs us all. Suspicion of negligence, at least, to be offset by copious CPD (continuous professional development) endorsements, or carefully archived evidence that one is adhering to one's PLP (personal learning plan . . . me? I'm off for a wander in the East End) or suspicion of abuse, at worst, all to be dealt with by the multiplication of complaints procedures. And while we are on the subject of the aforementioned violence that emerges through language, through an intrusion of a particular vocabulary, try, as a car journey game, to catalogue any abbreviations that have become the name itself (one such example would be CPD) that are not incorrigibly associated with authority and control; for example, FBI, CIA, MI5, DHSS, UKCP . . . one exception, something more benign, is that blighted zone, the NHS. An immediate effect is that all that is other, alternative, or singular is consigned to the periphery, the wild of the wilderness, and left to perish. Or at least that is the prevailing fantasy. So what can thwart this homogenizing regulatory power? Certainly not movements or initiatives that set up analogous lists with the invariant: an inside and an outside, all a spurious offering of shelter from the storm. Such enterprises may have some small scale political impact, but their symbolic or social impact is almost nil, as they can only meekly engage in a mimesis of the problem, all continuing to be subordinated to the system. Let us allow Beckett's indifference:

"What does it matter who is speaking?", the subject always standing as an obstacle, an impediment that will always distract from the discourse: in other words, a fiddling while psychoanalysis burns.

But, of course, I am preaching to the converted here, or at least I hope that I am. The history and the potentialities of psychoanalysis are manifestly disrupted, disfigured even, and the claim is that we are engaged in a pernicious self-mutilation. As I proposed, the terrain is occupied, but so are the conditions for analysis, indeed to analyse the manifest paucity of, to use Derrida's favourite word in the French language, "resistance" to all of this. The violence of the new vocabulary is so overwhelming, so insistent, that at times it seems impossible to think psychoanalysis differently. Psychoanalysis and its place as one of the chapters in the history of trance now appear to have become subject to a potentially fatal state of hypnotic seizure, a community mesmerized by registration. It exerts an extraordinary fascination, and more and more energy is jubilantly poured into chasing down increasingly complex systems of control and surveillance, the rationale for which, no doubt traced out in its myriad forms in other papers, is a moral condemnation mixed in with the holy alliance against abuse; abuse having become the micro-political fixation, while at a macro political level it is, of course, terror with so-called environmental disasters trailing in its wake . . . bird flu anyone? But this, at a conscious level, is on a par with an overwhelming but entirely unconscious desire to play a part in the mutilation of the superpower that psychoanalysis has become. Whatever the theoretical or formal allegiances, whatever the differences, psychoanalysis has become the same sort of people thinking the same sort of things. One is this imperative to register and the other is that it would be an impossibility to inaugurate or carry on a training that would not be handcuffed to a registering body, impossible not to have as a final destination the Holy Grail of eligibility for precisely this registration. And yet, this leads to such an orgy of disfiguring bureaucracy that it lends itself to the speculation that at some, no doubt disavowed, level, there is a secret delight in this uncontainable self-dispossession.

For psychoanalysis has become a superpower. Under the auspices of the ruling dictum of western individualism we are all subject to the demand that we know who we are, the assumption being, via the myth of interiority, that inside us all resides a truth, in part an unconscious truth, and that truth is sexual. It saturates our world and we are kidnapped by it. And, in order to track down this truth, the truth of our desire, which can only emerge in language, we have to listen; to listen to what we ourselves are saying, and, as an instance of the ubiquity of psychoanalysis, we need look no further than acknowledging that the notion of "the Freudian slip" is hardly talking shop. Of course, it would be absurd to suggest that psychoanalysis inaugurated this thinking. Foucault locates it as stemming from the Judeo-Christian confessional, when the ancient obligation of knowing oneself became the monastic call to "confess each of your thoughts". His claim is that this was the origin of the contemporary hermeneutics of the self, and that psychoanalysis is now the top-dog set within the confines of these concerns.

If we accept that psychoanalysis, as the dominant, indeed dominating, discourse, is in this position of a superpower, analogous to the symbolic place of the Twin Towers, then we can allow that this has become unbearable, and is in itself responsible for the violence that is endemic throughout our world (of course, I am limiting the term "our world" to the microcosm of the psychoanalytic community). Freud was entirely prescient with regard to such things: no one can avoid having destructive fantasies towards any power that has become hegemonic to such a degree. And violence and desecration are now what haunt the scene. The mild and truly pathetic version of this would be the spurious spites and spasms of the trade wars over who is entitled to call themselves what (pathetic not because Joe Public couldn't give a hoot, we are all shrinks in their book, but pathetic because it is so suffused with the self-aggrandizing self-interest of our wretched egos, always already pathetic, however much we are all entangled in just such considerations).

At times it may look as if "they" did it, as if it was always the others, but actually it is we who wished for it, and, seemingly, continue to do so. For, unless this is acknowledged, what is going on becomes almost accidental, a seemingly arbitrary act, or merely the murderous phantasmagoria of a handful of paranoid ego maniacs (the Pokornoys, the Deurzen-Smiths of our world) at the higher echelons of the UKCP, the BCP. But, of course, this is not an accurate reading of the situation; the contagion is everywhere. All are infected and to merely propose ignoring the emetic utterances from the cardinals of these regulatory bodies would be futile. We have to acknowledge its ubiquity, like that obscure object of desire; everywhere there is a lust for this catastrophic occupation. We cannot avoid recognizing a deep-seated complicity, a deep-seated but utterly disavowed collaboration, with regard to this self-mutilating desire for registration, although this is always already posited as elsewhere. What we are left with, fetishized, no doubt, are these computerizable lists and handbooks of practitioners. These representations have become our primal scene: everything stems from this, and everybody strains against the unbearable possibility of being left out. And they have utterly transformed the culture, as we bear testimony to an uninterrupted profusion of banality, a seamless flow of sham information (competencies? excellence? singularity?). And yet there is a curious ambiguity in all this. Identity and inclusion is now exalted, but, paradoxically, these lists, by taking identity and multiplying it to infinity, facilitates a diversification and a neutralization, all subject to the unforgiving law of equivalence. Our community of psychoanalysis consumes these lists, it absorbs them, is absorbed by them, and offers them up for consumption. And we sit back and watch as psychoanalysis eats itself up.

Any location of this passionate distaste, a hatred even, of the dominant ideology that psychoanalysis has become simply in those who elect to end up on the other side of a world order moves beyond the CBT merchants and the toxic psychiatrists. Nor can it be limited to that small cluster of supplicants who feel short-changed, disinherited, or exploited . . . and, of course, this can happen. Yet, despite the implications of transference, psychoanalysis is always an activity between consenting adults. Rather, we might glimpse that, amid those of us who so manifestly share in the advantages of this privileged enclosure that psychoanalysis has become, are some who are similarly, if unconsciously, implicated. We all have a malicious desire in our hearts. And, curiously, there is something on the side of health in all of this. For there is an almost inevitable ambivalence culminating in an allergic reaction to each and any dominant or definitive world order. And psychoanalysis takes its place as precisely this: a defining order. There can be no call for the suggestion of a death drive, or some destructive instinct. Nor can we claim that what is going on is the result of perverse but unintended intentions; after all, you will hear repeatedly from those who are utterly cognizant of the effects, "But what is so wrong with this way of proceeding?" Inexorably, and with an impeccable internal logic, the increase in the power of the definitive order will be co-existent with the desire to destroy, to disfigure it. They go hand in hand, and may be all the better for it, if it did not involve a setting up of these contaminating, regulatory, self-mutilating powers. Deconstruction is not to be conflated with a nihilistic desecration.

Psychoanalysis, far from being on its knees, is in the position of the Almighty, in the place of the big Other, taking up the situation vacant in our secular age, is in the place of God (and sees what an orgy of violence religion has brought forth). Psychoanalysis has become an Empire of the Good: the way, the truth. It proposes a narrative of divine omniscience, no doubt veiled by Freud's recourse to the "navel of the dream", that which will ultimately resist the closure of comprehension, the bit of the dream that we just do not get. Psychoanalysis (and remember Freud muttering to Jung and Ferenczi on the boat to America, "We are bringing them the Plague") was always deeply implicated in imperialistic tendencies. And now, as a way of thinking ourselves, it holds a monopoly to such an extent that it was only a matter of time before these impulses to reject, to do harm to such an all-powerful system would become manifest.

After all, we get so much from psychoanalysis. My earlier analysis of this narrative of compulsive collusion proposed that what we were witnessing was a hysterical flight from the "too much", the surplus enjoyment that is always on the side of a brimming over, that lies at the heart of the psychoanalytic tie . . . the greatest amount of fun you can have with another while still keeping your clothes on (well—football has its moments). Hysteria always proposes a substitute narrative, in this case one of these unrelenting calls for control and containment. And, while I am loath to let drop such possibilities entirely, it appears that something more insidious is in play. We find ourselves in a situation of considerable gratification, for all is potentially given to us, we are the privileged beneficiaries of the dominant discourse. And through this we are bound by a symbolic debt that, humiliatingly, is impossible to repay. To the "positive transference" (psychoanalysis never lets go, remember) there will be the inevitable response in the form of a "negative countertransference". In other words, a violent abreaction to this captive life, this privileged enclosure, to this saturation of our lives. It is a transferential or hypnotic effect or fall-out, in that we fall out with ourselves, because of the humiliation involved in being unable to extricate ourselves from these insistent and dominating certainties. Inevitably, this is denied, but, as we all know, what is denied runs wild. And this reversal, this turning upon ourselves, is via this grand confinement of regulation and registration. All of which has incontestably run amok. And so we play out (unconsciously) the impotent denial of our self-hatred and the unfaltering flow of disavowed remorse. Registration is the debased form of a counter-gift, in the forlorn hope that it might cash out as a sacrificial offering that might appease these virulent anxieties. The obscure object of our resentment, what we have come to detest in ourselves, is precisely this excess of power and comfort. This abuses us, forcing us into an abyss of despair, and so drives us to rage furiously against potential abuse. Always elusive, always elsewhere.

There have always been the two Freuds, always already in conflict: the one who wanted to get psychoanalysis recognized as a science; the one who craved respectability and set up conditions for training and inaugurated institutes. For this Enlightenment Freud, psychoanalysis was a form of expert knowledge about the workings and misworkings of the mind, with particular emphasis on the unconscious. The analyst was someone who knew how to go about providing the so-called patient with a cure for unhappiness, although to suggest any guarantee of this would engage in a particular fraudulence. The second Freud, which might be called the post-Freudian Freud, becomes an ironist of the Enlightenment project. Now there is a fuller recognition of the slipperiness of words, of the impossibility of a complete self-knowledge, of the impossibility of expertise. In other words, psychoanalysis came to embrace the idea that, in so many instances, people do not and cannot really know what they are doing or why they are doing it. And, inevitably, psychoanalysis itself cannot escape from this recognition. It is hardly a novel idea that this prompted the emergence of particular schools, the promotion of certain orthodoxies, and the unleashing of specialist vocabularies in order to shore up this faltering sense of failed expertise. The difficulty is that, by turning psychoanalysis into any kind of authority, something of the heart of the project, that psychoanalysis is fundamentally anti-authoritarian, gets catastrophically lost. After all, it is the task of any analyst to disabuse the so-called patient not only of the idea that this particular analyst is in any position to know the answers, but also of the idea that there were any answers in the first place. No master figure of authority to provide answers or to guarantee meaning; rather, to suggest that there are no guarantees at all. But the difficulty is that while we are engaging in the potential gratifications of self-congratulations, of how clever we are to have extricated ourselves from this claustrophobic set of demands, we have taken our eye off the ball.

While at the micro level of the consulting room we have, one hopes, successfully disrupted and dispersed the fiction of our authority, at a macro discursive level psychoanalysis, with its hallmark of the "Freudian subject", emphatically remains the "only game in town". Given this surplus of power, when no alternative form of thinking ourselves appears remotely possible (although with Foucault we can place our bets that one day something other will emerge), what other possibility is there but to turn on ourselves; to turn these regulatory insistencies on ourselves, tighter and tighter like an incorrigible tourniquet that inexorably drains the life blood out of the system. All this poses a seemingly insoluble challenge: if there appears no genuine possibility of thinking ourselves otherwise, then the inevitable and entirely predictable responses to this, inbuilt, as it were, at least as a structure, if not the explicit content, appear equally unsusceptible to exchange. For such as it is, in its absurdity and its self-loathing, it appears to be the verdict that this community has passed upon itself.

And it is not that I come with any answers, but it does seem unlikely that any single track counter-thinking, all united in some general historical action as a positive alternative, seems genuinely about to happen. Possibly all that can thwart the system is singularity, but not as an alternative, not as oppositional . . . merely taking up some other order, neither for better nor for worse. Somehow, it is not addressing a particular political reality as much as avoiding it. And that may be as good as it gets.

Reference

Strathern, M. (2000). The tyranny of transparency. *British Educational Research Journal, 26*(3): 309–321.

PART II

RESPONSES

CHAPTER SIX

How does "the state" regulate?

Leslie Chapman

The British Government is proposing to regulate the practice of psychotherapy through the Health Professions Council (HPC), an established regulatory body that already oversees the regulation of professions such as art therapy, biomedical science, and speech and language therapists. After a long period of debate, this proposal was announced in the White Paper *Trust, Assurance and Safety—The Regulation of Health Professionals in the 21st Century* (Department of Health, 2007), which lays out in some detail the government's plans for regulating a range of health professions, including psychotherapy and counselling. The main focus of the White Paper is on regulating general practice, but the principles appear to apply to other health professions.

The term "state regulation" is rather a misnomer, if it is taken to mean that there is an "external" entity ("the state") that "imposes" regulation on various professions and practices. Rather, I argue that psychotherapy is itself very much constitutive in the construction of the discourse of regulation, which I link closely to the idea of risk management. I refer to the White Paper as an example of risk-based regulation, which seems to be the preferred mode for regulating health professions. I conclude by looking at the possibility of challenging and deconstructing such a discourse through using a psychoanalytically informed theory of ideology.

In order to develop these arguments, I begin by examining the theory of the "psy-complex", a set of ideas developed mainly within sociology, and which helps to undermine the notion of a "monolithic state" that presides over and regulates society. The psy-complex is defined by David Ingleby as:

> . . . an ensemble of agencies, including clinical, educational, developmental and industrial psychology, psychotherapy, and social work, whose discourses are not confined to particular sites of professional intervention, but which traverse the family, school and work place—indeed, the "social" itself. [Ingleby, 1984, p. 43]

There are two characteristics common to all the psy-professions, and it is these characteristics that can perhaps best define the psy-complex as a whole: first, that all the psy-professions have a notion of the *psychological:* they define a domain of human existence as psychological, and thus the province of their own expertise. The second characteristic is that the psy-professions all attempt to regulate this psychological domain by various means: for example, through the use of psychotropic drugs, counselling, occupational therapy, and so on.

The governing of the soul

In a number of writings, Nikolas Rose analyses the growth of psychiatric and psychological discourse during the twentieth century (Rose, 1985, 1986, 1989). He argues that the spread of psychiatric and psychological ideas started quite early on in the century with the recognition among doctors and psychologists of the phenomenon of "shell shock" in the First World War. As this came to be seen as a psychological rather than an organic problem, this helped break the domination of organic psychiatry.

In the inter-war period, other "problem" populations also began to come under the psychiatric and psychological gaze: for example, maladjusted children in the 1920s. And, during this time, the notion of mental "illness" developed, which helped legitimate the formation of mental hospitals and clinics, such as the Tavistock, rather than asylums.

The outbreak of the Second World War helped to strengthen the power of psychiatry and psychology, as by this time the problems of "shell shock" and other psychological problems were being taken seriously. Both during and after the war, the psychological gaze spread into other areas of social life, e.g., industry, education, the family. The post-war period also saw the growth of psychiatric social work and clinical psychology. In essence, this gaze helped to effect the psychologization of life, in the sense that human relationships and social life became a set of psychological problems—with psychological solutions.

Rose argues that psychotherapy plays a key role in the psychologization of life, and identifies four key elements within its practice: a subjectification of work, whereby work and career are redefined in terms of a personal fulfilment and psychical identity; a psychologization of the mundane, whereby experiences such as marriage, divorce, childbirth, house-buying, etc., become a series of "life events" which can be approached within a framework of personal "coping" and "adjustment"; a therapeutics of finitude, whereby personal reactions to existential events such as death and tragedy are redefined in terms of pathology and normality and are seen as opportunities for personal growth; and a neuroticization of social intercourse, whereby social life becomes redefined in terms of "relationships"—both interpersonal and intrapsychic.

For Rose, the psy-complex is a network of control and regulation. However, unlike some Marxist/critical theorists, he rejects the idea that the psy-professions are simply instruments of state and capitalist control. Instead, he utilizes a Foucauldian concept of discursive practices, whereby the ideas, values, physical interventions—and even architecture—constitute both the work of a particular profession and the construction of its subjects.

The management of normality

De Swaan (1990) analyses the psy-complex through the lens of the management of normality, and, in particular, looks at the process by which human troubles become problems (which can then be "managed" by experts), and how this links to a process he describes as proto-professionalization.

The shift from troubles to problems is about a redefinition of human experience—what were once seen as everyday troubles of human existence are now seen as problems to be solved by professionals. This process is linked closely to the rise of the helping professions, and particularly to the rise of the psychologically informed professions—including psychotherapy. As De Swaan argues,

> The entire area of troubled modes of experience and interaction has become the working terrain of the fairly new profession of psychotherapy, and in circles of people who are closely related to it, laymen have begun to recognise their troubles as psychic problems, whereas they were previously accustomed to speaking of bad behaviour and evil moods, of sin and of illness, of deliriums and rage, of bewitchment or destiny, of the usual imperfections of human existence . . . [*ibid.*, p. 101]

Proto-professionalization is the process by which human experience becomes psychologized, and by which "lay people" incorporate the ideas of professionals—in this case psychotherapists—and start to redefine their everyday experiences in these terms. And the more people are proto-professionalized, the more likely they are to seek help from the relevant professional, which in turn strengthens both the profession's clientele and its influence on wider society.

It is interesting to note, particularly in the context of state regulation, that De Swaan considers psychotherapy to be an incomplete profession, in the sense that psychotherapists come from a variety of backgrounds, including well established professions, but have yet to succeed in establishing psychotherapy as a profession in its own right.

> . . . there is an occupational circle of psychotherapy, divided into various schools, which is professional in many respects but has not yet succeeded in closing itself off to the adjacent professions and struggles to guard its borders. The umpires in this conflict are the state's subsidizing agencies. [*ibid.*, p.105]

Psychotherapy and regulation

The examination of the psy-complex is a useful way of introducing a more fundamental point about the nature of the "state" and questions concerning regulation and control. As indicated earlier, Rose uses the idea of discursive practices to theorize the psy-complex, and, more specifically, to show how such practices construct and regulate their subjects (patients, clients, pupils, etc.). In order to develop this argument, he draws heavily on Foucault's concept of power, and I now briefly outline Foucault's key arguments, and how they can help redefine the whole notion of the "state" and "regulation".

The nature of power and regulation

The term "state regulation" appears to suggest that there is an entity called the "the state" that is preparing itself to regulate the practice of psychotherapy (along with other "emerging professions"). Often, this entity is described as if it were an Other, "external" to the professions that it wants to regulate and control. However, I would argue that this is based on misunderstanding regarding the nature of the "state". The "state" is not a monolithic "Other" that imposes itself on psychotherapy (or any other practice, for that matter). Rather, it is a complex network of institutions and practices that exercises power through acting on the actions of other actions, in order to modify them.

> The exercise of power is not simply a relationship between partners, individual or collective; it is a way in which certain actions modify others. Which is to say, of course, that something called Power, with or without a capital letter, which is assumed to exist universally in a concentrated or diffused form, does not exist. Power exists only when it is put into action, even if, of course, it is integrated into a disparate field of possibilities brought to bear upon permanent structures. [Foucault, 1982, p. 219]

In this view, power is about influencing or guiding the *conduct* of individuals. Foucault uses the term "government" to describe this process of influence—in its much broader, sixteenth-century meaning, when it referred to the way the conduct of individuals or groups might be directed. This included:

> . . . the government of children, of souls, of communities, of families, of the sick. It ("government") did not only cover the legitimately constituted forms of political or economic subjection, but also modes of action, more or less considered and calculated, which were destined to act upon the possibilities of action of other people. To govern, in this sense, is to structure the possible field of actions of others. [*ibid.*, p. 221]

This, in essence, is Rose's argument: the psy-complex is just such a process of influence, governing, in this instance, the souls of the population. Psychotherapy, as a discursive practice, "produces" governance and regulation through its actions. It constructs, governs, and regulates its subjects (patients/clients) through its practice. In this sense, psychotherapists could be seen as agents of "the state", even if they are in private practice.

However, psychotherapy, as a discursive practice, also governs and regulates *itself*. However, this is not in the normal sense of "self regulation", which still implies an "us and them" situation ("them" in this context being the "state", the "government", etc). Rather, it is more a case of psychotherapy evolving into a more complex network of power and governance relations (which could perhaps be described as a process of professionalization).

There has been a flurry of activity among the various organizations that offer support and guidance to psychotherapy, and, in many instances, act as accreditation and quasi-regulatory bodies in their own right. Such organizations include the UKCP, the BACP, and the British Psychoanalytic Council. Several of these organizations are expanding, and taking on new staff, and all are now involved in the debate on statutory regulation. Much of this activity seems to be in response to the anticipated statutory regulation—but ironically this activity is, in itself, helping to constitute the process of regulation. To understand why, we need to examine another important concept that is a recurrent theme in the White Paper: the idea of risk management, and, more specifically, risk based regulation.

Risk management and risk-based regulation

Power (2004) examines the rise of the phenomenon (and industry) of risk management. He defines risk management as a set of organizational practices for dealing with uncertainty, and that constitute part of a wider regime of organizational discipline and accountability.

Power acknowledges the notion of the "risk society", but is sceptical that this can be interpreted in terms of life being somehow riskier than it was in the past. Rather, it is the idea that a growing number of outcomes are amenable to human decision making and intervention, and, as a consequence, the public are increasingly looking to politicians and managers to make decisions regarding such interventions, and are also demanding greater accountability from such decision makers.

There are two significant themes connected to the emergence of risk management. The first is about communication with the public, and is linked to a growing sophistication in research on risk perception, with greater stakeholder involvement in risk management, and with a growing preoccupation with managing public expectations. Much of this concern is to do with what Power calls "secondary risk management", which is about protecting reputations. There is also a growing focus on managing the perceived legitimacy of regulatory activities and decisions.

The second theme is the emergence of risk-based regulation, and, as we shall see, this is a central principle of the White Paper. However, this is not simply a case of "the state" or "government" taking responsibility for the regulation of risk in various aspects of everyday life, for example in medicine or psychotherapy. Rather, risk-based regulation is about regulatory bodies harnessing existing private control activities, which alleviates such bodies from a great deal of responsibility: "regulatory organisations can be relieved of much of the economic and epistemic burden of detailed rule-making, and can focus on overseeing the design and functioning of local systems" (Power, 2004, p. 21).

In other words, much of the work of regulation is actually done by the profession or organization itself, through utilizing its own risk management or control processes. The role of the regulatory body is to ensure that agreed standards are defined, implemented, and adhered to. So, the more that organizations such as the UKCP and BACP develop and strengthen their own regulatory and control systems, the more they are facilitating the process of "statutory" regulation.

The sub-text of risk management is that politicians and managers accept that life is risky, and that things can go wrong. However, it is not necessarily expedient to publicly admit this, and therefore the focus shifts to devising systems and processes, often developed in consultation with external stakeholders, *that give the appearance* of taking risk seriously and being able to manage it. This is about managing expectations and protecting the reputations of the organizations involved in risk-creating activities.

The philosophy of risk management, and particularly its theme of risk-based regulation, features strongly in the White Paper. In his Introduction, the Chief Medical Officer begins by stating, "The primary purpose of professional regulation is to ensure patient safety" (Department of Health, 2007, p. 13). The Health Secretary, in her Foreword, begins by writing about the trust that patients have in health professionals. She also notes, "For any consideration of the regulation of health professions, the preservation of that trust has to be the starting point" (*ibid.*, p. 1). The substance of the White Paper is concerned with how to ensure that trust is maintained, through a framework of risk-based regulation, and covers such issues as: assuring the independence of professional regulators; ensuring fitness to practice; tackling concerns at both local and national levels; the role of regulatory bodies in education; and, of particular relevance to psychotherapy, the issue of emerging professions.

It is unclear how the HPC will work with the various "umbrella bodies", such as the UKCP and BACP. However, there are a number of indications in the White Paper that the Government intends to utilize as far as possible existing regulatory and control functions within the professions, employers, and local service commissioners. Examples include NHS clinical governance arrangements, and the use of existing disciplinary procedures within organizations. At the same time, it is clear that the government will be seeking to enhance and strengthen such arrangements where appropriate. Overall, though, the thrust of the proposals appear to be in line with the general principle of risk-based regulation; that is, that as far as possible existing regulatory and control functions are utilized, and the role of the regulatory agency is to set standards, support their implementation, and to ensure they are adhered to.

Deconstructing regulation and risk management

So far, I have been developing an argument that suggests that psychotherapy, far from being an unwilling "victim" of state regulation, is, in fact, an active participant in the process. The (emerging) profession of psychotherapy is deeply enmeshed within a complex set of ideas, institutions, and practices, which together constitute a complex network of control and regulation—one that is evolving and growing more complex all the time.

Where does this leave psychoanalysis? As far as it is considered to be part of the discourse of psychotherapy (a contentious issue in itself!), then it is part of the psy-complex, and thus part of the network of control and regulation referred to above. However, there is also another possibility: that psychoanalysis can be used *deconstruct* such a discourse, and particularly that aspect concerning regulation and risk management. One way to do this, I suggest, is to draw upon a set of psychoanalytic ideas that have been used to develop a critique of ideology. In the final part of this paper I briefly outline the key ideas of three authors, who are generally regarded as being the key "anchor points" for a psychoanalytic theory of ideology: Althusser, Laclau, and Žižek. I will then consider how these ideas could be used to help develop a critique of statutory regulation.

Althusser (2001) presented three theses about ideology. The first thesis is that ideology is a representation of the imaginary relationship of individuals to their real conditions of existence. The crucial point here is its rather subtle distinction from the Marxist "false consciousness" view of ideology, in which it is seen as a distorted representation of reality. For Althusser, there is nothing "distorting" or "imaginary" about the representation *itself*—rather, an imaginary relationship is represented *through* ideology. The second thesis is that ideology has a material existence. The argument here is that ideology exists in its practices; it is not a separate realm of ideas. This opens up the way for ideology to be linked to the theory of discourse and discursive practices. The third thesis is that ideology interpellates (or "hails") individuals as subjects. It is through the process of interpellation that individuals come to recognize themselves as subjects. The concept of interpellation is perhaps useful in understanding how the psy-discourses "hail" their subjects, and helps to explain how individuals come to "recognize" themselves as "psychological" subjects with "psychological" problems.

Laclau (1990) argues that it is through ideology that there is the attempt to "fix" (or hegemonize) meaning; it represents an attempt to construct an intelligible totality, and the notion of "society" is itself an attempt to "fix" such a meaning. All political systems, be they totalitarian or liberal democracies, attempt to create a stable totality, and all fail, because there is always an excess of meaning around the structure. Laclau also challenges the Marxist notion of ideology as "false consciousnesses". He argues that this notion is based on the idea of a fixed identity of the subject, and implies both a positive and non-contradictory concept of identity. However, this fixed identity cannot be sustained, because social agents are decentred subjects, and, thus, the notion of false consciousness becomes untenable because there is no "true consciousness" to start with.

For Žižek (1989), ideology is a social fantasy. It is not false consciousness of a "real" social existence; rather, social reality *is* the fantasy sustained through ideology. Another important aspect of ideology as fantasy, is what Žižek describes as its "inherent transgression" (Žižek, 1997, pp. 18–27). By this, he is referring to the "gap" between the symbolic fiction that we call "reality", and which includes laws, customs, etc., and the fantasy itself. Ideology "works" precisely because it points to something beyond itself, a trans-ideological kernel promising something beyond everyday reality.

How can such ideas be used as a basis for a critique of state regulation? A possible starting point is to regard the whole discourse of statutory regulation, which includes the discourse of the psy-complex, as an ideology—in the sense that this concept has be elaborated by Althusser, Laclau, Žižek, and others. In particular, I would suggest that statutory regulation, as a form of risk management, can be seen as a managerial and political fantasy (that is, ideology) of control, which masks a failure of control. As society becomes more and more complex and unmanageable, politicians and managers seek new myths and fantasies to reassure themselves—and the people they are (supposedly) governing—that they are still in control. Risk management is an example of this kind of fantasy. The rise of the "audit culture", which is closely linked to risk management, is another example. It is essentially an admission of failure by governments and managers; they can no longer govern, so instead they audit. This is an argument explored in greater detail by Cooper and Lousada (2005).

The ideology of risk management and risk-based regulation is an attempt to hegemonize, or "fix" a discourse (and legitimate a narrative) of management and control, which, like all other attempts at hegemony, ultimately is doomed to failure. It is an attempt to create the illusion that politicians and managers are able to operationalize, measure, and manage uncertainty by ensuring that risk is redefined in ways that *can* be operationalized, measured, and managed. Furthermore, this ideology is aimed not primarily at protecting patients/clients, but rather to manage expectations, and to ensure that the reputations of organizations involved in "risky" activities, whether as providers, commissioners, or regulators, are protected.

By way of a conclusion, I would like to suggest that psychoanalysis can be used to pose some very awkward questions about the nature of regulation and risk management. These would include: what is the anxiety that stands behind the desire for regulation and risk management? Is it about protecting in the interests of patients/clients, or is it more about protecting the reputations of psychotherapy organizations and individual practitioners? What is the nature of the fantasy (ideology) that constitutes the discourse of regulation and risk management in the face of an ever-growing *lack* of control? To what extent are psychotherapeutic bodies, including training institutions as well as "umbrella" and quasi-regulatory ones such as the UKCP and BACP, complicit in constructing this fantasy/ideology, and to what extent is this related to their own desires for greater recognition, "professionalism", and to be "in control"? And, finally, what are the contradictions in this fantasy/ideology?

References

Althusser, L. (2001). Ideology and ideological state apparatus (Notes towards an investigation). In: *Lenin and Philosophy and Other Essays*. New York: Monthly Review.

Cooper, A., & Lousada, J. (2005). *Borderline Welfare: Feeling and Fear of Feeling in Modern Welfare*. London: Karnac.

De Swaan, A. (1990). *The Management of Normality: Critical Essays in Health and Welfare*. London: Routledge.

Department of Health (2007). *Trust, Assurance and Safety—The Regulation of Health Professionals in the 21st Century*. London: Department of Health.

Foucault, M. (1982). The subject and power. In: P. Rabinow & H. Dreyfus, *Michel Foucault: Beyond Structuralism and Hermeneutics* (pp. 118–125. Brighton: Harvester.

Ingleby, D. (1984). The ambivalence of psychoanalysis. *Radical Science, 15*, 39–71.

Laclau, E. (1990). *New Reflections on the Revolution of Our Time*. London: Verso.

Power, M. (2004). *The Risk Management of Everything: Rethinking the Politics of Uncertainty*. London: Demos.

Rose, N. (1985). *The Psychological Complex*. London: Routledge & Kegan Paul.

Rose, N. (1986). The discipline of mental health. In: P. Miller & N. Rose (Eds.), *The Power of Psychiatry* (pp. 43–84). Cambridge: Polity.

Rose, N. (1989). *Governing the Soul*. London: Routledge.

Žižek, S. (1989). *The Sublime Object of Ideology*. London: Verso

Žižek, S. (1997). *The Plague of Fantasies*. London: Verso.

CHAPTER SEVEN

Psychoanalytic training in a culture of competencies[1]

Vivien Burgoyne

The United Kingdom Council for Psychotherapy (UKCP) is embracing the language of government and economics: now commonly used words such as "competencies", "consumer", "skills", "outcomes" are signifiers of state organization and intervention. These terms, which are used by government departments such as the Department of Health (DoH), are being taken up by some of the member organizations and individual members of the UKCP. The UKCP document, *Mapping of Standards of Proficiency Which Distinguishes Psychoanalytic Psychotherapy: Knowledge, Understanding and Skills*, uses these terms. Those who support the terms of this document argue that all this is necessary in order to lend to our profession an added legitimacy against rogue practitioners. In agreement with the DoH, it is argued that such standards would further protect the vulnerable patient or analysand. This involves a very delicate element in the work. It is claimed that drawing up lists of competencies, skills, and outcomes that trainees and clinicians must all adhere to would provide "accountability"—in the current jargon—to the consumer. When discussing these questions recently with individuals at a UKCP meeting, the name of Harold Shipman (the North of England doctor who murdered many of his patients) was frequently invoked as an example of the risks patients are left open to if we fail to reach agreement.[2]

It is worth considering some of the consequences of the push to prioritize a uniform agreement in the face of such complex issues. In a recent article (2007), Jacques-Alain Miller points out that, contrary to previous eras, we now live in a time where it is considered essential that scientific medicine is in absolute agreement with itself, and he links this demand to the increasing calls spreading across Europe for agreement to the regulation and quantification—not only of the psychotherapies and psychoanalysis, but also of other professions. Miller argues that registration is a concomitant of the "contemporary mode of the management of society", which reduces the subject merely to a number to be counted and ranked in a register (*ibid.*, p. 9). There are many arguments that are being made against the current moves towards registration, and it is not my intention to summarize them here. However, it is clearly important that those individuals who are seeking out a therapist or an analyst do have some way of verifying the practice of those whose help they seek, and I will return to this point later. I want to add a perspective that is both historical and political, and that has clinical implications. These thoughts come out of my reflections on having had three very different analyses, from having undertaken two trainings, and from having a long-standing clinical practice.

When I first found Lacan in the mid 1970s, psychoanalysis was just returning to the light of day having been analysed, criticized, and often dismissed by many feminists and intellectuals. Such critics found in the psychoanalysis of Freud and many of his followers who gathered within the International Psychoanalytical Association intentions, unconscious or otherwise, to normalize, control, and contain analysands and return them to an ideal of conformity as represented by the nuclear family. This critical analysis went hand-in-hand with an analysis of the structure of western societies and cultures as dominated by men and masculine forms of thought, which were often discussed in terms of a patriarchal order.

Some of these analyses contained arguments I agreed with. In the 1960s and 1970s, as now, much psychoanalysis was theoretically reliant on developmental and biological theories that were far from proven. Susan Isaacs, in her paper "The nature and function of phantasy" (1948), which continues to exert enormous influence since its first publication, had no hesitation in using induction as a methodology to develop her theories. She writes that "Unconscious phantasies are always inferred, not observed as such; indeed, the technique of psycho-analysis as a whole is largely based upon inferred knowledge" (*ibid.*, p. 74). She underpins this thesis, using inductive inference, from a theory of "genetic continuity" as an established fact rather than as theory:

> Experience has already proved that throughout every aspect of mental (and no less physical) development, whether in posture, locomotor and manipulative skill, in perception, imagination, language, or early logic any given phase develops by degrees out of preceding phases in a way which can be ascertained both in general outline and in specific detail. [*ibid.*, p. 77]

From this starting point, she argues that the "essence of Freud's theory of sexuality lies in just this fact of detailed continuity of development" (*ibid.*, p. 78).

It is perhaps worth reminding ourselves that not all psychologists agree with this position. Jerome Bruner, for example, questions the assumption that human behaviour lies in the biological substrate. He argues that "it is culture, not biology that shapes human life and the human mind . . . It does this by imposing the patterns inherent in the culture's symbolic systems" (quoted in Muller, 1990).

Susan Isaacs' position on methodology is utterly counter to Freud's, who uses a deductive methodology (though, here, the strength of Isaacs' work is that she does acknowledge her methodological position). Without going very far into this distinction, it is worth noting that, in "Instincts and their vicissitudes" (1915c), Freud clearly separates out the relation between biology and psyche by placing a gap between the two domains. He makes a distinction between the drive (*Trieb)* and instinct (*Instinkt)* and argues that the drive is "the psychical representative of the stimuli originating from within the organism and reaching the mind", and that it is "a measure of the demand made upon the mind for work in consequence of its connection with the body" (p. 122). In other words, the mind has to recast or reconstruct the order of bodily stimuli. Although at different times in his work, including in the paper I have just quoted, he clearly expresses a wish to find the relation between biology and the psyche, he does not rely on biological explanation to support his psychic theories. Such a separation allows him to use deductive reasoning in his theoretical formulations, which has very different implications from inductive thought. The consequences are far reaching, as Lacan would show.

Induction is still a dominant methodology in psychoanalytical theories and such theories simultaneously tend to leave out questions concerning the *subject* of psychoanalysis. In the 1970s and 1980s, I attended a number of seminars on the value of infant observation in psychoanalytic thinking, where it was said categorically that unconscious phantasies in the infant could be observed, and therefore validated by the observer. It was claimed, for example, that the incorporation of aggressive and hostile biting phantasies towards the mother could be directly perceived in the breast-feeding infant. The push towards statutory registration specifying competencies, which all trainings are supposed to comply with, falls into a similar trap. In itself, there is nothing new in certain sections in the field of psychoanalysis fighting against the diluting of the radical nature of psychoanalysis by those who want to rely on biological reductionism and an empirically generated basis of scientific practice. However, once more, these positions seem to have consolidated themselves and gathered renewed strength around the current political demands for a set of competencies.

When I first started training in the late 1970s, there was no consideration given to the particularity of the patient. Trainees were told not to engage with patients about the nature of the work and not to respond to questions during consultations. At that time the term "patient" was the fashion. There was also very little, if any, recourse to organizations that would disseminate information and enlighten would-be patients about psychotherapy or psychoanalysis as a means to address their suffering. As a trainee, I was advised by my supervisor not to reply when asked questions by patients about my qualifications or orientation, other than sometimes perhaps make some sort of grunt as an acknowledgement that the patient had spoken. According to this style of work, the one piece of information I might communicate was a request from the patient to free associate. At that time there was no Lacanian training in England, and so I had chosen the Guild of Psychotherapists, which was very encouraging of trainees forging their own path. I had at this time a very orthodox Kleinian analyst, who herself was in training with the Institute of Psychoanalysis. The Institute had allocated me to her. When I wanted to discuss some reservations I had about accepting that particular analyst, it was made very clear by the office that the only choice I had was to accept or reject her. Furthermore, I was told that if I chose to reject her I might have to wait a long time for another offer. I accepted, but the repercussions of that initial process continued throughout the analysis. This orthodox Kleinian analysis sat very uneasily with the supervision I had with a founder member of The Guild. Later, I went on to a very senior and wise "Independent" tradition psychoanalyst at the Institute; and, later still, I finally found a Lacanian analyst and supervisors in Paris, who conducted the work in English. These different analyses have stood me in very good stead in my practice. There is, however, a very great difference between clinical experience and theory, and this gap is one that, as clinicians, we need to struggle with.

The training I undertook at the Guild allowed me the freedom to find and struggle with my own path and in that sense the transference to the organization and to the individual "teachers" was very different to that found in many organizations. There was quite a visible lack of cohesion among the practices of the Guild members, who considered themselves to be individual craftsmen and women, which allowed different theoretical orientations to live side by side. The cost, however, was the side-stepping of any serious and rigorous comparison of positions. At that time I had just completed my first degree, in political philosophy, where we were taught to think comparatively about the different questions we were working with. We had to explore competing theories, examine closely their differences and similarities, their incompatibilities and antinomies, and think our way into the perspectives of those we disagreed with. This was not a comfortable experience. By the end of the first year I felt utterly disorientated, for all my previous ways of thinking about the world had been thrown in the air. Nowadays, degrees are mostly very different. They are not at all structured around the possibility of researching questions, but "modularized", and at the mercy of bureaucrats and administrative personnel, whose decisions are based not on questions concerning knowledge but on questions of finance and audit. The current logic is that soon there will be universities with no lecturers. Let us hope this is not the fate of psychoanalysis!

In England, in the training of clinicians, there has been a tradition of a single-theory approach. When confronted with irreconcilable theoretical differences, the solution found by the Institute of Psychoanalysis was to divide itself into three groupings.[3] Subsequently, when confronted with differences, there has been a long history of organizations splitting into separate sub-groups or even distinct organizations. From its foundation, the Guild attempted to structure into the organization a way of negotiating and managing difference, with much success; yet, when it comes to transmitting theory and clinical practice, it, too, has not been immune from difficulties. One of the main difficulties is that some trainees make a bet that it is possible to take a bit from this theory and a bit from that theory. The difficulty with such a pick-and-mix approach is that some parts of the mix may well be utterly incompatible with others; some of them may also have quite different consequences for clinical practices. Such a way of approaching theoretical questions often reinforces a combination of rivalry and fear. My experience of teaching Lacan is that when people feel threatened by what they find in Lacan, it is because Lacan's approach puts in question something at the level of unquestioning belief. There are, of course, others who disagree with Lacan, but who are willing and able to discuss their critique of his work.

In the past twenty-two years, the Centre for Freudian Analysis and Research has been at the forefront of generating a debate between organizations within the UKCP. However, we need to address the fear, distress, and even sense of personal risk that can irrupt when individuals find the basis of their orientation in their professional work, their lives, their psyche, undermined. This risk is very close to the kind of vulnerability that our analysands confront when undertaking an analysis. It seems to me that the rush in some quarters to embrace the requests of government for a "mapping of competencies" is a very likely indicator of some considerable anxiety. As we all know, it is extraordinarily difficult to find a way to verbalize such points in any group without merely inflaming the situation; added to that, the UKCP is now a large organization, which exacerbates the difficulty. So what are we to do? The "mapping of competencies" document, together with the push towards statutory registration, which appears to some to offer a strengthening of the position of the therapist, seems far more likely to generate a form of dependency or even enslavement to the politically led, dominant ideology of centralized mastery.

Recently, a very senior leader of an American multi-national body spoke gently against the Bush–Blair attempts to enforce so-called "western values" on Iraq and other parts of the world. He made the point that the recent period of "terrorist attacks" needed to be understood in a much broader historical context. He argued that history shows that "terrorism" becomes redundant when people involved discover that such large scale destruction and mayhem is not in their longer term interests—economically, socially, politically, and financially. This position allows both a historical perspective and, crucially, a subjective perspective, which introduces the possibility of dialogue. I am giving here a very quick and simplistic account of what he said. However, I want to emphasize that this man speaking on the radio, seemingly in common with other spokesmen from many multi-national companies, has recognized that change does not come about by way of the imposition of violence.

Centralized mastery can also appear as a very quiet form of violence—it is a way of gathering power in the hands of a few, of isolating people and of rendering them impotent. Centralized mastery threatens the very existence of psychoanalysis's most important discovery—that of the subject of psychoanalysis—and it smothers desire. Lacan's conception of the subject emphasizes what Freud identified as the contingent and the accidental elements that gives to any individual their particularity, if only we can negotiate and own them. No wonder there is a current fashion raging among many disciplines to find biological solutions to human difficulties: an obesity gene, an addiction gene, an antisocial gene, and so on.[4] Such a path to the solution can provide relief to a subject who feels at risk in the current political climate of thought (and thought police). A biological explanation for human behaviour absolves us from making any acknowledgement of the part we play in our own individual predicaments and suffering, a responsibility that Freud discovered *was* the human predicament. Although our political leaders would probably not recognize what I am saying, and may even be shocked by such an accusation, there seems to be an underlying wave of assumptions that threatens the very existence of the subject, as it constructs the mistaken ideal and belief that happiness, satisfaction, and comfort are the bases of "the good life".

We do need to find a way to retain the radical Freudian discovery of the unconscious—and that of the Lacanian subject—and to fight to retain our independence of thought and work. We have to do this because psychoanalysis is not in any way compatible with the ideological listing of "competencies". At the same time we also have to find a way to address more than just our allies. So, in all of this nonsense, there is something that needs to be considered; and I write "needs" with some care. There is something here that needs addressing in our trainings.

First, and it seems a small point, but clinically the ramifications are huge, analysands and would-be analysands have a right to know—if they wish—something about the work of their analysts during the process of choosing and deciding upon an analysis and an analyst. They need information, often hard to come by unless you are already moving in such circles. Second, the way in which the analyst responds has clinical consequences in relation to the development of the transference and will have a bearing on the strategy and the tactics of the analyst in the work of the analysis. Third, however problematic the questions of complaints and so on are, it is in the interests of psychoanalysis to think about ways in which psychoanalysis can be accountable not only to itself, but also beyond itself.

Arguments that are esoteric and only comprehensible within a field, and sometimes just within a particular theoretical orientation, fail both themselves and their chosen conceptual framework. It is no good saying to many non-Lacanians, and to those who know nothing much about psychoanalysis, that it is reasonable to expect from a psychoanalysis disappointment, frustration, and despair. Just as it is no good to underplay the benefits of psychoanalysis, it is no good to overplay them either—rather, we need to tread the tricky line between the two. Psychoanalysis can, and frequently does, improve our quality of life. So, how may we present to our colleagues, would-be analysands, and, particularly, the general public, the "impossibility" of giving a guarantee of outcome—which was the very first point that my first supervisor emphatically made to me—while at the same time being able to show that psychoanalysis could benefit many? Accountability is generated by a good knowledge of the range and field of psychoanalysis, and not just by the comfort of being able to speak merely within the logic of one theory. Comparative thinking can introduce something more akin to a Socratic dialogue.

So, we are back to the value of comparative thinking, and it is in the light of the foregoing argument that we should not be so shocked by the currently proposed suggestions for training. The current language that the UKCP uses to formulate its proposals, as many have pointed out, entails attempts to reconstruct questioning and research in terms of already given answers. But can we not change that? The "mapping standards" document proposes comparative research and questioning. If this position is taken seriously, it leads in the direction of enabling the individual practitioner to find their own answers to their own questions, which in turn would facilitate a capacity to speak about psychoanalysis in a way that could be grasped outside of the practitioner's small orbit. As I have already said, comparative thinking is not the equivalent of a simple pick-and-mix approach. It requires us to be willing to put in question our most closely held beliefs. In *Seminar I*, Lacan emphasizes the importance of the analyst recognizing that how, what, and when we speak can produce changes in the analysand:

> The ideal of analysis is not complete self mastery, the absence of passion. It is to render the subject capable of sustaining the analytic dialogue, to speak neither too early, nor too late. Such is the aim of a training analysis [Lacan, 1988, p. 3]

It is crucial that we attempt to sustain a dialogue with other psychoanalytic traditions and retain our passion, because otherwise we cannot develop our work, and because otherwise psychoanalysis itself will wither and disappear.

Notes

1. This chapter is the written version of a talk given at Centre for Freudian Analysis and Research in September 2006. It was a contribution to a round table discussion with members, trainees, and other participants.

2. Recently, I was told by a senior nurse manager that it is increasingly common for trainer-nurses supervising student nurses to forbid them from any hands-on contact with the patient, and to restrict their participation in the clinical part of the training to observation alone. This is because trainer-nurses can now be held accountable for the mistakes made by their trainees, which, if taken to the extreme, could mean that in the situation of a court case, they could be sued for the trainee's misdemeanours.
3. Susan Isaacs' paper was one of the papers initially given during the "controversial discussions" of the British Psychoanalytical Society, and which ended with a "gentlemen's agreement" that resulted in the division of the society, at first into two, and later on into three, groupings. For a brief, but clear account see Kohon (1986).
4. Dr James LeFanu, a medical doctor and a journalist for the *Sunday Telegraph,* is extremely critical of the high news profile given to gene research in the hope of cures to a vast array of known medical conditions. He says,

> there is every reason to suppose that susceptibility to illnesses such as diabetes or arthritis should run in families, just like red hair or blue eyes. But they are clearly not inherited diseases, and the search for their genetic "cause" within the context of that insoluble riddle, is a hopeless enterprise. Put another way, there must be a reason why one person gets diabetes and another arthritis, and it will be very important to find out what that might be. But the answer does not lie in the genes. [LeFanu, 2007, p. 18]

References

Freud, S. (1915c). Instincts and their vicissitudes. *S.E., 14*: 109–140. London: Hogarth.

Isaacs, S. (1948). The nature and function of phantasy. *International Journal of Psycho-Analysis, 29*(2): 73–97.

Kohon, G. (1986). *The British School of Psychoanalysis: The Independent Tradition*. London: Free Association.

LeFanu, J. (2007). We don't understand our genes. *Sunday Telegraph,* 10 June.

Lacan, J. (1988). *The Seminar of Jacques Lacan: Book I, Freud's Papers on Technique 1953–1954* (notes by J. Forrester, Trans.). New York: W. W. Norton.

Miller, J.-A. (2007). The era of the man without qualities. *Psychoanalytical Notebooks, 16*: 7–42.

Muller, J. (1990). *Acts of Meaning*. Cambridge, MA: Harvard University Press.

CHAPTER EIGHT

Of teaching and the university discourse

Lorenzo Chiesa

In his closing paper to the 1970 congress of the École freudienne de Paris (EFP), dedicated to teaching, Lacan proposes that the aim of teaching is not "to convey knowledge", as we normally assume, even when we "contest" the existing methods of teaching (Lacan, 1971, p. 206). According to Lacan, teaching "bars" knowledge (*ibid.*); knowledge is already present before any form of teaching is established. In other words, knowledge is the unconscious that knows without us knowing that *it* knows; teaching is generally nothing but an imaginary barrier: teaching teaches us how *not* to know. As Lacan himself specifies in a convoluted way in the written version of the same paper, entitled "Allocution sur l'enseignement",[1] "Le savoir est chose au monde plus répandue que l'enseignement ne se l'*imagine*' ("Knowledge is something more extended than teaching could ever *imagine* it to be") (Lacan, 2001a, p. 298, my emphasis). This is the reason why teaching is an imaginary "obstacle" to the possibility of "knowing what we are saying" (*ibid.*).

If knowledge is *not* the transmission of knowledge, how should we then account for this apparent transmission? For Lacan, the everyday relation between teachers and those-who-are-taught, like that between a lover and a beloved, is not a transitive one. Indeed, it does not express a direct object (teaching). In general, there is no such thing as a transitive action, or relation. At best, the transmission of knowledge is a "transitional action" in which there is "reciprocity" (Lacan, 1971, p. 207). Reciprocity excludes transitivity in order to allow transit: that which is in transit is not an object. The transmission of knowledge is not the passage of knowledge between two discrete human beings, but one possible way in which they mutually superimpose their imaginary alienation in the other.

Having said this, Lacan nevertheless suggests that one *can* actually be taught. One cannot be taught by an alleged transmission of knowledge, yet one can be taught by "a lot of different things", Lacan says, such as "gestures" and "acts" (*ibid.*, p. 208). Put differently, one can be taught by the signifiers of the formations of the unconscious, which do not necessarily have to be vocalized; "Je ne peux être enseigné qu'à la mesure de mon savoir" ("I can only be taught commensurately with my [unconscious] knowledge") (Lacan, 2001a, p. 299). At this stage, Lacan even acknowledges that maybe "teaching could be put to a different use" (Lacan, 1971, p. 206): this would be possible only in so far as we identify the teaching subject with the very division of the subject, the fact that he is split between statement and enunciation. "I'm not saying wherever one finds $ there is a teacher, but it's only *there* that there can be one" (*ibid.*, p. 210). In other words, teaching necessarily presupposes the barred subject, yet the barred subject does not necessarily entail the possibility of teaching. It all depends on which structural position the function $ occupies in a given discourse (Lacan, 2001a, p. 300).

For instance, in the university discourse, the function $ occupies the position of production and cannot teach anything. To cut a long story short, the function $, the division of the subject, cannot teach in the university discourse because it is isolated, unable to actively relate to all the other functions, or, as Lacan succinctly has it, "the machine has jammed" (Lacan, 1971, p. 211). Most importantly, the machine that has jammed is the very machine that aims at producing surplus knowledge. In the university discourse, "everything circulates in [one] direction" (*ibid.*), Lacan says, that of the alleged transmission of knowledge between S2 ("scientific–expert knowledge") (Žižek, 1997–2006) in the position of the agent and *a*, the *astudés*, students reduced to "obligation" and "stupidity" (Lacan 1971, p. 211), in the position of the other that works. Thus, Lacan is able obliquely to suggest that a different, non-unidirectional use of teaching is one that necessarily does not "serve" the university discourse, which in its turn "protects" bourgeois capitalist society (*ibid.*, p. 206). (As Lacan affirms elsewhere, the accumulation of knowledge is a precondition for the accumulation of value.)

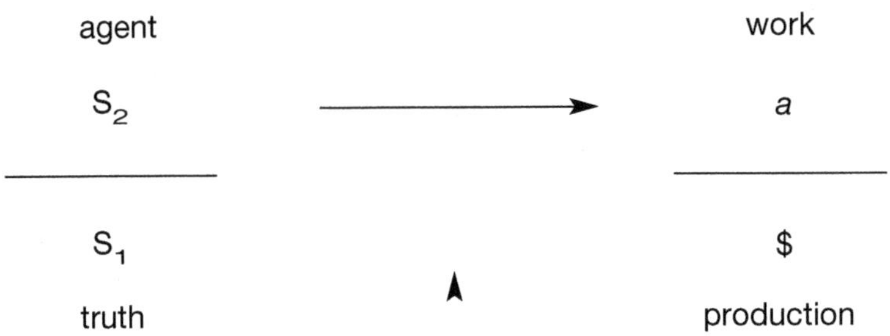

Let's take a step back. I believe that the most crucial question of Lacan's paper, which he explicitly formulates, is: "How should we behave with regard to knowledge when we put ourselves in the position of the teacher?" (*ibid.* p. 208). Two of Jacques-Alain Miller's seminal papers on Lacan's specific approach to teaching, "Topology in the teaching of Lacan" and "Teachings of the case presentation", seem to be tackling precisely this issue. In "Topology in the teaching of Lacan", Miller argues that "topology cannot be taken out of Lacan's teaching" (Miller, 1999a, p. 79). This statement should be understood in two overlapping ways: first, topology as used by Lacan is not an independent discipline.

> [Lacanian] topology can be useful only if it is merged with his teaching. It is not a discipline *sui generis*. We cannot have specialists in Lacanian topology who would consider it as the *Innenwelt* of an *Umwelt* which would be the whole set of his teachings. [*ibid.* pp. 83–84]

In other words, topology is not a special knowledge that would provide us with a *clavis universalis* able to solve all the riddles of Lacanian theory and practice.

Second, and most importantly, one cannot speak of a Lacanian teaching without including in it its topological component. Hence, according to Miller, Lacan's teaching is *per se* intrinsically topological; teaching and topology is one and the same thing in Lacan's work. More precisely, this means that teaching has necessarily to do with what Miller himself names "internal exclusion", the "paradox [of] a point that is at the same time central and exterior" (*ibid.*, pp. 81–82). This topological point, the position that must be occupied in order to make teaching possible, is, as in Lacan's 1971 paper, none other than $, the very division of the subject caused by the fact that he is a speaking being. As Miller has it, "topology is introduced with the signifier"; conversely, one can formalize the subject of the signifier, "a subject without substance", only in so far as one elaborates a topology (*ibid.*, pp. 85–87).

"How should we behave with regard to knowledge when we put ourselves in the position of the teacher?" If Miller's first article explores the paradoxically extimate position of teaching as such, its *a priori* topological status, the second article, "Teachings of the case presentation", examines the relationship between the extimate position of the teacher and the knowledge supposedly transmitted and accumulated by the university discourse. Why did Lacan not abstain from the old-fashioned psychiatric practice of presenting psychotic patients to his students? Miller's answer is straightforward: because he deemed this teaching, the presentation, to be profoundly subversive with regard to the psychiatric establishment. This teaching was subversive thanks to what we could approximately define as its topological structure: it undermined the psychiatric establishment from *within* since it was internally excluded *in* it. "To repudiate and negate [the psychiatric *doxa*] pure and simple, amounts to simply disavowing it and being even more under its dominion. One needs to be more astute" (Miller, 1999b, p. 157).

In other words, Lacan did not repeat the mistake made by the anti-psychiatric movement for which anti-institutionalization was the ultimate aim. What the imaginary logic of anti-institutionalization really intended to achieve by means of a "psychotisation of society" was ultimately a "psychiatrisation of society", Miller says (*ibid.*, p. 160). The anti-institutional teaching of the likes of Laing relied on an imaginary identification with the psychotic that tacitly presupposed the preservation of the very binary logic of psychiatric exclusion, the replacement of the customary attempt to adapt madness to society with the attempt to adapt society to madness (*ibid.*).

In opposition to this, Lacan's presentation of patients remained "essentially dependent on the university discourse", Miller argues, but only in order to demonstrate that the teaching obtained by presenting patients was rather the teaching *of* the patients, that which the patients themselves taught (*ibid.*, pp. 158, 164).

What does a psychotic teach? He teaches us that "he is caught in language, like us, or even more than us" (*ibid.*). The psychotic is $ like us but more evidently than us. This is why, according to Miller's account, after having diagnosed an unproblematic case of, say, paraphrenia, Lacan was able to exclaim, "But he is perfectly normal!" (*ibid.*, p. 156). In doing so, Lacan turned an unambiguous classical diagnosis into a suspension of meaning that, for his perplexed students, inevitably underlay the following open question: "How is it possible not to be mad?" (*ibid.*, p. 163). This is the teaching *of* psychotic patients. How is it that so-called "normal" people do not realize that they are split, $, and consequently spoken by the Other? Most importantly, this teaching is made possible only by the fact that Lacan asks his patients to produce their knowledge—which is all they know, Miller specifies—in the very place where the academic knowledge of psychiatry is usually transmitted and accumulated.

If the presentation of patients can teach us something *thanks to* the fact that it depends essentially on the university discourse, according to Miller, "this perfectly proves that it is not enough to shut up and listen in order instantly to enter the analytic discourse" (*ibid.*, p. 158). Put differently, entering the analytic discourse—in which, as Lacan claims in his 1971 paper, "the teacher is the psychoanalysand" as $ and the analyst teaches only in so far as "he finds himself in the position of the psychoanalysand" (Lacan, 1971, pp. 213–214)—is far from implying a sudden desertion from the university discourse in which $ can still teach in a number of different ways, for instance by means of the presentation of patients. Psychoanalytic teaching should not be anti-institutional. If we bear in mind that the university discourse is, for Lacan, the contemporary embodiment of the discourse of the Master, or, better, its distortion, this amounts to saying that psychoanalytic teaching is not diametrically opposed to the ruling discourse of the existing state. Psychoanalysis can subversively teach from within the institutions of the academic–bureaucratic state, the "jammed" Master that relies on a "knowledge [the function S2 in the position of the agent] whose truth [occupied by the function S1] is to preserve forever in an unyielding way the signifier of the master as such" (*ibid.*, p. 212).[2]

The isolation of $ in the university discourse is the other side of the (hypothetically endless) preservation of the Master, S1, in the position of truth. Yet $ is, after all, not completely silenced. A Lacanian academic should let $ speak by relating to the general university discourse in the same topological way as Lacan himself related to traditional psychiatry. Against the background of the specifically psychiatric case of the presentation of patients, we should ask ourselves the following question: in what ways can $ teach within the academic discourse, the discourse of the bureaucratic state that is "jammed"? I would suggest that one can put forward at least three complementary hypotheses:

1. $ teaches whenever a teacher teaches the dis-accumulation of knowledge, or, to put it with Dany Nobus, whenever one "teach[es] students how to treat knowledge acquisition as a process 'in failure'". Having said this, I am far from convinced that we have so far been able to identify concrete strategies to follow this path.
2. $ teaches whenever the teacher experiences the psychoanalytic effects inherent in teaching. As Jean Oury suggests in one of the debates that took place during the 1970 congress of the EFP,

    > exposing oneself to teaching produces analytical effects on the teacher [in as much as] having to explain something to a difficult audience [Oury refers here to Vincennes] can have an effect of diffraction that can make appear the very mechanics of enunciation.[3]

    Lacan openly subscribes to Oury's point. Bluntly put, whenever my students do not understand what I am teaching, especially if they do not understand what I take for granted in my knowledge and its alleged transmission, and I understand that they do not understand it, the subject of enunciation obfuscates temporarily the subject of the statement. On these occasions, far less frequent outside of academia, one talks to a brick wall and hears one's own voice speaking.
3. $ teaches whenever we practise what Lacan names anti-philosophy.

In the remaining part of this paper I would like to focus on this last point. In order to argue in favour of the possibility of an *anti*-anti-institutional psychoanalytic teaching I have so far availed myself of Miller's interpretation of Lacan. At this stage, I intend to suggest that in the 1975 short text "Peut-être à Vincennes" Lacan himself comes to a similar conclusion, and thus overcomes his 1971 paper according to which teaching and the university discourse were *de facto* incompatible. In his 1975 article, Lacan does not limit himself to outlining the four disciplines (linguistics, logic, topology, and antiphilosophy) that should be taught at Vincennes as a propaedeutics to the formation of the analyst. He rather goes as far as emphasizing the fact that the psychoanalytic "experience" should give these "sciences" a chance to "renew themselves". "What this is all about is not only helping the analyst by means of the sciences disseminated in [the university], but that these sciences may find . . . an occasion to renew themselves" (Lacan, 2001b, p. 313). The university discourse is not meant to be superseded by the analytic discourse; the latter does not simply establish itself to the detriment of the former. In other words, thanks to the contribution of psychoanalysis, linguistics, logic, topology, and antiphilosophy should be able to destabilize *and* renew the university from within.[4]

We should now make an important specification: if linguistics, logic, and topology are the three traditional disciplines that should be preserved only after having been renewed,[5] antiphilosophy is rather the discipline that offers itself as the very method of renovation. What is antiphilosophy for Lacan? Certainly, it is not what philosopher Alain Badiou claims it is; according to him, antiphilosophy means a "hostility to philosophy" that ultimately privileges a "silent, supra-cognitive or mystical intuition" (Hallward, 2000). Neither is antiphilosophy simply a catalogue of the imbecilities inherent to the history of ideas. True, in "Peut-être à Vincennes", Lacan refers explicitly to both imbecility and the history of ideas, but he articulates their relation in a much more refined manner. Antiphilosophy is strictly related to *teaching*. Initially, antiphilosophy is the "patient inventory" [*recueil*], Lacan says, of the imbecilities that the university discourse "owes to its *supposition educative*", its alleged ability to transmit knowledge. It is only at a second stage that such an inventory will make it possible to uncover the "eternal dream" on which the history of ideas relies, the belief in the possibility of accumulating knowledge (Lacan, 2001b, pp. 314–315).

To conclude, I propose to start such an antiphilosophical inventory by looking at some of the imbecilities that the educational assumption of the university discourse intends to transmit with regard to the notion of plagiarism.

> Paraphrasing means putting another person's ideas into your own words. The best way to do this is to make notes from the original by writing a few words or phrases, then making your own sentences. Unfortunately it is sometimes extremely difficult to write a sentence which is significantly different from the original. In that case, you can use several of the following strategies; using just one could still lead to plagiarism. Vocabulary: change individual words using synonyms (a thesaurus and dictionary can help) (NB. you may not be able to change terminology which is very specific); change nouns into verbs; change adjectives into adverbs. Sentence structure: change active sentences into passive sentences; change the order of the subjects in sentences with several clauses; change sentence length by joining or splitting ideas.

Our first reaction upon reading these official university guidelines could well be that of the friend courtesy of whom I entered into possession of this material: "Fantastic logic! Guys, here is a mechanism not to think (a kind of micro-handbook for academic fraud), but if you don't follow it fully, we'll fail you!" On the other hand, we may add, if you do comply fully with these guidelines, at the end of your academic education you will be able to sign the following declaration: "This doctoral thesis is my own work and contains no material that has been used before in any other degree".

Having said this, is it not possible to investigate this logic further by means of what Lacan, precisely in his text "Allocution sur l'enseignement" (2001a), defines as *la distance du pastiche au plagiat* (*ibid.*, p. 304)? Is it not the case that today's academia encourages pastiche, that is, paraphrasing according to the writing "styles" established by university regulations, in order to defend itself against the re-emergence of the structural truth of its discourse, i.e., plagiarism? Plagiarism intimately informs the university discourse, and, as Lacan points out, is "closed to any other [discourse]" (*ibid.*). It is only for the university discourse that knowledge is the master who will always be the *same* master. If only the transmission of knowledge were really possible, "a knowledge whose truth is to preserve forever in an unyielding way the signifier of the master as such", the ultimate paper jam, this would amount to nothing else than plagiarism.[5] Lacan sensed this paradox as early as his first 1931 academic paper; in a footnote that reads as a sort of abridged antiphilosophical manifesto, he states the following: "To avoid the charge of plagiarism we should really acknowledge our teacher Clérambault as the source of every expression we use" (Roudinesco, 1997, p. 25).

Notes

1. The written version substantially differs from the original paper (see Lacan, 2001a).
2. More specifically, Lacan affirms that his psychoanalytic School, the École freudienne de Paris, should be understood as "a hole with respect to the institution" (1971, p. 216).
3. See "Intervention sur l'exposé de M. Montrelay et F. Baudry: Sur l'enseignement de la psychanalyse à Vincennes", at www.ecole-lacanienne.net/pastoutlacan70.php
4. It is nevertheless important to emphasize that, starting with its title, "Peut-être à Vincennes" is written in the conditional mode.
5. Conversely, it is precisely because the (transitive) transmission of knowledge is not possible that Lacan is able to repeatedly maintain that "there is no property of ideas" and plagiarism does not exist (see for example, Seminar XIII, "L'objet de la psychanalyse", 1965–1966, unpublished, lessons of 23/03/1966 and 30/03/1966).

References

Hallward, P. (2000). Ethics without others: a reply to Critchley on Badiou's *Ethics*. *Radical Philosophy*, *102*, July/August: 27–30.

Lacan, J. (1971). En guise de conclusión. In: *Lettres de l'École freudienne*, no. 8. www.ecole-lacanienne.net/pastoutlacan70.php

Lacan, J. (2001a). Allocution sur l'enseignement. In: *Autres écrits* (pp. 297–305). Paris: Seuil.

Lacan, J. (2001b). Peut-être à Vincennes. In: *Autres écrits* (pp. 313–315. Paris: Seuil.

Miller, J.-A. (1999a). La topología en la enseñanza de Lacan. In: *Matemas I*. Buenos Aires: Manantial.

Miller, J.-A. (1999b). Enseñanzas de la presentación de enfermos. In: *Matemas I*. Buenos Aires: Manantial.

Roudinesco, E. (1997). *Jacques Lacan*. New York: Columbia University Press.

Žižek, S. (1997–2006). Jacques Lacan's four discourses. www.lacan.com/zizfour.htm

CHAPTER NINE

Regulation or ethics as the basis of psychoanalytic training

Del Loewenthal

Jean Laplanche speaks of starting a session with a young person with the words: "... your parents want this, but we don't care, we will talk of other things, of whatever you want" (1992, p. 6). I am taking this to represent a place where psychoanalysts work—in areas that our society does not want to think about. So, the work of therapy and therapeutic organizations involves holding a paradox. But then what happens to this space if the state wants to regulate it? There again, when are psychoanalysts and their organizations helpfully protecting the necessary space to carry out the work from external attack—and when are those arguments more about the ontological preceding the ethical? Furthermore, are self-regulating professions necessarily a better alternative? How can we determine what is best?

Should psychoanalysts place themselves more with sex workers, photographers, or freemasons, or should they attempt a more respectable authorization as with doctors, psychologists, and academics. Which group stands most chance of being ethical practitioners? How can one decide? Which side of the rim, if any, should we be playing from? Now Laplanche argues that "... psychoanalysis has to put all socially adapted aims—that is the whole notion of self preservation—in brackets. This is why it can never be a profession" (*ibid.*). He says one of the great problems is subjection to an external law; but would it be useful, indeed possible, if psychoanalysts were subject to ethics as an attempt to put the patient first. This might be inferred from the French philosopher Emmanuel Levinas' ethics of the relational (Levinas, 1969; Loewenthal & Snell, 2003, pp. 150–160). Is there a difference about being subject to an external law enforced by the state and subject to a form of ethical practice where one puts the other first? If our very being, the state, our own theoretical orientation and/or club membership can all get in the way of truth and justice in the moment with one's patients, how can we put the other first, (assuming we want to)? Ethical codes, whether from statutory or regulatory bodies would, by definition, be putting these first; but, in arguing against statutory regulation, is there also the danger that psychoanalysts are really putting themselves first in the name of their patients?

In the UK, the White Paper "Trust, assurance and safety—the regulation of health professionals in the 21st century" (Department of Health, 2007) includes psychotherapy, counselling, and counselling psychology in what is taken to be an attempt to provide greater protection to the public (at the time of writing it is not clear whether in this context psychoanalysis is considered part of psychotherapy). Perhaps there are characteristics of psychotherapeutic organizations which are more similar to trade associations, leading to practices that this White Paper, when implemented, should deter. There are many different responses, though, to regulation: for some therapists, being identified as a health professional is seen as giving them a status they deserve, yet, for others, any notion of a medical model defeats the purpose of the therapy. Postle (2007), for example, questions whether one can legislate for the humanity required in therapy. But can psychotherapists otherwise be trusted to be subject to their patients' interests before their own?

The place of the state in our work raises many questions about the creation of new forms of abuse; including what could be seen as psychotherapy's role in protecting the public through being essentially subversive. An example of this is apparent in training programmes in my own university, where a sense of community is increasingly at odds with the consumerist culture of education. It would appear that consumerist relations replace what were once considered human relations—we are more likely to respond to our students, as indeed our clients/patients, in a way that protects ourselves from litigation and may enhance our business in some senses, but deprives our students/patients/clients of the good that can emerge from the relational where the teacher/therapist/community feel a responsibility for the students'/patients'/others' responsibility.

So, the place taken up by therapists and their teachers might be considered abusive in terms of the teachers'/therapists' compliance to the dominant discourse. Also, will the attempt, through the White Paper, to find commonality in trainings prevent the ability for therapists to create a space where thoughts and feelings can be explored without censorship from a form of state control? There are many questions: who determines whether the training of therapists meets the need of the population(s)?; when is the course culture (regarding both what is learnt and how) something for the broader society to aspire to?; and who decides this? Yet, are "market forces" not another form of state control? When is a therapy oppressive and when is it liberating? How does what we offer fit the different perspectives of our culture, and should it? When do we successfully adapt to what is good and when do we successfully resist the bad—and how do we decide what is good and what is bad?

These issues are complex, involving, for example, not only the very nature of the therapeutic endeavour, but questions of identity for therapeutic communities, as well as larger dominant and minority communities, and questions of individual and collective identity (Hofstede, 2001) that post-modernism has thrown some light on—even though it may initially cause more disturbance. A visit to New Zealand raised these questions in terms of post-colonialism; whether it be Pakeha (European), Maori, Samoan, or Asian, there is no simple way out—which language does one use? Which experience does one privilege? Will wherever one comes from lead to some form of cultural domination? Perhaps such questions are becoming increasingly problematic for all of us in the so-called global village, with its apparent opportunities and problematics, but should we consider more where we are coming from, and where we are attempting to project our own anxieties about anxiety into abuses that might be protecting the public against professional violence but could be doing the complete reverse? One implication from Levinas is that we consider such issues through psychoanalysis as a practice of ethics, such that ethics as practice is not extraneous to psychoanalytic practice or theory.

While we may well abuse our patients far more through our theories than the potential exploitations that are more usually referred to, I do also want to speak of those notions of abuse that our society seems, often inappropriately, preoccupied with. Though, there are some occasions when the response from professional bodies might inflame such preoccupations. In my experience as, previously, an executive member of a national umbrella organization, I have met many people whom I enjoyed being with, but I increasingly felt I was part of an organization that had been set up with the purpose of being institutionally unethical. For example, an unpleasant experience occurred when hearing about a patient who had spent considerable time and effort getting her case heard, but when it finally got to the executive board the therapist resigned from the umbrella organization and was able to continue as a therapist in his member organization, which has the umbrella organization on its headed notepaper. There again, another national training organization printed the photograph of someone who, on her first day as a trainee therapist, said the wrong thing, admitted to this, and I think became a scapegoat for the members of that organization. However, these organizations are trying to change and it is, of course, possible for member organizations to have rules whereby a member cannot resign when a case is pending and that to be removed from the register of the umbrella organization would mean removal from the member organization. But if one has such rules, who creates and enforces them? And when can engaging in such activity be to defend psychoanalysis and when are we inappropriately using this to defend ourselves? There again, how, if at all, should we be organizationally concerned about ethics? It could be argued that we no longer expect multi-nationals, for example, tobacco companies, to protect the public, so why should anyone expect this from psychoanalytic companies?

Well, despite Laplanche's advice, there is a professionalization process, rather than heteronomy, gathering momentum in the therapies. This professionalization process might be linked to notions of autonomy—originally the right to prescribe but perhaps more not to be prescribed to, not to be subject to. Of course, psychoanalysts, through their trainings in such autonomy, like others, can become more abusive. For example, what Letiche (1990) suggests in "Five postmodern aphorisms for trainers" (Letiche, 1990, p.230, based on Baudrillard, 1990) might be adapted for the training of therapists:

1. "An examination of what is said reveals the banality of the text" (even though messages may seem to be communicated). "Anything can be aesthetic, can belong to a look; nothing really means ... In a society lacking in proscriptive authority, these aesthetic signs of authority however empty they may be, will be grabbed and exploited for all they are worth" (Letiche, 1990, pp. 230–231). To what extent is this happening with therapeutic labels where, for example, some counsellors now call themselves psychotherapists and some psychotherapists call themselves psychoanalysts?
2. Choice is at very best half choice: "... if the system breaks down and people really try to choose, violence surfaces". Can psychoanalysis resist both the pressure to provide therapy as a means of social control and the pressure to cease really offering psychoanalysis where it increases individual and group awareness of people's pain and suffering?
3. By improving the interaction with patients, one lessens the level of individual action. One imprisons the patient in his or her own narcissism. "The person might be made content, effective, and even creative". The individual receives the image that s/he, in turn, projects onwards. "There is no place for example for alterity" (Levinas, 1969).
4. Deliver us from thought. Where the psychoanalyst and her/his organization stops and the patient starts is not clear. Hence, it is as if the possibilities for consciousness are determined: could this lead to no imagination, no unconsciousness, and no tacit dimension?
5. Doubt not ... catastrophe is inevitable ... Does psychoanalytic knowledge contain its own negation? How often does psychoanalytic training, like other "... training tells what is to be done, it does not reveal how to doubt" (Letiche, 1990, p. 238). How many trainings genuinely teach students how to doubt their psychoanalytic Gurus? (Or such aspects as the training organization's approach to statutory regulation?)

But could the situation be even worse for psychoanalysts than other professional groups? Perhaps, for some, enfolded in the desire to be a psychoanalyst is the hope not to be hurt again. And do such attempts to create situations in which we are not "subject to" lead to the particular structuring of therapeutic organizations? As a variant of the old teacher training joke: to what extent, if one cannot be subject too, does one go into analysis—and if one cannot be subject to that, one becomes an analyst—and if one is still troubled, one trains analysts and expects control rights on any ethical procedures! I am not disputing that good can come out of this in the space created for the relationship with the patient, but is the attempt to not be regulated also in part driven by something else that is not always helpful? Now it may be that psychoanalysis should not be regulated by the state—though there are many who are tempted, and perhaps hope, as with some other professionals, that the use of long words and even a bit of Latin may create the status others have, and sufficient therapeutic space. I think, in an era of consumerist managerialism, that punters—whether potential students or patients—would probably (wrongly) initially choose state regulation with competency-based outcomes so that you can apparently know in advance what you are going to get! There are those who would prefer some form of self regulation. But if a trainee wants state regulation—or a therapist wants a self-regulating profession primarily because *they* (in contrast to the case for psychoanalysis) do not want to be subject to an other—is this ethical?

Is another alternative, which carries the risk of contraction, to stay outside, to recognize that we will/should always be on the fringes of society; and that, by definition, our work will involve opening up a place to talk about that which our society does not wish to think about? I have tried to think of Levinas's work on notions of putting the other first as a way of exploring this, and I have previously considered this in terms of these groups who may be on the fringes of society; for instance, photographers, whose training is often similar to psychoanalysts in that it is lacking in the radical, yet interested in what is on the margins (Loewenthal, 2006).

I have devised a framework, at best grossly over-simplifying some implications of Levinasian ethics for photography and psychoanalysis: this "ethical window" is a two-dimensional model, one axis concerns whether the psychoanalyst puts the psychoanalyst first or the patient. The other axis is whether the patient puts the patient or the psychoanalyst first. In bringing this second dimension, neither reciprocity nor symmetry is intended; "I'll put you first if you put me first", but is an attempt at a societal perspective. However, both dimensions seem needed for "responsible relatedness" to exist (Gans, 1997). Again, for the psychoanalyst to put the patient first is a complex notion. It does not necessarily mean doing what the patient wants, or denying the need for the psychoanalyst to be in a position of strength, as both would not necessarily be putting the other first.

If Levinasian ethics is about considering implications rather than defining standards, one suggestion is that if we put our concerns about being regulated first, rather than the other, then we are at best privileging a position that is to do with giving a primacy to autonomy at the expense of others and our society in general. In contrast, the positioning of psychoanalysis with regard to other external laws by a heteronomy that is putting the other first might indeed be what is most appropriate. There again, perhaps any attempt at schematization shows how, as Levinas (1969) suggests, true justice can only take place on a case-by-case basis in the moment with another, and anything else (including my Levinasian frame-up) is more to do with the violence of late modernism.

I am not disputing that psychoanalysis opens up a special space that needs protecting from regulation. We are already in an era where, in my experience, a young person can be falsely reported by his therapist for possible family links with Bin Laden, or where patients can be worried about speaking of ordinary problems regarding tax deductions for fear of being reported for money laundering! If we are to keep appropriate confidentiality, how are we to do it? One way is to stay as clear as possible of regulations, and, where individual groups obtain the trainees and patients on reputation, it would not matter what they called themselves or what their training standards were; and ethical practice would be determined by the therapist and the training organization on a case-by-case basis.

Even assuming such carry-ons would in future be allowed, to what extent would psychoanalysts themselves be able not to be recognized as professionals? In some ways this may be easier for those therapists who are recognized as professional doctors, lecturers, etc. (although I am not suggesting that it is a requirement).

There is also a problem for new courses on the "block" whose programmes are not recognized by someone who can show their lineage back to Freud. Is the attempted professionalization process of now a new group using the description "psychoanalysts" in part based on the French, calling themselves psychoanalysts while still allowing patients "time to breathe" on only a three times per week basis? Yet, is this any different to the likes of barbers becoming doctors and then projecting their inadequacies on lesser forms of professionalization? But, if we go down such a professionalization route (now with competencies et al.), do we end up with the "worst of all worlds"? Do we, to safeguard our own position, compromise too much on the space for something other than state regulation to appear?

One choice is whether to accept or to work outside of the regulatory system. Yet, whichever we choose, there are ethical problems. If we work from within the system, does that mean we either end up not putting our patients first, or with colleagues representing us through double standards? This latter dilemma can be present both if we are on the inside or appear to have left the system but nevertheless live off it.

How can we learn what is appropriate? Levinas gives a primacy to putting the other first, albeit from a position of necessary strength. Such ethics as these can have implications for all practices and provides a case for not being confused with any claim to a special ethic of psychoanalysis or anything else that may have been designed in the hope that we are not subject to others. However, as with any theory, it is suggested that Levinas should only come to mind in terms of implications for practice. Otherwise his work can too easily be used as another totalising dogma leading to further theoretical abuse that is probably more rampant than anything the state has so far considered.

References

Baudrillard, J. (1990). *La Transparence Du Mal*. Paris: Galilee.

Department of Health (2007). Trust, assurance and safety—the regulation of health professionals in the 21st century. www.babcp.com/documents/white_paper_summary_feb2007.pdf (accessed 15 March 2007).

Gans, S. (1997). Lacan and Levinas: towards an ethical psychoanalysis. *Journal of the British Society for Phenomenology, 28*(1), January.

Hofstede, G. (2001). *Culture's Consequences: Comparing Values, Behaviors, Institutions and Organizations Across Nations*. Thousand Oaks, CA: Sage.

Laplanche, J. (1992). *Seduction, Translation, Drives*. M. Stanton (Trans.). M. Stanton & J. Fletcher (Eds.). London: ICA.

Letiche, H. (1990). Five post-modern aphorisms for trainers. *Mead, 21*: 229–240.

Levinas, E. (1969). *Totality and Infinity*. Pittsburgh, PA: Duquesne University Press.

Loewenthal, D. (2006). Cultural conflict, values, and relational learning in psychotherapy. In: L. Hoshmand (Ed.), *Culture, Psychotherapy, and Counseling: Critical and Integrative Perspectives* (pp. 205–225). Thousand Oaks, CA: Sage.

Loewenthal, D., & Snell, R. (2003). *Postmodernism for Psychotherapists: A Critical Reader*. London: Routledge.

Postle, D. (2007). *Regulating the Psychological Therapies: From Taxonomy to Taxidermy*. Ross on Wye: PCCS.

PART III

INTERNATIONAL CONTEXTS AND RESPONSES

CHAPTER TEN

The analyst's desire between singularity of the act and "a few others"[1]

Robert Lévy

I will try to reconsider a few elements developed by my friend Paola Mieli from the Après-Coup Psychoanalytic Association in New York. She confirms that what is currently going on within the psychoanalytic framework in the USA is that which always happens when one tries to "pose" selection criteria that obviously have nothing to do with psychoanalysis. This phenomenon is not new: the IPA has indeed always had those criteria, and, during one of the first scissions in France, Lacan himself participated in the elaboration of a certain number of criteria to select candidates for didactic analysis; they were very close to those presented by Paola. However, the novelty resides, perhaps, in the shift from IPA regulations to the regulations considered by the American state to constitute the national standard.

The Accoyer law forces us to reconsider a certain number of paradoxes upon which, I think, the originality of the subversive question of the positioning of both psychoanalysis and the analyst are founded. As far as his act is concerned, the analyst finds himself intimately linked to that which brings him back to his desire. He cannot be positioned in any other way than as a "not being there already". As for the *après-coup* experience, it cannot establish a community: here is a first paradox. This has to do with the analytic act itself, or, more precisely, with its particular dimension of irreducible singularity, an irreducibility of the act for which the analyst takes responsibility, yet without being able to answer or account for it completely. That is an important point, and it constitutes a second paradox concerning the analyst's position within which we work. Between the irreducible singularity of the act on the one hand, and the question of the institution on the other hand, there is a necessary tension that is not to be resolved and that founds the question of that which is properly psychoanalytic. Lacan has, in any case, left us with the co-ordinates of the analytic dimension within the institution.

The question is, thus, to know how a psychoanalytic institution that is not working against psychoanalysis can be conceived. It is possible to envisage the answer in terms of "non-solution" between, on the one hand, the "irreducible singularity of the act", and, on the other hand, the necessary "few others" (*quelques autres*), who can be the Association Law 1901 (*association Loi 1901*) or any other form of school. If the question of this tension on the side of the irreducible singularity of the act is resolved by saying that, after all, psychoanalysis can only be defined from this side, the analyst is then nothing more than a single person[2] in a world where he would be the only one to be able to truly authorize himself. If the solution is sought on the side of the "few others", for instance through an institutional organization that would be solely or essentially democratic, it is the question of the irreducible singularity of the act which then becomes null and void,[3] for there is no collective enunciation in psychoanalysis.

We will therefore have to deal with the regulations affecting psychotherapies by positioning ourselves in the same terms, bearing in mind that a regulation of the title "psychoanalyst" will be presented in a few years anyway; for it is obvious that once psychotherapists obtain a regulated "title", a "psychoanalyst title" is bound to come up after a few years for the same reasons as those provided by the state to justify the establishment of a regulation for psychotherapies.

The difficulty implied by this positioning and the questions that will put us in an uncomfortable position are the ones that require us to know how to maintain this necessary tension between the irreducible singularity of the act that founds the analyst within his practice, and his relation to the institution and to "a few others". It is a very important and complicated point, since the analyst's desire is not something that refers to everyone's desire. The analyst's desire, or the "desire of the analyst",[4] is more a function than anything else, a function in the sense that is closest to that which Frege calls a function in mathematics. The *désir d'analyste* is a function founded on a certain type of relation between the subject's identifications and his objects. As soon as an analyst finds himself in a position of identification with his object—and this can be pointed out in supervision—he is no longer in a position to offer a parenthesis that would be empty enough with regard to the identification with his object[5] and finds himself caught within an imaginary collusion, identifying with the patient's object(s). It is, time and again, such a position that one owes oneself to bring to light in what we call supervision or, in France, *contrôle*. It is also starting from this very point that I would define the difference between psychoanalysis and psychotherapy. Indeed, it is the analyst's job to maintain the place of object *a* empty,[6] so that the whole series of identifications to the patient's object can come to take this place of empty parenthesis provided that the analyst can open up this space for himself. But as soon as this empty parenthesis is filled with a new identification[7] (we have evoked that of the therapist, or the doctor's *raison d'être*, it can be any kind of identification), analysis stops and psychotherapy begins.

One owes to oneself, at a time when the question of the difference between psychotherapy and psychoanalysis is posed, to say clearly that psychoanalysis is in no way on the side of a kind of psychotherapy, whether it calls itself analytic or not. I have to admit, by the way, that I do not understand what is exactly meant by "analytic psychotherapy", if not what it originally was. Let us remind ourselves that the word—the expression—was introduced in France at a time when, because of the standards required by the IPA, those who were in didactic analysis but not yet accepted as psychoanalysts because they were still training, were, none the less, practising. Most of them were psychiatrists or psychologists and already had patients. In order not to be found guilty for having transgressed the IPA standards of that time, they entitled their practice "psychotherapy of analytic inspiration".[8] It seems to me that the issue has shifted over time and that the division today is clearly situated between psychoanalysis and the psychotherapies of all kinds. I do not believe that we would have much to say about psychotherapies, apart from distinguishing psychoanalysis as belonging to a different field, and that difference must be clearly maintained even if psychoanalysis can also have healing effects.

Notes

1. Translated by Ariana Cziffra
2. [Translators Note.] *Seul(e)* can be translated as "alone", "lonely", or "single". In my view, the entire question lies in this ambiguity: in other words, "how can the analyst be a single person, i.e., singular, and yet be able to relate to other single people, i.e., "a few others". If a single person can relate, he or she is not completely alone, however lonely the analytic act might be when it is being performed. We may choose to translate *seul* in any of the ways I am suggesting, depending on the kind of solitude, loneliness, or singularity we wish to emphasize here. In English, those three terms have slightly different meanings.
3. [Translators Note.] *Caduc/caduque* can also be translated as "obsolete" or "outmoded". In this case we may have rendered it as "irrelevant".
4. [Translators Note.] *Le désir d'analyste* is usually translated into English as "the analyst's desire", but it seems important to emphasize the difference between the "desire *of* the analyst" as a function, and the "desire of *the* analyst" (*désir de l'analyste*).
5. $ ◊ (a)
6. $ ◊ ( )
7. $ ◊ (a'), (a''), (a'''), ...)
8. [Translators Note.] Or "analytically inspired psychotherapy".

CHAPTER ELEVEN

The double denial and the double bind of psychologization: the Accoyer Amendment revisited

Jan De Vos

In October 2003, the French National Assembly passed a bill aimed at regulating psychotherapy in France. In order to safeguard the Frenchman in psychic distress against the charlatans, the Accoyer Amendment intended to restrict the practice of psychotherapy to psychiatrists and clinical psychologists. The additional tools to sweep clean the terrain of psychotherapy were general assessment and *quality control*. Senator Accoyer, convinced that he was doing the right thing for public health, must not have anticipated the upheaval he would cause. The psychoanalysts, especially, set up broad actions of resistance.

They reproached the Accoyer Amendment for imposing the strait-jacket of *quality control* on psychoanalysis. Jacques-Alain Miller, who headed the resistance, argued among other things that a diploma is not a guarantee against deontological faults or psychological weaknesses. Miller also stated that the *university discourse* as a whole is incompatible with the psychoanalytical praxis of the transference (Miller, 2004). So, the French analysts proclaimed that they would never accept an administrator who would decide which kind of therapy and how many sessions one is to follow. And, since psychic suffering is something that can neither be measured nor evaluated, it is not for the state to control what happens in a psychoanalysis; this is the responsibility of the psychoanalytical schools or organizations. The French psychoanalysts were firmly resolved, "we will have to fight for the Freudian cause—as citizens, in the circumstances of the 21st century, here, now, I, you, and you (and not someone else)" (Miller, 2003).

When psychoanalysts use the language of the revolution, one is tempted to ask whether so much unexpected activism is not a last flicker of a theory and practice in its death agonies. Isn't the word on the street that psychoanalysis is in decline? The Accoyer Amendment is then simply confirming the actual situation. But the French senator should have known better: not only sleeping, but also dying dogs are better left alone. In Flanders, where I live, certain politicians also felt compelled to streamline the psy-business. And here, too, tensions arose; Flemish psychoanalysts sharpened their pencils, made the necessary phone calls, and planned the battle meetings. There was this slogan: "Quality yes! Quantity no!", attacking the so-called *Quality Decree* in Flanders. Most strange that this slogan popped up, since this Decree, which imposed on every social institution a strict evaluative framework, was brought into practice some years before, with no public contestation whatsoever at the time! Considering the long-harboured tradition of splendid isolation and silence, one should proceed carefully when assessing the sudden agitation the Accoyer Amendment and the like caused.

The sharpest comment on the sudden presence of psychoanalysts in the public debate came from Slavoj Žižek, whose verdict on the French turmoil and its front man Jacques-Alain Miller, was that it all came down to *pseudo-activity*. Miller's socio-critical analyses were met with: "The intellectual misery of these reflections cannot but strike the eye" (Žižek, 2005b). Is this just polemics? I think not: if psychoanalysis claims to be subversive, then a questioning of the French resistance is justified to get a better sense of what it is that threatens psychoanalysis. Because the question is: isn't Miller preaching the revolution at the wrong gates?

Psychoanalysis as a placebo

In France it has been much discussed whether Miller was right to join forces with family therapists and the like. Those who defend

Miller say that even Freud considered psychoanalysis to be a psychotherapy, albeit the *primus inter pares* (Grigg, 2005, p. 71). For them, psychoanalysis and psychotherapy have a common enemy: the figure of the Evaluator and his suffocating tool of Quality. But do they really have an adversary in common? While Miller tried to unite the factions around the resistance to the quality discourse, it seems to me that the mainstream psy is quite happy with this discourse originating in the world of industry. Due to a lack of own paradigms, the psy readily shops around for some model on which to ground its questionable science. In Flanders, the *Quality Decree* for social institutions was, as said, not only uncontested for the most part, but actually received with wide open arms. The key idea—that *clients* are entitled to the best possible service and every institution should meticulously explain and write down how they realize this quality—finally provided strict rules and guidelines on how to work. One could not imagine how things were done before the *mission statements*.

Should we then endorse Miller's opponents criticizing his alliance with the psychotherapists and the psychologists? As they see it, psychoanalysis must go its own way, since it is something completely distinct from psychology and psychotherapy. But exactly the same argument is used by those on the same line with Miller: think about Maria Christian Aguirre resorting to the classic Lacanian quote that psychoanalysis is not a science like the others:

> Psychoanalysis today is not a science, among other things, because we cannot reproduce the experiment or clinical trials. We cannot divide our population in groups of two, one given therapy and the others a placebo and measured after a set period of time. What is the placebo for therapy? [Aguirre, 2004].

The problem is that Aguirre does not escape the boundaries of contemporary scientism itself: she stays within the framework of *experiments and clinical trials* to prove the distinctiveness of psychoanalysis. Should we not, on the contrary, understand Lacan as saying that psychoanalysis is in absolutely no way to be held accountable in such terms? In this way, anyone who has been in analysis can produce the answer to Aguirre's question: isn't the placebo for therapy nothing other then psychoanalysis itself? What is certain is that what Aguirre shows is that the claim for a different place for psychoanalysis equally serves as an argument pro and as an argument contra the alliance with psychology and psychotherapy. So, we are compelled to say that both stances find each other in the fundamental refusal of a real debate on the relation of psychoanalysis with the psy-sciences. It seems that psychoanalysis today flees the meta-position, but, as Rex Butler puts it, "it is only through the attempt to occupy the position of metalanguage that we are able to show the impossibility of doing so" (Butler, 2005). The strongest aspect of psychoanalyis is its metavision, we should not denounce this heritage, however problematical it is.

In my opinion, psychoanalysis will have to take a stand with respect to psychology and psychotherapy; neither compromising nor disdainfully ignoring them will suffice. For today's hegemonic discourse, so called post-politics, grounds its post-ideological "doing what's good for the people" in the scientific university discourse. So, if psychoanalysis wants to preserve any relevance in the face of this dominant scientism, it is not by soliciting for a special chair, or in a little salon set apart, or in the living room crowded with all kinds of social and psychological engineers. This would result in getting a seat in the corridor, the interlude before being kicked out. Betting on a place in the margin of the official hegemonic discourse condemns psychoanalysis to a non-space. Because current ideology, presenting itself as above the old ideologies, above all biased theories too, is all encompassing; it does not admit any sides of the road. Current state regulations are the coalescence of the state, economics, and science, proclaiming: "we do not know how you can become happy (what the Enlightenment did pretend) but, here are some 'good practices', 'evidence-based methods' that can help you"! Which is to be understood as *Du musst nicht, denn du sollst*! You do not have to, so you shall and you will!

So, anyone for a placebo? Instead of taking refuge in the margins of psychotherapy, or of neuroscience, depending which you would prefer as your favourite buddy, we should seek to establish another place, another Schauplatz, a subversive one. Psychoanalysis is the *consciously given* placebo for the scientific political and psychological correctness that promises us the ultimate Good.

Paranoia displaced and misplaced

We should be very sparing with the notion of subversiveness—all too easily claimed these days. Think about Jean-Claude Milner who, backing up Jacques-Alain Miller with respect to the Accoyer issue, wrote that the psy is in the line of fire from a threefold barbarism: scientism, the ideology of management, and the iron grip of the administrators. For Milner, the psy is the only buffer between these barbarisms and people who are having problems of "digesting life" (Milner, 2003, p. 9). But, one could ask, why does Milner give the part of the good guy so easily to the psy?

> Due to one of those twists of which history holds the secret, the disciplines of bad-digesting-life find themselves in the position where they have to engage directly in a confrontation with the new barbarisms. [*ibid.*]

Sounds heroic, no? But doesn't the argument that history holds a secret point to the opposite: of refusing to question the history of current social deadlocks—deadlocks in which the human sciences as such play their role? Let me refer to Alain-Gérard Slama, editor of the French newspaper *Le Figaro*, who made a remarkable intervention in a radio programme with Jacques-Alain Miller as guest. If Miller's main argument concerned the weight of administration on the world of the psy, then Slama twisted this around when he questioned what he calls the *psychiatrization* of the state and of public life. He claimed, for example, that no accident can occur without immediately establishing a "psychological cell" for taking care of the traumas; coping is obligatory. Slama also referred to the courtroom, where, during certain trials, psychologists are held ready should the jury break down while listening to so many atrocities. Slama described this as outright infantilization and sheer disrespect for the citizen (Slama, 2005).

Are we stuck with two contradictory analyses? A governmentalization of the psy-field, or a psychologization and psychiatrization of the field of the state? Perhaps we are not dealing with two opposed explanations that exclude each other, but with two phenomena that are each other's mirror image. The complaint of the French analysts that they are haunted by politicians and administrators is mirrored by the fact that the common citizen is subjected to the psy from birth until death: from the psy of the pre-natal courses to the psy of palliative care.

At the crossroads of those two explanations we have the Accoyer Amendment, where we see the postmodern state playing its role in neo-liberal globalization—that is, making the global system work by taking care of its human and affective aspects. What the French analysts missed in their ideology critique is that ideology has retreated from politics and found a hiding place in the social sciences. More normative than ever, they are where the kernel of ideology—denied by post-politics—resides, supplying the theories to back up the profitable medicalizing, psychologizing and infantilizing of the postmodern individual. Trying to negotiate within the given co-ordinates, the French analysts did not question the framework itself and denied the real political dimension at stake. In this sense, the French *colère* is a fight in the wrong arena and a missed chance. In a lecture with the provoking subtitle "Why many Lacanians are reactionary liberals", Žižek says,

> There is a cruel irony in the fact that Lacanian orientation lost its socio-political critical edge in the very moment when its representatives decided to intervene in the public political debates . . . There are situations in which the duty of the analysts is NOT to participate in debates, insofar as such participation, even if it pretends to be critical, means that one accepts the basic coordinates of the way the ruling ideology formulates the problem. [Žižek, 2005a,b]

Psychoanalysis's missed appointment with its Golem

What threatens psychoanalysis is essentially not an anti-psy or an anti-psychological discourse. In fact, Accoyer can be seen as the advocate of the mainstream psychological and psychotherapeutic praxis. Current omnipresent psychologization stands for the fact that it is not so much the Evaluator as the "psychological individual" that is haunting the subject of psychoanalysis. But is not psychology, and, consequently, psychologization, the child or the shadow of psychoanalysis itself? Mario Goldenberg has already called the psychotherapies the Golem of psychoanalysis (Goldenberg, 2003). Miller developed a similar idea when he stated that psychoanalytic free association lead to the widespread cult of speech, that eventually threatens to suffocate analytic discourse: the idea that talking can solve everything comes back "to haunt psychoanalysis" (Miller, 1999). But when it comes to understanding this going astray, this betrayal of psychoanalysis, Miller resorts to the classic idea of psychoanalysis being misunderstood by society. But what if it is not a misunderstanding? What if the current cult of speech understands the Freudian stance all too well, that it takes it to its logical extreme? Psychology and psychotherapy as the true heirs of Freud?

To explain this unorthodox idea, let us start with the fact that Freud had to undertake his *own* analysis. So, logically, he had to stumble on the difficulty that one cannot analyse the ground upon which one stands. Is it not exactly at this point that he invented psychoanalysis? In this way, the production of psychoanalytic theory could be seen as departing from Freud reaching the boundaries of his own neurosis, his own not wanting to know. And, a point that has been made before, it is this remainder, Freud's blind spot, that was passed on to his disciples, and then on to the next generations of psychoanalysts. But can we not say that this initial movement keeps repeating itself with every psychologist or psychotherapist who passes on to theory and/or practice? Because one can claim that their heresies, denials, or aberrations from Freudian theory are exactly based on Freud's own not wanting to know, and on his impossibility to know. They are not misunderstandings, but the amplification of the structural blind spot of psychoanalysis. The Golem is the figure on whose forehead the word "truth" is written. But it is of utmost importance to situate this in the context of modernity as such. It was Freud who, for the first time, tried to grasp the consequences of modern subjectivity. So, the rock on which Freud stumbled must be understood first and foremost in the problematic stance of the Cartesian subject as such. The subject of the Enlightenment embarked on a journey to itself at the point where the ontological foundation of man and society had perished, and this lack could not but keep on returning, being both the impetus and the goal (that is, to staunch it) of modern subjectivity. It is this paradox of the reflexive subject that led Freud to invent the unconscious and, hence, psychoanalysis. So, the blind spot should be focused in the first place not on Freud's personal psyche, but on the historical context of modernity. Freudian theory, as the articulation of the paradoxes of modernity, became then as such "incontournable". Every theory of the human being is inevitably a comment on psychoanalysis.

In other words, psychology and psychologization are the return of the repressed of the structural problem of psychoanalysis, and of modernity *tout-court*. The Accoyer Amendment, which has to be understood in terms of the phenomenon of psychologization, thus confronted psychoanalysis with its own truth, with something we do not want to know. And if Miller above all refused a genuine political analysis, and refused to understand psychologization as one of the central axes of today's globalized capitalism, we are led to the idea that perhaps this moment, this missed appointment of psychoanalysis with its Golem, repeats another missed moment: that of Freud missing the political meeting with modernity.

A never fulfilled promise

A final (Millerian, of course) detour is necessary to clarify these last conclusions. In "A fantasy" (2005), where Miller tries to deal with the problematic history of psychoanalysis, he states that the social discourse is no longer the other side of psychoanalysis but its accomplishment. Freud created the formal structure for a discourse capable of analysing the discourse of the master (which is finally also the structure of the unconscious). This interpretive and subversive power of the analytic discourse had decisive effects on society, culminating in the fact that it turned society in the direction of the discourse of the analyst. "Hypermodern civilization", still according to Miller, is equivalent to the discourse of the analyst where the *objet a* holds the dominant place in society; the *surplus-jouissance* commands and prevails upon the disorientated subject (*ibid.*). Thus, it seems that psychoanalysis itself engendered hypermodern commercial discourse and its celebration of *surplus-jouissance*. Must we, like the sorcerer's apprentice, react with a horrified "look, what have we done?"

But, doing so, we are overlooking the wreckage caused by our direct descendant, psychologization. And second, the problem of Miller's version of the story of psychoanalysis is not primarily that he rules out any socio-political or economic dimension. Rather, the tricky part is that he is telling the socio-politico economic story as if it was to be reduced to the vicissitudes of psychoanalysis. Taking all the blame so as to avoid the responsibility? The society-building capacity these days, however, lies foremost not with psychoanalysis but with the psy-sciences. Think about the *DSM* (the *Diagnostic and Statistical Manual of Mental Disorders*), which was not only proclaimed in different European countries as the only official list to be used in matters of diagnosis, but also, through the combined efforts of government agencies, academia, resource centres, and the media, these *DSM* classifications were brought into everyone's living room. Because of this, every parent considers his child's behaviour in the light of the checklist of the ADHD-criteria. It is the analysis of this strange synergy of the postmodern state and the psy-apparatus engaging in a thorough psychologization that is missing in the Millerian critiques.

However, is it not precisely this political dimension that surfaces—in a strange way—in the following lines of Miller.

> Lacanian practice has to deal with the consequences of this sensational success [of Freudian psychoanalysis]. Consequences that are felt to be of the order of a catastrophe. The dictatorship of surplus-*jouissance* is devastating nature, it is fragmenting marriage, dispersing the family and remodelling the body. [Miller, 2005, p. 11]

Is this not the return of the repressed political dimension? Because the similarity with the following lines cannot escape us:

> [It] has left no other bond between man and man than naked self-interest, than callous "cash payment". . . . It has resolved personal worth into exchange value, and in place of the numberless indefeasible chartered freedoms has set up that single, unconscionable freedom—Free Trade. In one word, for exploitation, veiled by religious and political illusions, it has substituted naked, shameless, direct, brutal exploitation. [Marx & Engels, 1848]

To which we must add just one more quote:

> . . . it imposes equally on everyone its own path to the acquisition of happiness and protection from suffering. Its technique consists in depressing the value of life and distorting the picture of the real

world in a delusional manner—which presupposes an intimidation of the intelligence. [Freud, 1930a, p. 84]

Here, I quoted Freud in *Civilization and its Discontents*, where he names "religion" as the force that restricts the play of choice and adaptation. Was Freud pointing his gun at the old forces, already on the verge of disappearing, so as to overlook the wreckage caused by capitalism? *Civilization and its Discontents* is, furthermore, precisely the place where Freud devotes a few critical lines on Marxism, along with a promise, never fulfilled, to come back to this, in his own words, important issue.

A double denial and a double bind

Is it not strange that the market, seen as the only *natural* way, should play on all levels but one; that is, on the level of the analysis of the social and the subjective problems? On that level it has to be denied by all means that the market is to blame. There the human sciences come in handy: in a globalized system ruled by the market, psychosocial analyses overrule every ideological and political analysis. But the first denial needs a second one in order to ground it: the denial of today's mainstream psychology of the psychic dimension as a possible and legitimate factor in the understanding of the human or the social. Everything is psychologized, on condition that we do not understand the human phenomena from the perspective of *the psychic as a cause*. Yes, we are psychologists, but no, the explanations are not psychological but biological and genetic. Psychology, departing from genetics, biology, and neurology, serves to deny the enormous consequences of globalization on the subjective and the social level.

This double denial is, in fact, based on a double bind. We should not be naïve and think that it is about the market and capitalism leading to inequality and that the human sciences are restricting themselves to smoothing out the hardest consequences of the system. There, the critique would be that the human sciences are only collaborating without daring to engage in a fundamental critique, without really attempting to humanize the economic capitalism and without trying to realize equality. But what if, as Žižek

(2005a) points out, in the heart of capitalism the idea of equality is inscribed, and that this is the very reason for so much inequality? Then the human sciences are to be situated at the place of the fundamental phantasm of capitalism: from cognitive to evolutionary psychology, there is this pseudo-ethical stance of equality, diversity, and well-being. This is the double bind of individualization and totalization, of the totalitarian grip of an alleged liberating discourse. Just consider how it is almost impossible to oppose the hegemonic discourse of the True and the Good: who could possibly be against emancipation, empowerment, or the strengthening of coping skills and social attitudes? The signifiers of the human sciences, present in many social and political arenas, have the very effect that every discussion gets numbed in the broad consensus. The discourse of the Good neutralizes every possible debate. So, one should not reproach the human sciences for being too scientistic, too cold, and too focused on quantitative data; no, they are all too human ... In this way, the neo-enlightened administrator such as Accoyer is a psychologist himself, presenting us with false choices.

References

Aguirre, M. C. (2004). Psychotherapy and evaluation. *Lacanian Compass, 1*(1). www.amp-nls.org/lacaniancompass1.pdf.

Butler, R., (2005). What is a master-signifier? www.lacan.com/zizek-signifier.htm

Freud, S. (1930a). *Civilization and its Discontents. S.E., 21*: 64–145. London: Hogarth.

Goldenberg, M. (2003). Psychoanalysis and its Golem. *Lacanian Ink, 22*(Fall). www.lacan.com/frameXXII6.htm

Grigg, R. (2005). Regulating psychoanalysis: why we should be concerned over the new psychotherapy legislation in France. In: B. Burgoyne (Ed.), *The Pathology of Democracy*. London: Karnac.

Marx, K., & Engels, F. (1848). *The Communist Manifesto*. Rendelsham: Merlin, 1998.

Miller, J.-A. (1999). "Did you say bizarre?" *Lacanian Ink, 15*(Fall): 8–36.

Miller, J.-A. (2003). Appel du 2 décembre pour la psychanalyse, Judith Lacan en Jacques-Alain Miller. *Le Nouvel Âne, 2*. www.wmaker.net/reseaupsycho.fr/index.php?action=article&id_article=120764

Miller, J.-A. (2004). Une déclaration de Jacques-Alain Miller. La guerre des palotins. *Agence Lacanienne de Presse*, Bulletin spécial, n° 3, 8 january 2004 http://www.forumpsy.org/Resource/ALP2_3.html

Miller, J.-A. (2005). A fantasy. *Lacanian Praxis, 1*: 5–16.

Milner, J.-C. (2003). Le grand secret de l'idéologie de l'évaluation. *Le Nouvel Âne*, 2.

Slama, A.-G. (2005). Intervention in the radio program *Les matins de France Culture*, 17 May. www.forumpsy.org/Jam_frCult.html.

Žižek, S. (2005a). Ignorance of the chicken, or, why many Lacanians are reactionary liberals. Lecture at the Centre for Research in Modern European Philosophy, Middlesex University. 26 May 2005, London, Audio file on http://gold.socialtools.net/view/Main/Zizek IgnoranceOfTheChicken (my transcription).

Žižek, S. (2005b). Respect for otherness? No thanks. Lecture at Birkbeck, University of London. 20 May. Partial transcription: www.elsigma.com/popup/popup_body.jsp?idContent=7870&color=209973&authorName=Slavo Zizek j&authorSurname=Zizek&authorEmail=

CHAPTER TWELVE

The situation of psychoanalysis in France

René Major

I am going to address the current reality of the situation of psychoanalysis in France, in relation to the public authorities and the regulation of its practice by the state. But, before I do that, I shall give a brief account of the history of psychoanalysis in France, because certain contingencies in the attempt to regulate it can only be understood in the light of this history. What is of particular interest in an examination of the French situation? Well, in spite of several years of government insistence on this matter, state regulation has always encountered not only active opposition from a significant proportion of psychoanalysts and psychotherapists, but also difficulties of a legal nature.

Even though the establishment of psychoanalysis in France was relatively slow in relation to other European countries and to the USA—the first psychoanalytic society was founded in 1926—it is the only country in which it was rapidly and widely embraced in all sectors of cultural and artistic life. From the outset, Freud's thought was not spread by the great figures of the medical world, as it was by Ernest Jones in England, Ferenczi in Hungary, or Karl Abraham in Germany, but by literary figures, "intellectuals", as they have been called since the Dreyfus–Zola affair. All these figures were steeped in a tradition dating from the French Revolution, which viewed madness through the eyes of reason. Baudelaire, Rimbaud, and Lautréamont had already distinguished the authentic subject from the appearance given to him by his identifications, proclaiming, "I is another" ("*Je est un autre*"). Equally, the interest aroused by Freud's early work focused on speech and language, the interpretation of dreams, jokes, and slips of the tongue. In the 1920s, many writers experienced analysis for themselves: Michel Leiris, Antonin Artaud, Georges Bataille, and Raymond Queneau, for example. Prestigious literary reviews, such as *la Nouvelle Revue française*, with André Gide and Jacques Rivière, served as a forum for a style of writing which took the Freudian revolution into account, as did the surrealist movement around André Breton, and even the review *Philosophies*. A writer of Romain Rolland's ilk was surely closer to Freud than any eminent physician interested in the therapeutic applications of the Freudian method. If we compare the affinities woven between Freud's thought and the medical world, and the way it meshed with the thinking of contemporary writers such as Stefan Zweig, Arthur Schnitzler, or Thomas Mann, it is more along the lines of an equivalence with the latter that the closest connections were initially established in France. There were, however, a few exceptions, notably Marie Bonaparte, a non-physician, who did an analysis with Freud and played an important role in setting up the first Institute of Psychoanalysis in France, as well as facilitating Freud's exile to England in 1938.

The second generation of psychoanalysts in France demonstrated more clearly that there were two trends: the one, under the aegis of Sacha Nacht, which became more and more identified with the medical tradition, and the other, with Jacques Lacan, who, although himself a physician, was steeped in philosophy and literature, which developed more and more with the momentum of the sciences of language and the formalizations of logic. This distinction is too schematic, because, of course, the two trends did not fail to influence each other. But it is true to say that psychoanalysis remained almost exclusively Freudian, without any competition from the schools of psychotherapy that flourished in other countries. At least, that was the case until recently.

Lacan certainly made a significant contribution to the wide dissemination of psychoanalysis in French culture, and also to the considerable increase in the number of psychoanalysts. The divisions at the heart of the psychoanalytic movement were not contained within the bosom of a single society, as was the case for a long time here in the UK for the Kleinians, the Anna Freudians and the Independents. The numerous splits that occurred worked in favour of the expansion of psychoanalysis, and this has been even more the case since Lacan's death, because some twenty organizations have emerged out of his Ecole, dividing those who followed his son-in-law and heir, Miller, and the numerous groups that separated themselves from them with a great deal of resentment, claiming the teachings of Lacan for themselves. Today, of all countries, France has the highest per capita number of psychoanalysts, and, until now, the practice of psychoanalysis has been, to my knowledge, more free than anywhere else in the world.

Psychoanalysis not only enjoyed a great degree of freedom, but also held a privileged position: it is still often discussed in the daily press, and in weekly and monthly reviews; it occupied a particular place in the universities, it was regarded as prestigious in literary and philosophical circles. But perhaps all this blinded it to the threats that have been building up for some time. Where did these threats originate? First and foremost, in the power of the medical establishment, in trends of neo-positivism or scientism, and connivance with power vested in a state more and more concerned with issues of control, dominion, and evaluation in all spheres.

The history I have sketched out for you explains, at least to some extent, the positions taken up in the wake of the first draft legislation brought before the National Assembly in 2003. I should mention, incidentally, that the Etats Généraux de la psychanalyse, held in Paris in July 2000, took up a position opposed to any form of state regulation of psychoanalysis, and had already argued in favour of the setting up of an Institute of Higher Studies in Psychoanalysis, modelled on the Psychoanalytische Hochschulen proposed by Freud in "The question of lay analysis" (1926e). If we look at the accounts published in 1927 in the *International Journal*, we can see that these are by and large the same debates as those being taken up today, with the same emphases, and just as contentious. But Freud's position is both the most radical and the most defensible from a psychoanalytic point of view: it argues that psychoanalysis cannot be legitimized by any kind of institutionalized practice. There is no qualification that constitutes a guarantee for the psychoanalyst, who has unceasingly to justify his competence and his legitimacy, neither of which can ever be assured. Anything that purports to assure his identity and to comfort him in this way can do nothing other than increase the risk of his acting incompetently. Freud repudiates on principle anything that would make psychoanalysis subject to medicine, to religion, or to the sciences as such, or the state, which might claim to assure the interests of society, or even to psychoanalytic associations, which might lay claim to powers of legitimization. If psychoanalysis has to be unceasingly reinvented, it cannot be satisfied with anything that is capable of being institutionalized. Freud's fear that therapeutic considerations would take precedence over psychoanalytic thinking, over the "science" that it developed independently of its therapeutic applications, has become a very real threat in today's world.

This threat was taken seriously in France, and that is why the "Forums psy" organized by Miller, which brought together not only analysts but also well-known intellectuals, had a degree of success. But on the one hand, the intellectuals, such as Lévy or Sollers, are marked by their influence on the media, and their tendency to seize every media opportunity. On the other hand, because of the hostility to any initiative by Miller, as much on the part of the "Lacanians", who did not follow him to the École de la Cause, or who have left it, as on the part of the IPA analysts, a movement has emerged among analysts that has attempted to reunite those who would wish to be recognized by the state, directly or indirectly, while hoping that psychoanalysis can have a special status within the law. The Société psychanalytique de Paris, the oldest organization, affiliated to the IPA, on this occasion allied itself with the anti-Millerian Lacanians. I will not go into more detail about this situation, which must already seem quite confused.

I was one of those who, in "le Manifeste pour la psychanalyse" and the "Front du refus" opposed any kind of regulation, or any dealings with public authorities.

After numerous comings and goings, between the National Assembly and the Senate, a law was finally passed in August 2004 that, to sum it up in a few words, was concerned solely with the status of the psychotherapist, giving the right to practise to medical doctors, chartered psychologists, and psychoanalysts whose names were on a list registered at their local prefecture. Others had to undergo a training in clinical psychopathology. Once the law was passed, we had to wait for "decrees of application" in order for it to come into effect. These decrees are being drafted now, and the projects are being discussed by various representatives of the groups of analysts, psychologists, and psychotherapists of all sorts, producing nothing but dissatisfaction for virtually all concerned.

In more general terms, we have to say that the question of regulation concerning "mental" health has arisen in Europe under pressure from all those who aspire to the status of psychotherapist. But what has been minimized, if not ignored, is that, at the same time, the medical authorities, which have always been cautious, even suspicious, with regard to their traditional monopoly concerning health in general, have never been able to contemplate losing the slightest degree of their hold over anything defined as "therapeutic". These authorities have found themselves in a position of objective complicity with a state that is more and more set upon extending its control over all aspects of the life of its citizens, in the name of an ideology of security. Witness, in France, the recent reports by the Institute of Medical Research (INSERM), which on the one hand established that cognitive–behavioural therapies obtain far better results than psychoanalysis (most of the members of this committee were behaviouralists), and on the other hand that the behaviour of children should be monitored and recorded from the age of three years in nursery schools, in order to detect future delinquents, and to subject them as early as possible to treatment with medication.

Well, in France, as I have shown, the experience of psychoanalysis and psychoanalytic thinking have never been confused with any therapeutic project as such, even if the therapeutic virtues of psychoanalysis, which we all agree are manifest "into the bargain", are recognized, that is to say, through the analysis of the underlying conflicts that have made the compromises of symptoms necessary for a while. So, everything that psychoanalysis and its concept of the freedom of the subject strove to leave behind them over the decades, that is to say, the conditioning of subjects to adaptation, whether familial, social, or political, has now returned with a vengeance in the guise of biopolitical projects of technologization of human relations in order to reduce them to manipulable substrates according to the interests of political control and a market economy.

The meaning of the word "therapeutic" in terms of health is the restitution of a former state, the "*restitutio ad integrum*", which clearly does not accord with psychoanalytic practice. Freud, as early as 1926, feared that therapeutics would come to destroy psychoanalysis as a science. If, as Romain Rolland wrote, he had spent the major part of his life in deconstructing his own illusions, and those of humanity, it was not so that his heirs could devote themselves to becoming slaves to some sanitizing or political ideology.

Today, in the face of these threats that are bearing down on psychoanalysis, to consider what is called "psychoanalytic psychotherapy" as a modality of psychoanalysis, as is maintained by the groupings of psychoanalysts who are in favour of the law, is to consent to become "state psychotherapists" and to abandon, at least to a significant degree, the critical function of psychoanalysis in relation to any power whatsoever, including the power that psychoanalysis itself may end up exerting. I therefore consider that resistance to psychoanalysis comes nowadays as much from psychoanalysts as from those who fight against it. Consequently, it has developed an auto-immune disease that is attacking psychoanalysis itself, a disease that is destroying its own antibodies, its own resistance to external destructive agencies.

So, where are we now in terms of this struggle, this combat, against the public authorities, against the return with a vengeance of therapies designed to produce compliant subjects, in this struggle which causes divisions among psychoanalysts themselves? First of all, the reports produced by INSERM, which I mentioned earlier, caused a huge public outcry. Then, faced with projects designed to apply the law, the psychoanalysts, who were divided, may be on the road to making a common stand. In fact, this project means that candidates for the title psychotherapist would need to acquire a Master's, which would include teaching on four types of psychotherapy: cognitive–behaviouralism, systemic psychotherapy, integrative psychotherapy, and analytic psychotherapy. The psychoanalysts can see just how they would be stitched up. Those who teach at the universities would also see their role reduced to a smaller and smaller one, and their situation become practically untenable.

With regard to this latter eventuality, we had also foreseen at the Etats Généraux de la psychanalyse in the year 2000 the setting up of an Institute of Higher Studies in psychoanalysis, independent of the public authorities and of the universities. The Institute was inaugurated in 2003 with a debate, "Why war?", on the eve of the American intervention in Iraq. This Institute provides for ten intersections of psychoanalysis with philosophy, literature, the life sciences, political science, the law, religious studies, history, etc. We are attempting to put into practice the programme outlined by Freud in 1926 and 1927 for the multi-disciplinary formation of analysts in addition to the usual personal analysis and supervision.

Concerning "the decree on the application of the law" with regard to the title of psychotherapist, our intersection psychoanalysis–political sciences–law produced a ten-page document that I sent to our Minister of Health to show that "the project of the decree on the application of the law" was likely to be rejected by the Conseil d'Etat because it remained, on several points that we enumerated, legally indefensible. This letter to the Minister was an open letter, widely circulated on the internet, on the website www.ihep.fr. The Minister has already made it known that he did not wish for any kind of confrontation, and that he would wait and see.

So, this is where we are. The future remains uncertain. We have existing laws that mean that some of the "decrees with regard to application of the law" take a long time to appear, and other existing laws that mean that the decrees never even see the light of day. If you ask my opinion, all I can do is encourage psychoanalysts to promote the highest possible standards of training (formation) and to continue on all levels and by all possible means to resist state regulation. Because, in the majority of European countries where regulation has been implemented, it has brought nothing positive for psychoanalysis. Freud's preferred position on this was clear. It is far better to inform and educate public opinion, and leave it to each individual to speak to whomsoever he sees fit. Because anyone is a charlatan if he practises psychoanalysis without competence, whether he is a medical doctor, a psychologist, or even a psychoanalyst recognized by a psychoanalytic institution. The institutes can try their best to offer the best possible training, and to transmit the psychoanalytic experience in the best possible way. What they cannot do is offer any sort of guarantee. Nothing is less analytic than to guarantee an analysis in advance, by any title or certificate whatsoever. Each analysis is unique, each time it has to be invented anew. Only the analysand can say whether there is, or has been, what we can really call "some analysis", if the bonds of the transference that assured it have really been dissolved. An analysis is the experience of freedom and responsibility.[1]

Postscript May 2007[2]

Nicolas Sarkozy (elected President of the French Republic on the 6 May 2007) responded to the question posed to him about future decrees specifying how the law concerning psychotherapists will be enforced with this letter, reproduced below. The content of this letter sums up where we are on this question now, and it shows that Sarkozy has taken into account all our observations on the matter (observations that can be found on the *Institut des Hautes Etudes en Psychanalyse* website, www.ihep.fr/reglementation). No other European country has, until now, succeeded in respecting by law the existing practice of psychoanalysis (including the title of psychotherapist for those psychoanalysts who claim it) provided the administration in charge of applying these standards actually understands fully all that is required. We will continue to be involved in ensuring that this will be the case.

Nicolas Sarkozy's response to the Fédération Française de Psychothérapie et Psychanalyse, dated 19 April 2007, is as follows:

> Mr President,[3]
>
> I have been paying full attention to your letter concerning regulation of the title of psychotherapist.
>
> It is true that cancellation of the amendments made to the law on medication by the *Conseil Constitutionnel* logically maintains the legislative text in conformity with its initial form, as originally promulgated on the 9th of August 2004. The law aims, as you had also wished it to, at avoiding the sectarian deviations that can potentially take place in this particularly sensitive area in which people seeking therapeutic help are extremely vulnerable. Attending to this issue, the law provides for the requirement that there should be training that aims at avoiding a situation in which people

who are not trained are still able to claim the title of psychotherapist. In addition, collaboration with universities makes it possible, as you have rightly emphasised, to ensure requisite pedagogical standards are maintained. Universities signing the convention will allow for the naming of training bodies involved in those conventions and, beyond the requirement for regulation, will leave them with full freedom in the pursuit of the teaching which they take to be their legitimate activity. *As far as psychoanalysis is concerned,* and in accordance with the meetings that took place with all the psychoanalytic bodies, *I must make it clear that there is no question, either in the law or in the decree projects, that universities would be responsible for the teaching of this activity.* With respect to the validation of professionals that are already practising at the time of the publication of the decree, it is indispensable, as you have also emphasized, for the relevant committees to be composed of qualified professionals. Finally, I note with satisfaction that you wish for psychotherapists to furnish themselves with a common code of ethics. I can only encourage you in this direction, so that the code of ethics in question can be applied (by endorsement of the law) to all practising psychotherapists.

I sincerely hope that those points will serve to answer your questions.

Yours faithfully,

Nicolas Sarkozy

Notes

1. Translation of main text by Lindsay Watson.
2. Translation of postscript by Ariana Cziffra.
3. In this letter addressed to the President of the FFPP, the italicized emphases have been added by René Major.

Reference

Freud, S. (1926e). The question of lay analysis. *S.E., 20*: 179–258. London: Hogarth.

CHAPTER THIRTEEN

Regulation, ethics, and freedom

Jalil Bennani

I address these questions from my personal experience in Morocco, where psychoanalysis is fairly new compared with European countries. We will see that, wherever we might be in the world, and despite cultural differences, our questions are universal and common to all. First, I provide a brief history of psychoanalysis within a Moroccan context, and go on to describe the evolution of psychotherapies and psychoanalysis in Morocco up to the present day. Finally, I give a personal perspective on psychoanalysis, transmission, and culture.

Psychoanalysis in Morocco

The practice of psychoanalysis in Morocco is a fairly recent phenomenon. It was introduced in the late 1940s by a group of French psychoanalysts led by Rene Laforgue, who was one of the founders of the French psychoanalytic movement. He came to Morocco to regain the freedom to practise and do research, which he had lost in France. He had no Moroccan patients and did not have much to do with the traditions of the country. This is why there was no transmission of the art of psychoanalysis. However, in Western North Africa (the *Maghreb*), Morocco was the only country to which psychoanalysis was introduced during the colonial period.

Moroccan psychoanalysts started to appear on the scene in the 1980s, and over the past few years a transmission has been taking place at last. The Moroccan Psychoanalytic Society (SPM) was set up with practical and theoretical training and with its own rules for best practice. Most of the Moroccan psychoanalysts have done their training in France. It is important to point out at this stage that when we talk about transmission we are faced with questions about filiations. Transmission takes into consideration different schools of thought. In France, we know that most psychoanalysts are opposed to an "order" of psychoanalysts and are still opposed to the type of regulation that has affected psychotherapists and soon could include psychoanalysis. It is well known that psychoanalysis is under attack from "scientific" ideology and behavioural psychology. We know that psychoanalysis is continually reinventing itself. This "reinvention" comes about with each treatment, but, in order to have transmission of best practice, culture and language must be taken into account.

The historical and cultural context in Morocco concerns the relationship between magic or religious practices and so-called scientific practices. In the past, many outcasts were considered to be possessed (*mejnoun* in Arabic)—victims of either magic or sorcery. Healers could then be called upon to exorcize demons or lead the patients to the tomb of a saint whose "divine grace" (*baraka*) was capable of performing miracles. "Illness" of this kind was often associated with the phenomenon of possession. The role of the demon (known as *jinn*) as an outside agent is very important: he is at the root of these phenomena and is thus the causal agent. Traditional medicine uses saints, magicians, sorcerers, and clairvoyants to exorcize the patient. These figures provide answers to questions that scientific medicine does not even ask: to consider whether *jinns*, for example, are responsible for an illness. The family and social environment follows the patient through his or her illness. In a traditional society—when it is not dictatorial—members of a group feel the need to find out the causes of the illness, whether they are social, psychological, supernatural, or appeal to notions to do with fate or destiny. When traditional medicine fails, only then do patients go to see a doctor.

A psychoanalyst in the city

When I returned to Morocco in 1981 after training in France, there was no official organization, no institution, and no psychoanalytic school. Patients did not have access to psychoanalysis. They simply went to their doctor to sort out their psychological problems. As psychoanalysis was practically non-existent, I myself was neither known nor recognized as a psychoanalyst. There was no question, therefore, of state control of our practice. I was authorized to exercise as a psychiatrist. At the outset, many people did not know the difference between psychoanalysis, psychotherapy, psychology, and psychiatry. Many of them could have seen a traditional therapist before coming to my office. As a psychiatrist and a psychoanalyst I could receive anyone; I could listen, analyse, and interpret anyone's demand and desire.

Psychiatry, psychoanalysis, and the different psychotherapies are in continuity with each other and they presuppose a break with traditional methods. Continuity, since we are still interested in the symptoms and method of treating the patient. It also requires a break with the past and with "tradition", since we utilize scientific or rational methods and apply these methods to the symptoms. I can illustrate this with a typical example—that of the "evil eye". The notion of the "evil eye" is that of looking at someone and causing them to be ill or cause bad luck to befall them or their possessions. Fear of this evil eye, by itself, can cause illness. In this tradition, it is someone else who has brought the illness upon those who suffer; but, for the psychoanalyst, the illness is the fear itself, which is projected on someone thought to be responsible for it.

I could very well receive patients who would speak to me in much the same way as they would address the holy men, the saints they would traditionally consult. The patient believing him or herself to be bewitched is in search of someone who might be persecuting them and is asking for treatment to make the demon placed in him or her go away. Many patients have already tried traditional methods before consulting me. They know, sometimes intuitively, that the answers or treatment, if we can say that, will not be the same—no promises or cosmic interpretations are given; instead, they are asked to consider their personal implication in each symptom.

In our culture, psychiatrists and psychoanalysts can therefore be considered as being on the same level as healers and magicians. Explaining the differences between these practices and psychoanalysis is the best way to fight quacks and sects. We must, therefore, insist on the ethics of our practice: for the psychoanalyst, it consists of that which our function confers upon us, to listen and interpret without interfering in the patients' personal lives, without influence or suggestion. We also have to emphasize the difference between psychoanalysis and psychotherapy; that is, that psychoanalysis is not adaptive and cannot be evaluated according the scientific or bureaucratic maxims favoured by state authorities.

Psychotherapies and psychoanalysis

In 1992, I created the Moroccan Association of Psychotherapy in order to bring together psychiatrists and psychologists who treat suffering without recourse to medical practice. Gradually, psychotherapy has become the main method of treatment—to listen and to treat individual psychic illness.

It would be interesting at this stage to reflect on the etymology of certain key terms. In Arabic the word "psychotherapy" can be translated as "*ilaj anafsi*" which means "treatment of the soul". "Soul", in Arabic *an nafs*, relates to the multiple psychic aspects of being, its internal equilibrium and its link to other beings. An analogical relationship is established between the individual psyche (mind), language, and the universe in which he or she exists. This *an-nafs* is not only rich in semantic implications but also in ancient history, evoking representations of human suffering as existed and were described before the arrival of Western science. Each culture has its own representations of mental illness, and these precede psychiatry.

Over the past three decades, science and medicine have been developing at a steady rate. This development has gone along with the steady growth of the pharmaceutical industry. Immense progress has no doubt been made, but there is no chemical answer for every problem or illness that might occur. All along, patients have sought something other than a medical solutions for their illnesses. They have needed to be listened to and to find a solution to their problems with the help of the supportive actions of those who listen to them. Gradually, as a practitioner, I have become recognized as a therapist who does not systematically prescribe medication but who is there to listen and interpret.

In parallel to the development of psychotherapy, psychoanalysis is becoming a field in itself—it is already so, but, as I have noted, previously, in Morocco, people did not make a distinction between the two. Today, there is a realization that there is a distinction between psychoanalysis, psychiatry, and psychology, and the number of patients asking for psychoanalysis is increasing. Many practitioners have themselves undergone a personal psychoanalysis, and have worked on theory and the practice of supervision.

On a social level, the democratization of the Moroccan society has made considerable advances, allowing freedom of speech and freedom to meet. We are witnessing social transformations with the lifting of certain taboos and the emergence of the individual within the group. In order to exist, psychoanalysis has to take place in society; and in 2001 no restrictions were imposed on the creation of the Moroccan Psychoanalytic Society.

The Moroccan Psychoanalytic Society

The Society was set up after many years of recognition of the need for it. My colleagues and friends encouraged me to set it up, as they wanted to submit themselves to psychoanalysis. Also, those undergoing psychoanalysis and those who had finished psychoanalysis needed a theoretical framework to underpin what they were doing in their current practice, and so wanted me to organize more training. Therefore, the aim of the SPM is to train psychoanalysts, to develop the discipline and to provide the context for best ethical practice. Ours is the first such society to be set up in a Northern African country and, after Lebanon, only the second in the Arabic world. It has taken a long time to come into existence. Why, you might ask? There are several reasons for this. First of all, the fact that this practice was little known and there were too few psychoanalysts to create a society or an association. But, apart from that, if we consider notions of free speech and association, Morocco was not yet ready for such a society. For psychoanalysis to come to maturity with the creation of our society, it needed to be recognized as a viable discipline; this was made possible by the first practitioners of our discipline in Morocco. A long-lasting structure needed to be set up—there was a need to meet, reflect, and organize theory and training.

I proposed a system of training that involved inviting one or two analysts from France, for several days on a monthly basis. This inevitably raises questions concerning transmission and resistance. But I could already see that, as soon as the process had started, it would provide a springboard for further development. The future of our society, the SPM, would depend on it.

To begin with, my colleagues and I decided to use existing practitioners as trainers. These were people who expressed a desire to undergo personal psychoanalysis. Having undergone an analysis, they themselves would be subjecting others to it, which would prove a sound basis for them to become trainers of other prospective psychoanalysts.

Finally, we made the decision not to become affiliated to any other association or school of thought. We had to exist through our own work first of all, and not through some other school or policies dictated from outside. Rather than simply copying what others have done, this choice allows us to be more inventive and favours a real transmission of our personal knowledge to our trainees.

How to reinvent psychoanalysis inside a culture?

My first wish was to think about treatment, and then to train and set up the society in order to train others. It is known that the desire of the analyst is a function, that which makes the analysand into an analyst. The change occurs when the analysand wants to practise in the same way as her analyst. However, when I say "as her analyst", I am only thinking about the "function" of being an analyst. Only when she practises does she become an analyst; before this stage she cannot be recognized as such. But the question of when the analysand actually becomes the analyst should be left open. When the state imposes rules, it ignores this fact, reducing our profession to the sort of discipline that may be guaranteed by a degree or diploma. Freud himself insisted on this point against a reduction to state-determined rules. Our profession cannot be measured or quantified in this way, and it would negatively affect our discipline to bend to that measurement and quantification of "outcomes", whether of psychoanalytic practice or training.

Whenever we submit ourselves to analysis, even if we are already established psychiatrists or psychologists, we change our way of speaking and our discourse. The symptom is no longer related to a medical "syndrome", but to repression and truth. The response to suffering consists of following what a patient says without trying to anticipate what is expected of them. My own patients consult me for many different reasons—they may be deeply worried or anxious, have some physical pain or be depressed, have phobias or obsessions. By listening to my patients I can try to meet their needs and desire. Our way of doing things is not the same as that of a psychiatrist. If psychoanalysis seems feasible, I do not prescribe medicine. This refusal of medical "science", as if were the only possible framework for treatment, has become standard practice for psychoanalysts in Morocco. To transmit psychoanalysis we need to reinvent it, and to reinvent it has necessitated finding new ways of approaching the unconscious.

Personally, I take into account two things—the psychiatric institution and the evolution of ancestral traditions in Morocco. Taking into account the institutions, individually, we have been obliged to reinvent ourselves within our own culture. Since Freud's time, psychoanalysts have continually been redefining the question of transmission: how do we transmit what we have learned? Transmission is not merely the reproduction of what our ancestors did. It is making use of the body of knowledge and experience accumulated and adapting it to our present-day needs. Trying to reproduce exactly what was done before would be to caricature and pervert the profession. What worked and was feasible once is not necessarily possible today. What is being learnt comes from the analysand, and transmission is that of an unconscious knowledge. The training received by the psychoanalyst comes from the unconscious.

If the unconscious is universal, it is through cultural particularities and social mutations that individual discourse is questioned by the psychoanalyst. We can take into account cultural specifics that are not considered as narrow particularities, but as "resistances" that need to be analysed before we may move on. Even patients' religious experiences, beliefs, and practices are *individual* experiences, as is, for example, Islam's notion of interpretation. The psychoanalyst accompanies the patient's words. The desire for *individual* expression, *without* a family member being present, is necessary. Thanks to this expression, each individual appropriates the language with which he or she can rebuild his or her life.

In our practice, we hear of young people who take liberties that go against what they have been taught, who do not hide behind an archaic vision that does not take into account the change in mentalities and the reality of society.

Conclusion

Why, then, is Moroccan society ready now to accept the existence of psychoanalysis? There are several reasons for this. There has been a certain democratization of Morocco and things have opened up more. We are seeing more individual freedom and an open acceptance of different points of view. A particular kind of individual subject is now emerging from traditional social ties. People are questioning tradition and ancient taboos. Furthermore, women—some of whom, incidentally, today are involved in the practice of psychoanalysis in Morocco—have always been at the root of major advances in society, against inequalities, for individual differences, for the opening up of society and for secularism. Bilingualism and even multi-lingualism (Arabic, Berber, French, English, and Spanish) encourage this openness.

Finally, we must underline the position of Morocco on a cultural and geographical level. Morocco is criss-crossed by other cultures and other religions. These cultural exchanges take place not only with the West but with Arab cultures, too. In Morocco, tradition and modernity run side by side. They are not in open conflict with each other. We can see this in the way Moroccan society has changed and is evolving. Changes produced by present global circumstances and many questions concerning identity, culture, language, and religion, are vital matters for researchers in different disciplines. At the heart of each of these disciplines, a place must be reserved for the individual dimension, which is inseparable from the social dimension. Psychoanalysis is faced with the difficult task of questioning the individual and his or her context, language, and culture as part of a symbolic universal field into which a different knowledge is woven. Psychoanalysis is a private practice "in intension", but in the public domain it is "in extension". In private, each treatment is a "reinvention". In the public domain it is not enough that a psychoanalytic discourse exists. In order for real transmission to take place, psychoanalytic discourse must be recognized and accepted by the culture. But this does not mean recognition by the state. State recognition does not guarantee "reinvention".

The analyst is only authorized by him or herself . . . and by some others—this conception of authorization elaborated by Lacan is well known, but sometimes misused by analysts themselves, who appropriate this idea but without recognition of the discipline or association to which they belong. As for state intervention in our discipline, this would simply stifle and put a brake on our creativity. We cannot be put into a strait-jacket, as each individual treatment cannot be quantified, controlled, or measured. The supposed protection that state control would give would only create layers of bureaucracy and obstacles to our creativity. Regulation and training must come from within the body of psychoanalysts.

In my practice, I am free, and patients are free to see any analyst they wish. What would be the impact on this if the state decided what the essence of psychoanalysis and its goals should be? If rules and training were to be imposed by the state, and if laws were applied, nothing of what I do would be possible. Freedom, ethics, and individual responsibility raise questions that go beyond psychoanalysis and that concern society as a whole. Regulation, guarantees, and control institute a change in social bonds and a different, regressive way of managing human relations.

CHAPTER FOURTEEN

Psychoanalysis and regulation in Japan

Kazushige Shingu

I approach the question of the particularity of psychoanalysis and regulation by briefly reviewing the current status of registration procedures for psychotherapists in Japan. The discussion then turns to consider the position of the "dead person" in Japanese Buddhism, which provides an analogy for the current position of psychoanalysis in Japan as it faces the prospect of state regulation. I conclude with some reflections on the transmission of psychoanalysis.

Current conditions of qualifications concerning psychoanalysis in Japan

The predicament of psychoanalysis in Japan is governed by the position of psychiatry as a medical profession, the practice of which is authorized by the Japanese state, and the role of clinical psychology in the recent drive to registration.

Psychoanalysts and clinical psychologists in psychiatry

In Japan, psychiatrists are paid for their psychoanalytic practice within the provisions of national health insurance. The length and frequency of sessions are specified within this scheme as forty-five minutes for one session, with payment for up to six times a month. The fee is also specified as 3,900 yen for one session, a very low amount compared with that in an average private psychoanalytic practice.[1] There is an academic qualification for clinical psychologists. So far, this qualification is not governmental, and so it is independent of the national insurance scheme. Instead, this qualification is based on an academic curriculum determined by psychologists in the universities, and it is that curriculum which is, in turn, regulated by the state. Qualified clinical psychologists vastly outnumber qualified psychiatrists. However, this does not mean that clinical psychologists find it easy to work psychoanalytically within the health service framework, and to get their fees reimbursed. It often happens that clinical psychologists work together with psychiatrists in a hospital or psychiatric clinic. In these cases, there is sometimes the option, though one that is only barely and formally compliant with the law, for a psychiatrist to refer their client to a clinical psychologist so that the psychologist may offer psychoanalysis within the frame of the national insurance scheme.

There is, in addition, an academic qualification of psychotherapists by the Japan Psychoanalytic Association (JPA), which is that of "psychoanalytic psychotherapist". Although this qualification is not administered by the government, in so far as it is an additional qualification that is only applicable to qualified clinical psychologists or qualified psychiatrists, it is fair to say that this qualification, too, is dependent on the state. Personal analysis (as a form of didactic analysis) is not stipulated as a necessary requirement to become a psychoanalytic psychotherapist, and the candidate needs only to follow the requisite academic curriculum and do therapy under supervision.

Qualification of "psychoanalysts", psychoanalysts of the kind recognized by the International Psychoanalytical Association (IPA) in many countries of the English-speaking world, is something that functions independently of these national qualifications, and on a very small scale. The IPA members in Japan form a small society, the Japan Psychoanalytic Society (JPS). Members of the JPS are usually also qualified as psychoanalytic psychotherapists by the Japan Psychoanalytic Association (JPA), and are usually thought of as being at the core of that Association.[2] The members of the JPS who are psychiatrists are actually quite indifferent to the issue of the state regulation of psychoanalysis; they are already regulated as medical doctors and this is not at all inconvenient to them. The JPS members who are psychologists (a handful of people) may be interested in this issue, but only as far as the qualification of clinical psychologist is concerned. Those members are the ones who are eager to be qualified and regulated by the state, as medical doctors are. In either case, JPS members do not seem to be very involved in state regulation for psychoanalysis as such, because what matters for them is the qualification provided by the IPA. As for Lacanians, there is no formal system for the training of such analysts. Lacanians in Japan are mainly psychiatrists and clinical psychologists, or they are academics who are not involved in clinical practice. This means that while the psychiatric and psychological Lacanians are practising in their own respective disciplinary fields (and governed by relevant training standards and codes of practice) the academic Lacanians are generally engaged in literary or philosophical works. Japanese psychoanalysis is thus scattered among other different dominant professions, and so diluted in the existing practices of psychiatry and clinical psychology.

The case of a clinical psychologist

Let us approach these issues by considering how a clinical psychologist might be able to practise in these conditions. One of my colleagues, a qualified clinical psychologist, is working in a psychiatric clinic. Sometimes the psychiatrist refers patients to him, and then he undertakes psychoanalytic psychotherapy. This is barely within the legitimate territory, but on the edge of the regime of national insurance. For this work, he receives a meagre 3,000 yen (and the psychiatric clinic holds back the remaining 900 yen for itself). This kind of arrangement is, as we have already noted, an exceptional case, and usually conditions for a clinical psychologist working in the context of a psychiatric clinic are not as good as this. It is just one example of how co-operation between psychiatrists and clinical psychologists within the framework of national insurance compensation for therapy actually works, how therapy carried out in the name of "psychoanalysis" actually functions.

A more common practice is that the psychiatric clinic will refer patients to an attached psychotherapeutic facility, and here a clinical psychologist may provide therapy for these patients outside the national insurance scheme. In that case, the fee is over 10,000 yen, and then the clinic often receives more than a half of the amount.[3] In these cases, however, the clinical psychologist's practice does not go under the name of psychoanalysis, and in general, it is referred to as "counselling". My colleague, who is given referrals by the psychiatrist (and so reimbursed through health insurance a small amount), is also working as a school counsellor four days a week. School counsellors are paid between 5,000 and 7,000 yen per hour, which is quite high compared with other regular teachers. Moreover, they are paid regardless of whether clients (those students who are referred to them) come for counselling or not. This means that to find a position as a school counsellor is preferable on financial grounds for clinical psychologists (and those who commit themselves to psychoanalytic work pay a high price for their commitment).

Psychoanalysis in clinical psychology

These institutional conditions are such that it is very easy for psychoanalytic practice in Japan to melt into the wider psychological context of the society. The term "psychoanalysis" is fairly well known to the general public, but it is not usually differentiated from the work of other clinical psychologies. We could say that the concept of psychoanalysis is pretty well amorphous, which is not to say that it is completely forgotten. When seminars on psychoanalysis are opened up to clinical psychologists and psychiatrists, there are many participants. We can see from such events that clinical psychologists and counsellors are actually quite eager to know what is happening between therapist and patient, between analyst and analysand. They feel themselves in need of a vocabulary that will enable them to render such a relationship knowable, and that will also enable the therapist to have a better idea of the social role of the therapist herself. Psychoanalysis is expected to provide such a vocabulary, and it is still one of the reference points of the broader psychotherapeutic community.

The pressing issue now is the state regulation of clinical psychology rather than psychoanalysis as such, and it is this that will have major consequences for therapeutic work of any kind. The organizations of clinical psychologists want to be qualified and regulated by the state, and there has been very active participation in negotiations by the different clinical organizations between the profession and the government. Many expect that state qualification and regulation of clinical psychologists will come about in the near future.

It is still important that there are psychoanalysts practising outside psychiatry and clinical psychology, however small their number. When psychotherapy is regulated by the state, what will happen to this minority, these psychoanalysts who are still not qualified as psychoanalysts by any formally recognized organization? Does the so-called "problem" of lay analysis then arise, in which the practice of those who are not already medically qualified is seen as a problem? It will depend on which precise terms will be regulated: if the law stipulates that "psychotherapy" should not be carried out by people other than a psychotherapist who is designated as such by the government, psychoanalysis in Japan will be in peril, for psychoanalysis will then be defined merely as a form of psychotherapy. At present, we can only hope that such a reduction of psychoanalysis to psychotherapy will not happen, and that a form of psychoanalysis that is independent of psychiatry and psychology will not end up being against the law.

The "dead person" and the position of psychoanalysis in Japan

The role of the law in clinical practice can be seen very clearly if we consider how Japanese Buddhism survived through an adaptation to state definitions of the role of an officially recognized religion. There are dire warnings here for psychoanalysis. The price Buddhism paid is not, as we shall see, a price that psychoanalysis should now be expected to pay.

A comparison between psychoanalysis and Japanese Buddhism

Lacan made the point that the psychoanalytic subject, the analysand, has a dead person as her partner. This partner comes repeatedly to the fore during analysis. In so far as this partner is symbolic or imaginary, psychoanalysis is able to speak of this dead partner within private practice, but the crucial question is: when they come to be "real", in the Lacanian sense of "real"; in such a case, can the partnership of the analysis with this dead person remain private? It is commonly assumed that there should be a public, societal dimension as far as a real dead person is concerned, and it is precisely here that psychoanalysis is susceptible to regulation by the state. State regulation of psychoanalysis, then, would be akin to a registered funeral.

Such a state of affairs was in fact the choice of Japanese Buddhism during its development (in which it came to restrict its function to the supervision of funeral procedures and registration of the dead, thus enabling it to be ratified and overseen by the state). It was owing to this strategy (state registration and so legitimation by the state), that Buddhism survived the intense conflict with pre-modern political powers and the modernization of Japan, but it is now suffering as a result, suffering from its own formalization. And it is in this respect that we can compare the process of state regulation of psychoanalysis with the status and predicament of Buddhism in Japan.

For Lacan,

> [T]he death instinct essentially expresses the limit of the subject's historical function. This limit is death . . . the subject being understood as defined by his historicity. Indeed, this limit is present at every instant in what is finished in this history. It represents the past in its real form; . . . the past which manifests itself in an inverted form in repetition. This is the dead person [*le mort*] subjectivity takes as its partner in the triad instituted by its mediation in the universal conflict of *Philia,* love, and *Neikos,* strife. [Lacan, 2006, pp. 261–262]

According to Lacan, the past in its "real" form is a dead person. As analysts, then, we in fact treat these dead persons. How do we deal with them? As analysts we are operating with death in quite a different way from that prescribed by the state in the world outside the clinic. If we were actually to find a dead person, in its "real" form and within a social "reality" as defined by commonly agreed norms, we would *de facto* immediately find ourselves involved in the public realm. Perhaps, this dead person might be implicated in a criminal case, or perhaps may be the result of an accident; in any event, it is a matter that must be decided publicly. If we were to treat our clinical practice as operating in line with those public conventions it would logically follow that, if psychoanalysis has a reason for being regulated by the state, it is because it deals with "real" dead persons. A psychoanalyst would then be liable to be called as a witness and may be required to attend court proceedings to testify there.

Let us take a different, genuinely psychoanalytic stance on this, and learn from the history of Japanese Buddhism. The position of being a witness to the dead person reminds us again of the history of Japanese Buddhism. In Japanese Buddhism, people are very much accustomed to equate the Buddha to a dead person. Buddhists see a Buddha in everyone we meet on the street. It is his death as well as mine. It is just as Lacan maintained in his commentary on the role of the object, it is "In you, more than you" (Lacan, 1977, p. 263), and it is thus that we see a Buddha in our fellow persons. We have another word for Buddha, *Hotoke*; if we hear this word *Hotoke* in a television detective programme, for example, we know that the police are referring to the victim's corpse.

"Being still alive, I am a corpse, every piece is dead in me, how nice it is to be like this and to be free in every act of mine," said a Japanese Buddhist monk. From all this, we know something of how Japanese Buddhism has dealt with death in its long tradition. Four hundred years ago, the *Shogun* determined that every family should belong to a temple, and it was assumed that the pedigree of the family should be maintained in temples. This was in order to eliminate the influence of Christianity, and to ensure the seclusion of Japan. Buddhism thus came to function as a registration office of death in Japanese society. It could, in this way, also stay true to its essential mode of existence, of dealing with death. But it chose too conservative and bureaucratic a mode of existence to remain a vital force in society.

And now, I think, the position of psychoanalysis is similar to that of Buddhism in earlier days in relation to Japanese society. Analysts often accept analysands when the latter are in mourning. We must remember that Freud himself was in mourning when he invented psychoanalysis. If psychoanalysis thinks that individual mourning should be processed in public, it should then logically be willing to be regulated by the state. But, if psychoanalysis wishes for individual mourning to remain subjective, it will follow another independent path, and this will also be a path different from that taken by Japanese Buddhism.

Japanese Buddhism is now reduced to being a practice concerned with the execution of a funeral in public. And this function is now far too "official" and superficial to provide a model for psychoanalysis. Buddhism, it should be said, preserves not only the ritual, but also many artistic treasures owing to this conservative tactic of survival. Buddhist temples are like museums. If we are curious enough, we can find many aspects of psychoanalytic mourning in the Buddhist arts and legends. These treasures may inspire psychoanalysts, but even then we have to understand that this is still not a psychoanalytic way of dealing with the dead. Even as we acknowledge the importance of Buddhism to psychoanalysis, we have to imagine how the state legitimation of Buddhism would spell the alteration of psychoanalysis as a practice if that attempt to conserve itself was taken as a model. So, then, the question arises: if it is not a "public" processing of the mourning that an analysand undergoes, is a *subjective funeral* possible?

A subjective funeral

I would say it is impossible but it *is* psychoanalysis. Let us remember Antigone. After her brother's death, the state refused to allow a public funeral to be conducted for him. However, Antigone wanted to execute a funeral for her brother. The express intention of the governmental power was that the corpse of her brother should be deserted and exposed to natural decay, that he should not have a funeral. Antigone's act of putting some soil on the corpse, giving the body funeral rites of some kind, was thus explicitly against the government.

In these conditions, Antigone herself did not know what she was doing; she insists that it is the state, not she, who is against the law of humanity. Human beings should be given a funeral and so she felt that, since her brother was not to be provided publicly recognized funeral rites, she must carry out the funeral rites herself. This she does; this is her "act". When her activity was uncovered, she was condemned to death. Now, should we conclude that she was sent to her death because she was too "humanistic", because she was too extreme in her respect for the memory and body of her brother? No. Rather, she was sent to her death because she executed a private funeral. As we have noted, it is commonly understood that a corpse should be made public, and this was the case in the city-state in which Antigone then lived. The state decided that the corpse should be publicly abandoned; it was a public decision about public matters. Antigone, on the other hand, tried to retrieve the corpse, to bring it into her own subjective realm and execute a kind of funeral that is impossible.

A subjective funeral here is therefore banned, or, in other words, it is considered to be nothing. But what can we do when the public funeral does not please us? When it is against our own will that our dear ones, or ourselves for that matter, should be subjected to the procedure of a conventional funeral, should we comply with the law? In such a case, why could we not execute a "subjective funeral"? This is not a trivial question. It touches on the matters of life and death, subjective life and death, with which every analyst has to deal. The question is quite serious.

In the dreams of analysands, I have come to witness numerous scenes where analysands are carrying a corpse. It may appear as a corpse as it is, explicitly represented as such, or the "corpse" may take a form of other objects, as the corpse of the subject of those dear to them. In such cases it is evident that the analysands are looking for a place where they can carry out a subjective funeral for these corpses. The analytic setting is a place where such a subjective funeral can be enacted.

It seems clear that for many of us a public funeral is insufficient or deficient. We need something more, or, perhaps, less. Recall that Freud was too late for his father's funeral (Freud, 1985, p. 202), and this lateness was one of the driving forces for him to write *The Interpretation of Dreams* (1900a). After a conventional public funeral, it is not only Freud but all of us who still have many things to do. This is psychoanalysis as a subjective funeral that state regulation cannot govern.

What is unanalysed is transmitted

The dead person in analysis, the partner of the analysand who is carried by them as they carry out the analytic work, must be the object that is transmitted in analysis. Or rather, if there should be such a thing as a transmission of psychoanalysis from generation to generation, it would be through this kind of corpse that the transmission should occur.

If a psychoanalytic treatment could really be said to be "perfect" and "complete", then psychoanalysis would not have to be transmitted to another generation. What is conveyed of psychoanalysis in the lineage of a human generation is its incompleteness or impossibility.

We could ask whether "Little Hans" was analysed to perfection. As every analyst knows, his analysis was terminated when he constructed an Oedipus complex of his own. However, although the aim of psychoanalysis is often understood to entail dissolution of this complex, not many analysts think that this particular analysis ended in failure. In what sense was it a success, then?

The completed Oedipus complex in Little Hans is quite singular. His Oedipal desire is fulfilled: he gained (imaginary) children whose mother is his mother, whose grandfather is his father, and whose grandmother is his father's mother. Freud writes:

> Things were moving towards a satisfactory conclusion. The little Oedipus had found a happier solution than that prescribed by destiny. Instead of putting his father out of the way, he had granted him the same happiness that he desired himself: he made him a grandfather and married *him* to his own mother too. [Freud, 1909b, p. 97]

Here, however, Freud forgets the infinite character of this procedure as the logic of the subject. Hans could have continued his operation *ad infinitum*. It is true that his father could have a spouse, and his grandfather, too, but the last or original father must then be a single man. If that original man at the end of the logical sequence had a spouse, there would be no possibility of this spouse being other than nature herself. Here comes a fantastic conception of a marriage, of an original man and nature (perhaps "mother nature"). It is this that remained unanalysed in Little Hans; and, just as Freud admitted that there was always something that was left unanalysed, it is this that remains as unanalysed in us as well. We continue to transmit this fantasized marriage down the generations. In Japan, this fantasy takes the form of animism. What is unanalysed will repeatedly be handed over as something to be analysed in the future; this may be a corpse of the primal father in the midst of nature, which psychoanalytic Antigones would like to cover with some soil without ever succeeding in doing so.

Notes

1. This is under £16, under Euro 23, and around the same amount in dollars.
2. For a history and functions of the JPA and JPS, see Parker (2008).
3. This means that the therapist will get just over £20 (or about 30 Euros or dollars), with an equivalent amount going to the clinic.

References

Freud, S. (1900a). *The Interpretation of Dreams. S.E., 4–5*. London: Hogarth.

Freud, S. (1909b). Analysis of a phobia in a five-year-old boy. *S.E., 10*: 3–152. London: Hogarth.

Freud, S. (1985). *The Complete Letters of Sigmund Freud to Wilhelm Fliess 1887–1904*. J. M. Masson (Ed.). Cambridge, MA: Harvard University Press.

Lacan, J. (2006) *Écrits: The First Complete Edition in English*. B. Fink (Trans.). New York: W. W. Norton.

Lacan, J. (1977) *The Four Fundamental Concepts of Psycho-Analysis*. A. Sheridan (Trans.). Harmondsworth: Pelican.

Parker, I. (2008). *Japan in Analysis: Cultures of the Unconscious*. London: Palgrave.

CHAPTER FIFTEEN

The Italian lesson

Gillian Clayton

It could be instructive to note, in various countries, which conditions have favoured the development of psychoanalysis and which have held it back: in Europe, at present, psychoanalysts are struggling to maintain their independence and the specificity of their theories and practice.

In her book *Why Psychoanalysis?*, Elisabeth Roudinesco (2001) puts forward the view that psychoanalysis can only develop in those countries that have a solid tradition of psychiatry, and are therefore capable of conceptualizing mental illness in ways that exclude ideas of divine possession, and also where there is a State of Law that is capable of guaranteeing the free transmission of knowledge. Italy, at the turn of the past century, was such a country, with Lombroso being its most famous psychiatrist (although his ideas were far from Freudian), and, in fact, it was Italian psychiatrists, studying under Kraepelin in Munich, who first brought Freud's ideas to Italy.

The first Italian psychoanalyst was Edoardo Weiss, a young doctor from Trieste, a pupil of Freud's, whom he first met in 1908, and a life-long colleague (Roazen, 2005). Psychoanalysis did indeed gain popularity among a few poets and writers—such as Saba, Svevo, Joyce—in Weiss's home town on the border with Austria, the most cosmopolitan Italian city, which was part of the Austro-Hungarian Empire until the end of the First World War. A small group of analysts then gradually formed, with their centre in Rome. In a letter to Weiss, Freud wrote in 1923 (Weiss, 1970), "Do not doubt that in Italy too the future belongs to psychoanalysis. Only you will have to wait quite a while" (my translation). These words were to prove prophetic, since the forces opposed to psychoanalysis in Italy were many and powerful. First, there was the predominant philosophical current of idealism (as expounded by Croce and Gentile); then there was the influence of the Catholic Church; later there was Fascism, which evolved into anti-Semitism; there was the general outlook of the scientific and clinical world and the universities, which was hostile; then, still later on, there was the influence of Communism.

In 1934, the Vatican prohibited the publication of the official psychoanalytic journal, the *Rivista italiana di psicoanalisi*. Although Mussolini was not personally opposed to Freud or psychoanalysis, once the Race Laws had been passed in 1938 and persecutions started, Weiss, who was Jewish, emigrated to the United States (in 1939). Jews were excluded from academia, teaching, and any public office, so that most Jewish analysts, the majority in the small Italian group, emigrated as well, and those who stayed in Italy found other ways of earning a living for seven years (David, 1990). So, whereas in Britain there was a large analytic community, with the lively Controversial Discussions taking place in London during the war, in Italy psychoanalysis all but disappeared from early 1939 until the end of 1945.

In 1945, the Societa' di Psicoanalisi Italiana (SPI), affiliated to the IPA, had six members, in 1955 it had twenty and in 1963 it had thirty. The Jungian group had fifteen members at that time (Vegetti Finzi, 1986). However, with the economic boom of the late 1960s and the 1970s, psychoanalysis came into its own: it was as if all the years of resistance to it had sharpened an appetite for it. When I went to live in Italy in the early 1970s, it was clear that there was a real interest in psychoanalysis, and a far less ambivalent attitude towards it than there was in England. Cesare Musatti, popularly dubbed the father of Italian psychoanalysis, though a mathematician before becoming a psychologist, was a much-loved and respected figure in the media. However, a very subtle change has been recently introduced, one that seems to leave the vast majority of analysts unperturbed, and the general public generally unaware. As a result, the practice of psychoanalysis has been dramatically and, it would seem, irremediably transformed. To my knowledge, the analysts most concerned, one could say alarmed, are mainly, although not exclusively, Lacanians.

On 18 February 1989, a law was passed in Italy—Law 56—that regulated the profession of psychologist. For twenty years this law, promoted by a senator who was also a psychoanalyst, Adriano Ossicini, had been prepared and discussed. (It should be noted, in passing, that resistances to psychoanalysis come from all quarters, including analytic circles.) The psychologists wanted to be recognized as professionals in the same way as other categories—doctors, lawyers, architects, and so on—with their own professional organization, or Order (*Ordine*). In Italy the *Ordini* comprise those professionals who have obtained a degree in a certain subject (law, engineering, commerce, etc.), then gained substantial practical experience (*tirocinio*), and passed the final state-controlled exam, written and oral, which covers the whole degree course (*esame di stato*). This latter qualification allows them to practise the profession that their degree has prepared them for, and their names are included in a registry (*Albo*).

I can still remember going to my local kiosk on the day that the law in its final version was to be published in a certain magazine (*Riza psicosomatica*—I only bought it on that one occasion), and reading it through with bated breath. To my great relief—and many like-minded analysts felt the same—the word psychoanalysis did not appear once in the text of the law: it seemed that this law had nothing to do with the practice of psychoanalysis and that we had been spared. However, this was an over-optimistic and naïve view of events, as I shall try to explain and develop. I believe there are valuable lessons to be learned from the way things went wrong in Italy, and we are still in time, in the UK, to make a difference when it comes to the question of state regulation of the psychotherapies.

If we look at Law 56, it is clear that its concern is to regulate the profession of psychologist, which is defined in the first article. I think that any analyst would struggle to think that this is a definition of his or her work or stance. Nowhere in the law is there a definition of the practice of psychotherapy. The translations that follow are mine.

Article 1

(Definition of the profession of psychologist)

1. The profession of psychologist comprises the use of tools for understanding and intervening in matters concerning the prevention, diagnosis, activities of enabling/re-enabling and support in the psychological sphere, directed to persons, groups, social organisms, and communities. It also comprises the activity of experimentation, research, and teaching in this sphere.

Of the thirty-six articles, only two (Articles 3 and 35) are devoted to the subject of psychotherapy; these are the ones that have affected the practice of psychoanalysis in Italy.

Article 3

(The practice of the profession of psychotherapist)

1. The practice of psychotherapy is subordinated to a specific professional formation, to be acquired after obtaining a degree in psychology or medicine and surgery, given by specialization courses of at least four years' duration that envisage (*prevedano*) an adequate formation and training in psychotherapy, and are activated according to the decree of the President of the Republic on 10 March 1982, no.162, in specialization schools of universities or in institutions recognized for such a purpose through the procedures in Article 3 of the above-mentioned decree of the President of the Republic.
2. Psychotherapists who are not doctors are barred from any intervention that is the exclusive competence of the medical profession.
3. After obtaining the patient's consent, the psychotherapist and doctor (GP) are obliged to share information.

Article 35

(Recognition of psychotherapeutic practice)

1. With reference to the contents of Article 3, the right to practice psychotherapy is granted to those who are members of the

Order of psychologists or doctors who are members of the Order of doctors and orthodontists, in possession of a degree for at least five years, and who declare, under their own responsibility, that they have acquired a specific professional formation in psychotherapy, who provide documentation of their formative curriculum, indicating places, times, and duration, as well as their scientific curriculum, with documentation as to the continuity of their psychotherapeutic profession.

2. The Orders will establish the validity of such certification.
3. The provisions of Sections 1 and 2 are to be applied until the end of the fifth year after the present law has been in place.

So, summing up: only those who had obtained a degree in medicine or psychology and who had frequented a state-approved specialization course in psychotherapy for at least four years, would, after the passing of Law 56, be allowed to practise psychotherapy, which is, however, not defined. And the definition of the profession of psychologist is such that many priests and teachers, rather than psychoanalysts, would recognize themselves as falling into that remit. Those psychologists and doctors who wanted their psychotherapeutic practice recognized had five years in which to provide the necessary documentation. Although the specific nature of psychoanalysis had been discussed on several occasions in the parliamentary debates preceding the law (Santacatterina, 1996), there was no mention of psychoanalysis in the text of the law. Many psychoanalysts decided that this law did not concern them; however, the vast majority applied to become members of the newly-constituted Order of Psychologists; there were various possibilities for practitioners without degrees in medicine or psychology to become members for five years after the law was passed.

One needed to be quite long-sighted to see where all this was leading. It was not until the new Order of Psychologists printed out forms, to be filled in by those who had already become members and who wanted to have their psychotherapeutic practice recognized, that the word psychoanalysis finally appeared. Specifically, in section M, under the heading "Methodological references", where it was the first of a long list, followed by "Psychoanalytically orientated psychotherapy, Analytical psychology (Jung), Individual psychology (Adler), Freudian psychology (Lacan)" (which, of course, is nonsense, as Lacanians always refer to their practice as being that of psychoanalysis), "Transactional analysis, Cognitive–behavioural therapies, Systemic therapies, Non-directive therapies, Hypnosis, Autogenous training and relaxation therapies, Sex therapies, Bioenergetic therapies, Group therapies, Psychodrama, Gestalt therapy and Other . . ."

It is interesting to note the strange bedfellow of hypnosis cropping up alongside psychoanalysis: the specific difference of psychoanalysis from all the therapies based on suggestion is ignored. Although in a general sense one could say that psychoanalysis is a form of psychotherapy, one also has to qualify that it is different from all other forms, in that it recognizes the power of suggestion but does not base the treatment on this, quite the reverse. By placing himself in the position of the one who is only presumed to know, by the patient (Lacan's *sujet-supposé-savoir*), but refusing to acknowledge himself in the position of Ego Ideal, the analyst allows the knowledge that is imagined to be in his possession to unravel and be extricated in the course of the treatment; at the same time the position he occupies for the analysand is progressively explored and undermined.

The way that psychoanalysis was surreptitiously regulated in Italy, leading to a homogenization of the psychotherapies, suggests that what was at stake was not only the regulation of the profession of psychologist, but also the marginalization of psychoanalysis. It is true that if Freudian ideas are accepted (and to my knowledge they have only ever been corroborated in more recent research), i.e., that there are unconscious thought processes that have a real effect on our conscious thinking as well as our bodily sensations and illnesses, then a great deal of psychology needs to be re-thought. It is the subversive nature of psychoanalysis that is so hard to tolerate; the very reason why it can only survive, let alone flourish, in conditions of democracy.

The current, highly ambiguous situation in Italy, as far as psychoanalysis is concerned, is, in my opinion, one that we in the UK should fight to prevent from occurring. It is regrettable that not one of the larger psychoanalytical organizations publicly spoke out against Law 56: the SPI and AIPSI (affiliated to the IPA), the two major Jungian societies, and the largest Lacanian school (linked to the *Ecole de la Cause freudienne*) could all have made a difference had they done so. In most, if not all, of these organizations there were many analysts opposed to compliance with this law. Whatever the reasons behind their decision to become state-approved schools of psychotherapy (and it is true that one could think that there were concerns for the future of trainees, as well as links with institutions, university posts, and so on at stake), the outcome has been that a long Freudian tradition of lay analysis has come to an end. This can only result in an intellectual impoverishment of the analytic institutions themselves.

Moreover, in Italy today a person who has spent his/her life as a student, at school and then university, may now, at the age of thirty or so, with little experience of life in the real world, practise as a psychotherapist. Yet, someone who has had a career in another field, say a teacher with a degree in philosophy who becomes interested in psychoanalysis at a later stage, will have to do a degree in psychology, which lasts a minimum of five years, a year's clinical work experience (usually unpaid), and then the minimum four years of specialization in an approved institution in order to practise. Or s/he could train with one of the few organizations that have not complied with Law 56, thus risking social exclusion and, possibly, a court case. Yet Freud (1926e) believed that no particular degree prepared a psychoanalyst to practise psychoanalysis. By conflating psychoanalysis and psychotherapy, Law 56 glosses over the specific training of psychoanalysts.

This really is the crux of the matter, and one that the College of Psychoanalysts—UK is rightly putting to the forefront. We might ask: what is it that forms or creates a psychoanalyst? How is a psychoanalyst made? Ever since it was founded by Bernfeld late in 1923, the Berlin Institute has been taken as a model for the training of analysts. That is not to say that there could not be others. What all institutions seem to agree on is that the training should comprise three aspects: a personal analysis, lectures or seminars concentrating on psychoanalytic theory, and supervision of cases, especially at the beginning of an analyst's career. Historically, this training has been provided by psychoanalytic institutions, without any necessary reference to universities or interference from the state (Safouan, 2000 [1983]). In my view, it is necessary that this should continue to be so. As far as the training of analysts goes, the emphasis should, I feel, be placed on the personal analysis. Following

Lacan, I would pose that there is no difference between a training analysis and any other: in some institutions a difference is made between a personal analysis and a training analysis, just as there are analysts who are labelled training analysts while others are not. I prefer the view that a training analysis is quite simply one that produces an analyst—something that cannot be known or in any way guaranteed in advance—and that a training analyst is one who finds him/herself in the position of having conducted an analysis to that point where an analyst is formed.

Although it was not a total success, I consider that the concept, if not the practice, of the *passe*, instituted by Lacan in the *École freudienne de Paris* (Lacan, 1968)—an institution that tried to rethink the question of analytic training—still has some mileage left in it. During this procedure an analysand who, during the course of an analysis, has taken the step of putting him/herself in the position of analyst, a kind of self-authorizing, bears witness to this transition or passage by speaking of his/her experience to two other people at a similar stage of their formation, who in turn report to a committee. The idea was that something of the nature of the phenomenon—the production of an analyst—might be understood and become part of the theoretical stock of the institution. What is interesting is the idea that we still have more to find out about what it is that turns an analysand into an analyst. To posit, as has already happened in Italy, and could happen here, that we know in advance what trajectory a person has to take in order to become an analyst—so many hours of analysis, so many years of particular courses, so many hours of supervision and training patients—is to lose sight of the idea that every analysis, and therefore every training, is unique and unrepeatable. I am not saying that these components of a training are not desirable or should be ignored, just that there is a real danger that we begin to actually believe in the importance of these kinds of accountancy. It is largely through the personal analysis that an analyst is formed and also that an understanding of theory takes place, through subjective transformations. Given that, in any analysis, much of the work will take place unconsciously, and that it is not always possible to observe directly how transformations have occurred, although it is possible to take note and theorize retrospectively, it follows that the analysand is never completely in control of his/her own analysis, and neither is the analyst. We should, I believe, oppose any attempt by the state to legislate and presume to control analysis. The criteria for an analytic training or formation can only be determined by the psychoanalytic institutions, which have the necessary experience and understanding. The transmission of psychoanalysis is complex and cannot be left to the universities (Freud, 1919j).

In Italy today, in order to carry on practising, all the 'psy' professionals now have to notch up annually a minimum number of credits (*ECM: Educazione Continua in Medicina*) to prove their continuous medical [*sic*] training. This can lead to shopping around for bargain courses—a maximum of points for a minimum of effort (Benini, 2004)—while other formative experiences, such as international conferences, or indeed, further analysis or supervision, will not count towards the total. Bureaucracy spirals out of control, as new jobs are created for those who then have to decide on the meting out of credits. Surely, as psychoanalysts, we should rather be concentrating on defining and practising an ethical position for ourselves and for our institutions (Perella, 1995)? Even if our work is not directly controlled by the state, as citizens we are still responsible for our actions and do not operate outside of the law, to which we are all subject. The enormous pity is that, paradoxically, had the Italian analysts not rushed *en masse* to get legal, then it would be clear in Italian society today that Law 56 does not necessarily apply to them (Molino, 2001; Santacatterina, 1996), as a few recent court decisions have shown.

In the UK, since there is no system of *Ordini* (whereby graduates in subjects leading to recognized professions, such as medicine, architecture, engineering, etc., after passing a final state exam are then entered onto a national register), it is unlikely that the practice of psychotherapy will be limited to graduates in medicine and psychology. What, then, might be the lessons to be learned from the regulation of the psychotherapies in Italy?

First, perhaps rather obviously, an open and informed debate is needed, which addresses the issues facing psychoanalysts; the differences between psychoanalysis and psychotherapy, for example (Contardi, 1990; Fondation du Champ Freudien, 1992). Can a psychoanalyst really be considered a "health professional"? The kinds of compromise that would be needed to fit into the regulatory strait-jacket could destroy the specificity of psychoanalysis.

There would not be so much an end to lay analysis, as has happened in Italy, but an end to psychoanalysis itself, as Freud conceived it.

Sadly, the history of psychoanalysis has shown how the various schools—one might almost say "factions"—of psychoanalysis have been caught up in the narcissism of small differences. Their lack of communication now prevents many of them from acting together for the right to continue to practise according to analytic principles. Today, the threats to psychoanalysis come, not from neighbouring schools that might have a slightly different theoretical perspective, but rather from centralized forms of control, as well as the powerful pharmaceutical companies, whose influence in the field of psychiatry and mental health care even extends to affecting clinical diagnoses. Interestingly, Bollas and Sundelson (1995) suggest that psychoanalysts have everything to gain from being generous, and should consider including psychoanalytic psychotherapists among their ranks in order to face the current emergency—presumably they mean those practitioners whose personal analysis was conducted with fewer sessions per week than recommended by a particular national IPA directive, but who nevertheless see their practice as psychoanalytical.

Finally, the essence of the psychoanalytic relationship needs to be explored in order to see how the current proposals for regulation might interfere with it, altering its very nature, so that it can no longer be called analysis. In the relationship between analyst and analysand there is always something other (Safouan, Julien, & Hoffmann, 1995). We might think of this in various ways: for example, as Lacan's Other, the place of the unconscious; or the function of the third person described by Freud (*die dritte Person*) to whom jokes are addressed; or perhaps the empty place that the analyst occupies (Lacan's object *a*), the space of desire. However, when the third element in an analysis becomes a real agency, such as an insurance company, a lawyer, or the state, to whom the analyst is answerable, not as a private citizen but by virtue of his profession, then the analyst is unable to place himself in that position that ensures the work of analysis, with the result that there is an inevitable *perversion* of the analytic relation: the presence of an Other (an Other of the Other, Lacan would say), *in the real*, instead of a *symbolic* one.

In order to preserve the integrity of psychoanalytic practice, I would suggest that the schools of psychoanalysis concentrate on outlining the practical, theoretical, and ethical reasons why the formation of analysts and their practice need to be self-regulated, according to the criteria established by individual institutions. That is, unless they prefer the "state-sanctioned respectability" that Bollas and Sundelson describe. Even if the aim of state regulation is to protect the general public, there is nothing in the government project that will protect it from "wild" psychoanalysis; this can only be the responsibility of psychoanalytic organizations.

References

Benini, F. (2004). Dal sonno della ragione nascono le Mucche Caroline ovvero. A proposito degli ECM. Brescia: Unpublished paper.

Bollas, C., & Sundelson, D. (1995). *The New Informants: The Betrayal of Confidentiality in Psychoanalysis and Psychotherapy*. London: Jason Aronson.

Contardi, S. (1990). La guarigione e la cura analitica. *Thelema, 2*: 31–44.

David, M. (1990). *La psicoanalisi nella cultura italiana*. Turin: Bollati Boringhieri.

Fondation du Champ Freudien (1992). Psicoterapia e psicoanalisi. *La psicoanalisi, Studi internazionali del campo freudiano*. Naples: La Moderna Stampa.

Freud, S. (1919j). On the teaching of psychoanalysis in universities. *S.E., 17*: 169–174. London: Hogarth.

Freud, S. (1926e). The question of lay analysis. *S.E., 20*: 179–254. London: Hogarth.

Lacan, J. (1968). Proposition du 9 octobre 1967 sur le psychanalyste de l'Ecole. *Scilicet, 1*: 14–30.

Molino, A. (2001). Italy's subjection of psychoanalysis: a case-study look at regulatory politics. In: A. Molino (Ed.), *Where Id Was* (pp. 178–181). London: Continuum.

Perella, E. (1995). *Psicanalisi e diritto*. Pordenone: Biblioteca dell' Immagine.

Roazen, P. (2005). *Edoardo Weiss: The House that Freud Built*. New Brunswick, NJ: Transaction.

Roudinesco, E. (2001). *Why Psychoanalysis?* R. Bowlby (Trans.). New York: Columbia University Press.

Safouan, M. (2000[1983]). *Jacques Lacan and the Question of Psychoanalytic Training*. J. Rose (Trans.). Basingstoke: Macmillan.

Safouan, M., Julien, P., & Hoffmann, C. (1995). *Malaise dans la psychanalyse. Le tiers dans l'institution et l'analyse de controle.* Paris: Arcanes.

Santacatterina, M. (1996). Dalla legge alla psicanalisi. Vicende recenti degli analisti italiani. *Scibbolet, 3*: 157–181.

Vegetti Finzi, S. (1986). *Storia della psicoanalisi* . Milan: Mondadori.

Weiss, E. (1970). *Sigmund Freud as a Consultant.* New York: Intercontinental Medical Book Corporation.

CHAPTER SIXTEEN

Psychology, psychotherapy, and psychoanalysis in Italy[1]

Anna Barracco

In Italy, the law that instituted the State regulation of psychology and psychotherapy, which, in this country, form a single profession, was introduced in 1989. When considering its preparatory work, which lasted more or less four years, one could say that the debate about the regulation of the professional act 'psy' has continued for more than twenty years. And, in some ways, the promotion of this law has fomented, rather than dissipated, this debate. Over the last four years we have seen a parallel debate in France, which started from the same presuppositions but was then elaborated in very different ways. I focus on the Italian law as a starting point for some crucial questions about the role of state regulation. What scenario existed when it first appeared? Which type of profession and professional reality pre-existed it? And what has its application produced? I say something, too, about the current scenario and the problems that remain open, and I insert my considerations also within the broader European debate concerning the reform of intellectual professions.

In Italy, the trigger to the explosion of the debate about the state regulation of psychotherapies was a sensational case that was widely covered by the media. In the mid 1980s, a notorious psychoanalyst was accused of exploiting a very wealthy patient—a dentist. The patient accused the analyst of having extorted large sums of money from him, of having led him to take part in various purchases, to leave jewels as payment, and so on. All this would have been possible, primarily thanks to the therapeutic relationship, the subjecting relation, the transference, the profoundly asymmetrical dimension in which he—a man who certainly could not be said to lack capacity to understand and consent—found himself by virtue of his therapeutic relation, a relation of dependence, an unequal relation, which the therapist, allegedly, had used to his advantage. More cases followed this, with more sensational revelations and more evidence, produced by provocative agents disguised as new analysands. The essence of what I want to tell you is already clear from these few prompters.

The problem was raised by the public in the first instance, and subsequently embraced by the professional associations, as a problem concerning quality assurance and the safety of service users. Often, a service user who requests a session does not know and is not required to know what he is actually requesting, what he may actually need. Further, often he does not know whom he will meet. Who guarantees the one who puts up a plaque with "psychotherapist" written on it? What trajectories underline that declaration, "able to practise", implied by this plaque?

On the basis of the possible bad encounter, the matter, then, is raised in terms of the necessity to put a limit to the a-specificity, the pure variability of the encounter, in order to defend the citizen from fraud and impostors. It is, therefore, a matter of instituting, by law, a body of knowledge and trajectories that may be recognized as necessary and sufficient to guarantee a substance for that plaque, "psychotherapist", which may allow the encounter to situate itself within a frame of reasonable predictability.

The Italian solution has privileged a very close link—a link that is even a little perverse, for reasons that I will explain in a moment—between academic training in psychology and professional and extra-academic training in psychotherapy. In fact, Article 2 of Law 56/89 establishes that a psychologist is anyone who has a degree in psychology, and subsequently attends a further one-year training and passes a state examination that grants him the right to practise the profession.

Article 3 establishes that a psychotherapist is whoever has obtained a degree in medicine or psychology, and, having gained the right to practise either of these through a state examination, attends a further four-year training in psychotherapy, and, having obtained a diploma in psychotherapy, requests to be registered as a psychotherapist through the relevant professional bodies—that is, medics through the Order of Medics and psychologists through the Order of Psychologists. Bear in mind that, in the main, schools of psychotherapy are private, and are granted a ministerial recognition that validates their training and equates it to that of a university.

So, for the foreseeable future, the law establishes that there are two professions: psychology and psychotherapy. Nevertheless, the profession of psychotherapist does not exist as such, in that it presupposes that one should be already a professional in another field: that of medicine or that of psychology. Thus, then, the law institutes an obligatory passage through the academic world, while also limiting this to degrees in medicine or psychology. Hence, therefore, psychotherapists are professionals—medics or psychologists—who share a further journey: an extra-academic four-year journey in private schools that, by law, grant a specialization in psychotherapy.

These schools emerge from the panorama of prestigious associations—psychoanalytic, as well as psychotherapeutic of different orientations—that, in Italy, from the 1940s onwards, had trained the first and second generation of psychotherapists, the epigones of the great schools. Many of these psychotherapists and psychoanalysts arrived via the most diverse routes, often taking up psychotherapy or psychoanalysis in their middle age, starting from academic and non-academic professions and formations very distant and different from one another.

In Italy, the great second generation analysts and heads of schools are graduates in Law or Mathematics, and, in some cases, hold no recognized degree whatsoever. And some also arrived after living for many years abroad. In some ways, until the 1980s, psychotherapy and psychoanalysis were more or less undistinguished, and were even considered one and the same thing. Therefore, in order to deal with the professional and social realities of this time, the law took a transitional position. That is, for an interim period, during which the conditions imposed by Article 2 were repealed, all those professionals who were already practising were able to enlist on the psychology register. In other words, so long as they could produce evidence of their professional practice and scientific curriculum, these professionals could be enlisted as psychologists even when they had not graduated in psychology, even when they had not graduated at all. Further, in some cases, by producing additional documentation, and with further derogation of the law, they were allowed even to enlist on the psychotherapy register. The result of this was a great rush. Indeed, taking advantage of these transitional norms, almost all psychologists around in those days enlisted on the register. And, then, almost all psychologists found themselves extremely at odds with what the law imposed. That is, thousands of registered psychologists had actually received no academic training in psychology whatsoever, and, in essence, were "psychotherapists".

So, in reality, the container "psychologist"—which had been foreseen as a founding container—turned out to be an empty one that was arbitrarily filled by an extremely diverse content. That is, it turned out to be a container filled with psychotherapists with the most diverse humanistic and scientific training, who had been able to enlist on the psychology register only thanks to their psychotherapy training and practice.

In addition, by an extreme paradox, many of these professionals were not admitted to the psychotherapy register. Consequently, they found themselves unable to practise what they had practised until then without first obtaining a degree in psychology. These professionals, then, were recognized psychologists who were not psychologists. And although they thought of themselves as psychotherapists and had been able to register as psychologists precisely because of their psychotherapy training, they could not access a psychotherapy school.

This paradox led to painful warfare within the category, warfare that lasted for more than a decade, and that, in many ways, is still not over. This entailed, also, a profound loss of professional identity, perhaps the only positive contribution that recognition and the constitution of an Order might have made. I think that this event—this tragic, and in many ways comical beginning—was in some ways over-determined by the very question of "regulation" and by some perhaps unsolvable difficulties.

Regulation aimed at creating a "knot" between academic and non-academic formations (humanistic, personal, directive); in other words, those that are proper to the psychotherapy "shops". This knot had been conceived—and this may be the first problematic aspect, the first mistake—in terms of a "first" and a "second". That is, first an academic formation (medicine or psychology), second a personal and professional formation. It sought to make psychotherapy a "specialization" rather than a profession, when, in fact, the basic formations differed profoundly one from the other. In fact, the prerogatives that were granted to a psychotherapist, a psychologist, or a doctor were very different indeed. Inevitably, from the very beginning, this created a profound sense of confusion and overlapping of planes.

Psychotherapy, then, was conceived as a subsequent and transversal specialization of two bodies of knowledge that differed greatly between them. In fact, the relationship between the knowledge–power of medicine and that of psychology was already marked. For example, one of the intentions of those promoting this law—mainly psychologists from within the public sector—was that of taking over a slice of power from the medics, who held power even within the great societies and psychoanalytic schools. Consequently, from the very start, there was a situation of extreme discontinuity: there was a psychotherapy practised by medics, who could also prescribe medication; and there was one practised by psychologists, who could not prescribe medication.

To the present day, the power relation between these two categories remains very unequal. If, on the surface, psychotherapy appears to be one, in reality, within the public and accredited structures, there are many limits imposed upon the practice and decision-making functions of psychotherapists who work in health institutions and are not medics. That is, psychotherapists who are medics immediately find themselves in a privileged position. This is so, despite the fact that it is obvious that the necessary bases for accessing the kind of formation and knowledge proper to psychotherapy are certainly not provided by a degree in medicine. What is more, very soon there was the realization that the exclusion of other formative foundations—such as philosophy, anthropology, linguistics, logics, law, or sociology—also impoverished the picture somewhat.

So, twenty years from its first application, today's law presents the following five problems. First, it subordinates psychotherapeutic formation to two academic trajectories; medicine and psychology. Neither of these is indicated as being privileged or particularly suitable for the subsequent stage. Second, it identifies a sole specialization—that of a psychotherapist, a psychologist or a medic—without clarifying the prerogatives of each; that is, without clarifying in professional and epistemological terms how the competence to administer an object—medication—may articulate itself against that of a lack of this same competence. On this question hinge, also, all the problems to do with the administration of other objects—for example, non-conventional therapies and bodily mediations or manipulations—and a conception of "therapeutic act" that is distinct from that of "medical act": for example, the prescription of a diet and the formulation of a diagnosis that use distinct instruments. Third, it does not give due recognition to the profession of psychotherapy's own autonomy, and, instead, turns it into a specialization. But, in practice, by making its access transversal to two worlds, two knowledge–powers so different one from the other, it turns it into a distinct profession because there is no autonomous subject that can represent it, since it cannot be represented either by the Order of Psychology or the Order of Medicine. It is, indeed, this very complexity that some recent judicial decrees highlight: the absence of an ethical code to which psychotherapists could make reference. Fourth, it precludes access to the profession of psychotherapy to all those professionals within the social, psycho-pedagogical, sociological, and anthropological fields, who, already enriched by a very interesting cultural baggage, may develop an interest in psychoanalysis or psychotherapy in their middle age. Provided that their trajectory could be validated, these professionals could very well have direct access to psychotherapeutic training but, instead, find themselves forced to undertake a basic academic journey that is both unlikely and unnecessary. Fifth, it does not identify and resolve the problem of rationalizing access to the profession in numerical terms. Indeed, in recent years, psychology graduates have increased to a very significant level. Further, within the next four years, the number of registered psychologists will have doubled. And the proportion of psychotherapists with a degree in psychology is four times those with a degree in medicine.

Thus, access to the profession is limited, in that there is a loss of riches that could be had by allowing access across a broader range of knowledge. But it is also indiscriminate, in that there is an explosion of people enlisted on the register and other specialist lists within a poorly delineated profession that is often perceived by young practitioners as a "health" profession when, in fact, it offers very limited opportunities in this sense.

One positive aspect of the Italian law is the extreme variegation of the schools and the kind of training to which these are inspired. In a way, even given the objectionable "funnel" that limits access to only two degrees, this has recreated the "democracy" and aleatory nature of the encounter for both the young trainee and the service user. In fact, in contrast with the Accoyer–Mattei law in France, the "Ossicini" law—that is, Law 56/89—has nothing that upholds or foresees the medics' supremacy in relation to the "reading" of the question, the formulation of diagnosis, and the subsequent referral to a professional. People may refer themselves directly to a psychotherapist, and this may be done with absolute autonomy.

It is true that, in France, the Accoyer–Mattei design has been literally demolished by a vocal movement that has subverted the terms of the debate, a subversion that has led to an idea of self-regulation in the hands of the category's associations and the psychotherapy societies. In Italy, the law made no allowances for this, which is for the better, and the way in which it has been applied has favoured, instead, a flattening of the debate. But if, on the one hand, at least on paper, a psychotherapist may practise only once he has enlisted on the registers, on the other he may take someone into treatment without first having to contact a health service. Nevertheless, it is true to say that there has been a loss of relation with a large part of the centres for acute disease, and when a psychotherapist works within a health structure his work is very likely to be subordinated to the logic and hierarchy of medicine (precisely as the French legal system conceived of things).

So, with this law, in Italy, too, psychotherapy as "other" formation, as "other" discourse on the subject and the living body, has paid the price of being flattened over and confused with the academic–scientific culture, and essentially sterilized. This is so, despite the fact that the various schools have held on to psychotherapy's inheritance, its soul, its ownership, and its self-awareness.

The war between the two "souls"—the scientistic and the humanistic–psychoanalytic souls—goes on. First it was between those without a degree in psychology, who had enlisted during the period of transitional norms, and those with a degree in psychology and public sector employees. Now it is with professionals who come from Europe, with a formation in psychotherapy founded on different academic bases; with counsellors who have new approaches to the relationship, new formative paradigms that bestride the terrifying void left by academia—which churns out young psychologists "devoid of quality", who possess a multitude of notions but completely lack any "doing capacity".

In our society, then, a growing demand for relational and mediational capacities goes hand in hand with a world of "psy" professionals that is profoundly divided; a world that is mostly incapable of catching from within itself the richness of the different approaches and of the stories from which these have originated. Therefore, today, Law 56/89 appears to be truly incapable of confronting the wind of legal–bureaucratic change in Europe; that is, the necessity to render visible professional and formative trajectories. Law 56/89 is a law founded on a pure authorizing principle. Yet, as a result of how it is constituted and the reality with which it deals, it is unable to guarantee a closed number and the selection criteria that may account for it. But this would require a completely new set of considerations.

I believe that for those who engage with the problem of regulating a profession, to create some rules, some standards, the question of quality assurance is fundamental. But I think that the Italian case—and, if even differently, the French case—fully demonstrates that establishing an academic and professional trajectory defined by the State is not enough to assure quality, guarantee adequate numbers, and make possible a demand for analysis. Nor is it possible to regulate psychotherapy with the programmatic kind of logic that could work for cardiology or other highly technical professions.

In Italy, the flattening of the "psy" professions over a scientistic and medicalized paradigm has led to an explosion of allied professions: counselling, family mediation, social work, psychopedagogy, professional education, practical philosophy, coaching. Of course some of these already existed, but today they occupy a very significant space within the horizon of relational professions. Inevitably, this raises the problem of how these professions may situate themselves in relation to "traditional" ones, such as psychology and psychotherapy. These are all professions that make huge demands in terms of training, active techniques for the management of emotiveness, group dynamics, and linguistic and expressive techniques.

Now a profound transformation of this law has become unavoidable. For sure, psychotherapy will have to free itself from the obligatory academic trajectory. Already, as a result of judicial adjudications, several European psychotherapists have had to enlist within the register despite their initial rejection by the Orders and the approved state organs.

Psychotherapy, then, will become a profession in its own right, with its own rules of access. The solution may be in terms of authorization, or we may head in the direction (which I would prefer) of leaving to the state only the assurance of minimal standards and to associations within the category the task of regulating for themselves, if even differently, the access and recruitment of trainees.

Either way, the problem of assuring as far as possible the visibility of professional trajectories, how acquired competencies may be transferred from one sector to another, how specializing trajectories may be identified within the huge wealth, cross over and multi-disciplinary dimensions that are proper to the field, will continue to be the task of, and an important commitment for, organizations and scientific societies. I believe that true accreditation and true legitimation will always be a function of the professional community. For sure, this will not be independent from the community's capacity to enter into dialogue with the public.

Note

1. Translated by Simona Revelli.

CHAPTER SEVENTEEN

1989–2005: That is, psychoanalysis against itself[1]

Mauro Santacatterina

The title of my contribution is "Psychoanalysis against itself", a statement that I am asking you to consider in its literal sense. Indeed, what has happened in Italy since 1989 proves that sometimes psychoanalysis goes, quite literally, against itself. You may think that the Italian case is a specific one and that this specificity is due to the fact that psychoanalysis came into the Italian language later than it did in the French or English languages. However, I will argue that even if it is particular, in some respects the Italian case is paradigmatic and could serve as an example of what English psychoanalysis must not be tempted to tolerate, and, still less, subscribe to. It is a case of a real and dangerous "paralogism", into which psychoanalysts from whatever state are in danger of falling. A paralogism, remember, is a logical mistake that starts from correct premises and leads to incorrect conclusions.

So, in the understandable attempt to defend one's own practice from the effects of state regulation, one ends up obtaining the exact opposite effect. At the time, only a few psychoanalysts had a sense of it being a mistake, and today, sadly, even they partake of a sort of conspiracy of silence around this issue. Of course, it is difficult to correct one's own mistake without running the risk of making an even greater one. In precisely this way, unfortunately, with regard to the regulation of their profession, the majority of Italian analysts continue to sleep undisturbed, awakening now only to regret either the scarcity of "classical" cases (our old friends, the dear old "neuroses") or of "didactic analyses" (that is, the supply of trainees). They seem unable to make a connection between the crisis of their profession and the lack of an adequate politics; or, better, the profoundly sad politics that they themselves have implemented.

My contribution is in three parts. The first concerns what has happened. The second section focuses on what is currently happening. The final section is about what I hope will happen, not only in the UK, but in other countries, too.

What has happened?

In Italy, the need to regulate "psy" knowledge and practices comes to the fore in the mid 1980s. The push to regulation comes from several directions; not least from the mass of graduates in psychology who wish to secure a workplace, and from the trade unions of the few psychologists who work within the public health service and wish to look a little like doctors. However, psychoanalysts, too, develop their own great stimulus. Psychoanalysts think that the time has come to "put their house in order", that is, to distinguish "serious and good" analysts from "fake and dishonest" ones. But, when the time comes to offer the legislator those criteria that may allow it to distinguish a serious psychoanalyst from one who is not, psychoanalysts no longer know what to say and the great analytical societies become embarrassed. This, of course, is a wholly predictable embarrassment, since we know that it is logically impossible to foresee, *a priori*, some general rules for psychoanalytic formation, since, if we did, these would be guaranteed by an external authority and, therefore, would be immediately falsified. For example, this always happens whenever one subordinates the practice of psychoanalysis to academic formation. To be sure, today psychoanalysis is taught in the universities, and sometimes even very well. But the teaching of psychoanalysis within universities is always preliminary, in other words, insufficient, as Freud clearly illustrates in his writings: analysis, Freud says in his defence of "lay analysis", cannot be learned from books, but only on one's own skin (Freud, 1926e). What does it mean that analysis is "learned on one's own skin"? To understand this one needs to undertake an analysis. But this answer will not be enough for the legislator. Or must it be? This is the crucial point.

In any case, at some point, the great societies withdrew from the debate that took place in preparation of the law, and so we arrived at the sadly infamous Law 56. Someone has a truly "genial" idea: the idea is to eliminate from the text of the law any reference whatsoever to psychoanalysis (something we see in the 1 June 1988 Italian Chamber of Deputies Commission, devoted to the matter). That is, there is a pretence that the problem—the problem on which today we are reflecting—simply does not exist. There is a pretence that there is no relationship whatsoever between psychotherapy (which everyone wants to see subjected to some norms) and psychoanalysis. And so, with the help of psychoanalysts, the decision is taken that in order to practise psychotherapy one must first obtain a degree in psychology or medicine and then attend a specialist school for a further four years. Obviously, this way of formulating training should have been totally rejected, in that it is anti-analytical. Instead, with very few exceptions, the great majority of analysts remain silent, because they think that they can turn a burning defeat into a jubilant victory. Or at least they think that the state regulation of psychotherapy will not cause any damage, since, they think, it will allow them to continue to do as they please, as free as birds. Indeed, having digested some minor worries, they even think that the contingency could become a tasty worm; that is, that they may even be able to utilize the signifier "psychotherapy" for analytic ends. In other words, the analysts had come to realize that the relationship psychotherapy–psychoanalysis is an "antinomy" (an irresolvable contradiction as analysed by Kant). However, since they had come to realize also that it is a difficult antinomy (and in some ways an embarrassing one, given that they, too, had wanted regulation), they think of exploiting it, of obtaining some gain from it. So, the antinomy transforms itself into ambiguity. After all, it cannot be such a bad thing if trainees study for a while at the faculties of psychology or medicine. From this moment on, all the schools—large and small—say, "Yes, it is good."

The current situation

Today, the formation of a trainee occurs very much according to the same modalities of thirty years ago. On the surface, very little seems to have changed. Each school governs its own training, applying its own criteria. There are very structured schools that entail passing a series of tests or preparatory stages. Other schools seek to model themselves as far as possible on renaissance workshops, "workshops of the soul", as Sergio Benvenuto punctually described them; for sure, this second modality of training is closer to the Freudian spirit. What has changed, though, is that a trainee must have a degree in psychology or medicine and that all schools—large and small—train in accordance with a series of rules established by the state. In other words, these must be specialist schools that operate within the terms imposed by the law: so, they have to teach human anatomy, statistics, testing techniques, and other disciplines, perhaps very interesting, but of very little use for the work of a psychoanalyst. Each trainee can thus be licensed first by the universities and then by specializing postgraduate institutions; afterwards, the idea is, they can really be taught "how to drive" through an "other" kind of training, which will be the real kind (comprising personal analysis, didactic analysis, and so on).

This is how the analysts have sought to exploit the situation. Indeed, those who had *authorized themselves* in their own analytical formation have now already implanted themselves within the faculties of psychology, teaching anything they are required to teach, as if it does not matter. And they have had at their disposal ample resources to create those institutions that were recognized by the Italian state. It was enough to have two rooms and a not-too-bright secretary who could answer the phone, and the deal was done. One could earn a living on keen trainees not once, but twice: first, by allowing them to have the qualification of psychotherapists; second, by allowing them to have that of psychoanalysts—pretending not to notice that, in this way, each professional title annulled the other.

Were it merely cynical two-timing that was enacted in view of the economic situation, something other than some analytical effects on the so called "supposition of knowledge", that might have been forgivable; but, unfortunately, this is not so. The consequences for the practice of psychoanalysis are much more profound. In fact, what happens is, on the one hand, a fraud to the detriment of the trainees, and, on the other, a savage ravaging of the credibility of Italian psychoanalysis, which had been conquered through great efforts from idealism, Marxism, fascism, and Roman Catholicism. This brings us to the situation in Italy today, in which analytical schools no longer have trainees, and, when they do, these are only "future psychotherapists", not "future analysts". Having obtained a driving licence, having been authorized by the state, these trainees turn the corner and try to make a living. And how can we blame them for this? And, so, here we have the paralogism to which I referred above. Even at the cost of the fraud and ravaging I have mentioned, psychoanalysts have wanted to accept a law that, in theory, could guarantee the survival of psychoanalysis during an historical moment that seemed to be turning against it. But the outcome, the effect of this choice, has been that of having authorized the agony of psychoanalysis—a slow agony perhaps, but certainly inexorable.

The most evident proof of all this is that today, in Italy, anyone can declare themselves an analyst, not only without possessing the requirements for psychotherapies established by Law 56 (which, incidentally, is absolutely right, since psychoanalysis is "lay" practice rather than a medical treatment, as Freud has shown us), but, also, without having undertaken any training whatsoever. In our country, there have been four court cases related to the "abusive exercise of the profession", which have all ended in dismissal of the cases. Four judicial outcomes concluded that the practice of psychoanalysis is free, which means, its practice does not require compliance with the state law's requirements. I, too, have marginally contributed to these outcomes. Much more so than I, however, have Ettore Perrella (Director of the Platonic Academy of the Arts), Rolando Ciofi (President of the Independent Psychologists Movement), Pier Francesco Galli (Director of *Psychotherapy and Human Science*), and Moreno Blaskovich. They went to court to defend people they did not know personally; they went in order to defend a principle: that of the freedom to analyse. But I am telling you that one cannot be too happy with this outcome either. Defending colleagues who have not wanted to conform to the law that regulates psychotherapy is absolutely right.

However, I also want to point out that lay psychoanalysis—in other words, psychoanalysis that is free from all rules of accreditation—is nothing but the reverse of the coin of regulation that occurs independently from the spirit, the tradition, the epistemology of psychoanalysis. Today, we have trainees already authorized by the state who have nothing really serious to ask, no opportunity to formulate a question for analysis; and then we have the "personal trainer", the "expert in public relations" or the practitioner of some other "noble" and ancient profession, who could also declare himself or herself a psychoanalyst, not only without having undertaken an analysis, but even without knowing who Sigmund Freud is. I myself was formed within a Lacanian orientation. Jacques Lacan used to say that "the analysts authorizes himself" but certainly does not "recognize himself". This formulation seems very clear to me.

What should be done for the future of psychoanalysis?

First of all, we must take very seriously current historically contingent factors, as a result of which there is a sense of necessity to regulate psychotherapy. Some think that this is a symptom of cultural regression, but it also hinges on the fact that there are some psychologies and some psychotherapies that may be taught according to university criteria; in other words, transmittable in a general way, with no regard whatsoever to the subject. Perhaps we dislike this, but such are the facts. Further, and this is the most important point I wish to make, we must be aware that the problem of regulation is a problem also for psychoanalysis. Neither Freud (see the so-called "committee of the seven rings" designed to maintain the integrity of his inner circle) nor all the others after him really managed to work successfully on this theme. Although he has written admirable pages on this matter, Freud himself did not go much further than the observation that regulation would emerge—as if by miracle—simply by referring to his theory: a position that, for us, today, is highly insufficient. Admitting to this perhaps could cause a scandal.

Still, today, it is not Oedipus that scandalizes but the theme of formation, a formation that in psychoanalysis occurs in a way that is altogether "subversive" by comparison to other cultural presuppositions that seem obvious and reassuring; except for the fact that this subversive character has never been explicitly declared, has never been "written". But, if so, what solution could we suggest? Only we analysts can agree on a solution that is "respectful" of the tradition that forms our point of reference. This could be a solution that may be valid as a formula—in other words, a bet, such as the famous "Trimethylamine"—and, obviously, as an avoidance of any "final" solution. Perhaps this is a point on which we must elaborate our mourning. That is, it requires the renunciation of those "easy solutions" on which many of us have leaned all too comfortably. One of these "easy solutions", very French, consists in believing that the demand for recognition should *always* be returned to the sender, as if the state were an analysand. How does one become an analyst? How may an analyst be recognized? The easy answer is, one becomes a psychoanalyst by becoming it: personal analysis, didactic analysis, supervision, and so on; as with a traveller who asks how far the destination is, the reply is the "keep going" that Freud has taught us.

However, now we must have the courage to admit that this admirable interpretation was effective a century ago, but today is not enough. At a concrete level, in each school, teaching occurs through a number of procedures, trainings, tests that go from the simple reading of texts to participation in study groups on particular topics; from listening to seminars to theoretical presentations by trainees; from research on specific topics to participation in group discussions, Balint groups, psychodrama workshops, and so on. To be effective vehicles of formation, all these activities need to be undertaken in a manner that is sufficiently "free"; in other words, they need to occur according to modalities and a timing that respect the individuality of each trainee. This, however, does not mean that these activities are not also very structured; in other words, that the various formative activities are not also "exercises" that need to be carried out according to some rules, precisely as it is in analysis. The *Grundregel*, the "rule of free association", is a sort of oxymoron. The analysand is invited to freely expose his or her thoughts only in order to discover their determined character, the automatism to which they are subjected. And the analysand's word resonates only within the setting. That is to say, the essential, structuring value of the parental ties is discovered only through incest. But, while we have at our disposal entire libraries on Oedipus and the setting, when it comes to the theme of this volume, this is not so. In reality, until now psychoanalysis has developed more on the clinical side. Freud, on the other hand, always said that the therapeutic dimension was only one of the possible applications of psychoanalysis, beside many others: for example, the pedagogical dimension.

In our way of thinking of formation—and, therefore, recognition—we feel the effects of a sensational delay, mostly accumulated over the last thirty years, so that we lean excessively on tradition. If I may give you a risky example, it is as if Freud had limited himself to formulate the Oedipus complex without offering a tangible proof of it by writing *The Interpretation of Dreams* (1900a), in the first instance, taking upon himself all the responsibilities and honours of his great discovery. The various groups—societies, institutions, associations—hold a huge richness within them, a richness they could begin to communicate and exploit (this time, rightly so), passing from a strategy of mere survival to a project of expansion and a true relaunching of psychoanalysis; to become what, after all, they have always been, agents engaged in researching the most precious good (for which the West has a huge hunger): subjectivity. They could then function as agents that may be able to operate as "agencies" of accreditation, to dialogue also with the state, and to provide useful directives for other professions, too. As I enjoy saying, in a somewhat provocative fashion, after all, the profession of psychoanalysis is a profession like any other, of course, as long as we remember the impossible dimension that is proper to all professions. "Profession" derives from the Latin *professio*, which means "to declare one's own rule", "to declare one's own faith", and, therefore, "to promise".

To clarify the rules of formation, rather than keeping them a "secret", which sometimes is even comical, could have a truly revolutionary effect. And I think that this move would relaunch also the theoretical work, which at times stagnates on the usual topics. "Free association" was the slogan of courageous pioneers. Today, we have the opportunity to reaffirm this slogan, as long as we understand that this is as valid for our own thoughts (that circulate in our minds), as for those of our analysands (who may decide to practise our profession). In other words, to have faith in free *association*, today, means to believe in the *free* association of analysts. Obviously, all this could happen only on one condition: that, at last, all the various psychoanalytic orientations begin to collaborate so as to achieve a common end.

If, indeed, the problem of formation constitutes today's resistance, as sexuality did at another point, well, we must deal with it as such. While today every psychoanalyst admits with no reservations to the sexual determination of symptoms, even his own (which means, to his capacity to cure through what has been his own suffering), when it comes to one's own professional qualification, this is not quite so. In reality, every analyst knows full well that every day he takes care of people who come to his office not because of his professional title, not because he is a psychiatrist, a psychologist, or a psychotherapist, and not even because he has been granted his title of psychoanalyst by some great Association. Are we ready to admit to this with sincerity, to admit that "being an analyst" is a decision taken on a daily basis, and that each one of us has come to occupy this position by following the contorted paths of our own lives, which have nothing to do with rigidly predetermined paths? And that some of us have come to psychoanalysis from medicine or psychiatry, but others from mathematics, philosophy, anthropology, or other humanistic disciplines? And that the diverse formative paths of the various schools are a great resource, rather than a limitation? The fratricidal war to win the primacy of the profession will only lead to our extinction. We Italians have not dared, have not tried to relaunch psychoanalysis, to "re-establish it", even though we had an excellent opportunity to do so. I place my hope in you British analysts. Starting from your reflections, I hope that psychoanalysis will begin to free itself from the "recognition complex"!

Note

1. Translated by Simona Revelli. I would like to thank Simona Revelli and Anthony Molino for their help with this contribution.

References

Freud, S. (1926e). The question of lay analysis. *S.E., 20*: 179–254. London: Hogarth.

Freud, S. (1900a). *The Interpretation of Dreams*. *S.E., S.E., 4–5*. London: Hogarth.

PART IV

LESSONS AND DIRECTIONS

CHAPTER EIGHTEEN

Global psychoanalyst?

Christian Ingo Lenz Dunker

When we observe the current debate on state regulation of psychoanalytical practice, two issues are raised. First: it is a question arising in many places across the world. It is important to note that the same pressure towards regulation of psychoanalysis is occurring, *at the same time*, in countries with differing socio-political conditions and distinct cultures, in relation to the application of psychoanalysis. In other words, I do not believe the problem can be reduced to the local contingencies of health systems that are quite distinct (for example, compare those in the UK, Brazil and the USA). Also, they should not be forced into a normative homogenization because of administrative adjustments in countries seeking economic or legislative integration. This temporal simultaneity, in the appearance of the question, cannot be explained entirely by the ideology of the abbreviation of the risk and of the security of the populations. In the end, understanding that there is risk in practising psychoanalysis is understanding, indirectly, that it is efficient, which is far from being the consensus among those who push for regulation.

The worst case scenario

This is not a question of state expansion into the maintenance of social well-being, but the unique point in which the state is interested in the capital, or the sovereign instance of utilizing power as violence, whether military or regulatory.

I would like to propose a little mental experiment, a conjecture that will take our problem to the next step. Consider the following scenario: (1) national criteria are established for educating analysts; (2) a control system for the application of these criteria is established; (3) the practical benefits and scope of psychoanalytic treatment (the ambit of psychotherapy, psychiatry, science, or technology) are delineated; and (4) the conditions for commercialization of this "service" in a secure and free market are determined. In other words, this scenario, which is quite probably the worst possible scenario, allows yet another extension. Even worse: what would come after the state? What will happen when states are forced to unify their regulations in accordance with the global market? Would we then have a single practical model for psychoanalytical education and application?

The objection could be as follows: no form of control is totally efficacious; there will always be, on the margins, contraveners or pirates who continuously break the rules or boycott what has been established. However, they will be the exceptions: those who have not studied psychology, those who have not received accredited training, and those who have turned against psychoanalytical associations. Probably, we will revive this same segregative debate: how do we regulate the charlatan psychoanalysts and the sub-psychoanalysts?

I hope that this conjecture makes clear how the problem of state regulation of psychoanalysis serves to illuminate how its impact is supported by segregatory logic, *currently happening*, and our place for charlatan psychoanalysts, sub-psychiatrists, and contraveners. This place of exception simply cannot be eradicated; it is a structural place when addressing the social implantation of psychoanalysis, as I hope that the "worst possible scenario" conjecture has demonstrated.

There are, however, two traditional strategies employed to handle this exceptionality. The first consists of reinforcing the barriers, like a small community that is apprehended and securely separated from society so as to maintain the functionality of its regulations. It is the policy of constructing walls inside walls inside walls. We then have a series of small communities with different solutions and varied resistance tactics, including minor compromises in relation to integration. This is the strategy of continuous negotiation and of resistance groups. This is the spontaneous solution that psychoanalysis encountered, in most countries, for the problem of its social insertion. In this case, the exceptionality is considered in the place of contradiction.

The second strategy consists of finding, within the community, a principle that becomes universal or that allows participation in a universal. This is the strategy employed by science and religion. We find a prevalence of this strategy in countries where psychoanalysis becomes a branch of psychiatry and even in those in which it is established as a university discipline. Here, it seeks to transform the exceptionality into a particularity, thus abolishing its structural place. The great risk of this procedure is that it exposes us to the passion functioning as the object of law, in this case reduced to regulating statutes. From many angles, including historical, there seems to be a consensus that when one becomes a psychoanalyst, one faces a question of instrumentalization of means and obedience to the rules of psychoanalysis that are actually unviable. This is evident, and we have to take into account that something expected of psychoanalysis is the questioning of the conformist attitude or the criticism of obedience to regulation.

In the first strategy, psychoanalysis adopts a para-political route; in the second, it adopts a meta-political route, if we take into account the categories proposed by Žižek (1999) and Rancière (2007). Para-politics is characterized by the reduction of politics to a system of alliances and agreements. Meta-politics is characterized by a reduction in politics to the level of demand administration. I argue that what we need, at this time, is really a policy that we express (proper-politics) that would be at the height of the response against the segregatory, which is expected from psychoanalysis in extension. Therefore, instead of these two strategies, I suggest a third that is loosely based on Lacan's thesis that there is no universal that does not contain in itself a negative existence. Facing this debate to regulate or not to regulate, we need a third alternative, and I propose that this could be based on a kind of rule that would be intentionally paradoxical.

This would be the pragmatic paradox we encounter in proclamations such as: let us establish as a fundamental rule that no fundamental rules should be established. I do not know if there are many examples of this as, generally, when one considers regulation or any type of norm, one becomes obsessed with the idea that it has to work both theoretically and practically. A good rule is usually one that includes the greatest possible number of exceptional cases and responds to the greatest number of political interests. My proposal is that we turn our thinking upside-down. I invite you to try this exercise, like the ones that Jorge Luis Borges and Ítalo Calvino had us try, that is, a kind of rule premeditatedly designed to reveal its innate paradox.

We have learned with the clinic that facing the superego and the sadistic maxim of the law, humour and irony are two important alternatives. We have also learned that witticism is not without consequences and that the interpretation of the structure is similar. However, I do not know if it would be possible to defend a regulation that contained a clear structural paradox. Why then, would we not be able to consider a route that was intentionally and explicitly deduced from this perspective?

A real case

I will now relate a real case concerning the question of state regulation of psychoanalysis that happened at the dawn of the new millennium in Brazil. You should know that psychoanalysis in Brazil is comparatively rather widespread. There are hundreds of associations, groups, and schools connected to a wide variety of institutions and theoretical orientations. Their presence in university courses, in both psychology and social sciences, is truly expansive. According to the state regulatory agency, of the ten primary scientific psychology reviews, five concern psychoanalysis. Brazil has already been defined as a high-consumption country for psychoanalysis, with the critical exception that this applies to the middle-class, which is far from the majority of the population. However, in the mental health services and our principal hospitals, there is a significant psychoanalytical presence, without having any expressly educational or controlling system by medical practice.

Despite the extensive consumption of psychotropic drugs, such as anti-depressants, which is growing at an alarming rate, there does not seem to be a great symbolic opposition to the practice of psychoanalysis. As in the case of France, both practices live in harmony, in contradiction to the major reports that insist that there is great rivalry. However, unlike the case of France and more like the situation in the USA during the 1970s, the widespread use of psychotropic drugs, sexual potency stimulants, or psychoactive weight-loss formulas, occurs "within the law". I hope that the example serves to demonstrate that regulation does not always protect the population against risk, but often is calculatedly created to "administer" contraventions to the law.

In Brazil, social assistance, both governmental and through private insurance companies, in the area of psychoanalysis is quite limited. The widespread and liberal practice of psychoanalysis is, therefore, probably influenced by the fact that it is often practised outside the normal canons, such as four times per week, and that it does not follow the European or American fee structure standards.

In other words, our psychoanalysis fits in with our peripheral status in the current geo-political environment: widespread, but difficult to qualify, probably interpreted by common sense as a type of psychotherapy. This wild psychoanalysis would be the perfect example for the regulatory furore, an easy victim of the need for regulation. However, the diversity and proliferation of associations makes this endeavour, internally, if not undesirable, then impractical. There is not a group sufficiently strong to impose itself upon the others, and the alliances, in general, are weak, whether because of inherent contingencies or unstable ties with international psychoanalysis associations or groups. The psychoanalytical associations are small and, in general, with no real national voice. The most recent initiatives in this area are, curiously, led by psychoanalysts.

The case I wish to relate occurred within this scenario. It concerns groups linked with evangelical religions currently spreading across Brazil. As with other groups, their enterprises include radio stations, universities, cinemas, newspapers, editorial houses, and even television channels. Two of these groups have become quite famous: the *Associação Nacional de Psicoanálise Clinica* and the

International Refoundational Psychoanalysis Association, which adopted the ridiculous rubric IRPA purposely to create confusion with the IPA. Adopting a strategy of integrating conversion procedures and religious teaching, such groups have spread, primarily in the poor periphery of the major urban centres and in the remote regions of the country. Their declared mission is to bring psychoanalysis to the masses; their goal plan is to "create" 5,000 analysts per year.

The didactic material for this work is bizarre: exact measurements for the construction of divans, methods to cure homosexuals, the use of psychoanalysis in exorcism rituals, the insertion of theological content in psychoanalytical theory, etc.[1] This psychoanalytical "education" may be done by correspondence course, including multiple choice testing. A "diagnostic" procedure that has become a tragic joke among the critics of this project is the following: to discover if a patient is possessed by the devil or is suffering from psychosis, the analyst should say the word "Jesus". If the patient reacts indignantly, he is possessed; if not, then he should receive treatment for psychosis.

Even here, the initiative does not seem to be new and has many precedents that we do not hesitate to place in order of difficulty, fraud, and manipulation of psychoanalytical discourse with ulterior motives. However, this is exactly the type of case that can be raised to demand regulation of psychoanalysis in the name of protecting consumers, the public health, and psychoanalysis itself. This type of scenario induces paranoid reasoning and incites demands for laws that would put an end to this type of barbarity and organize *jouissance.* In other words, against this terrorism we need stricter laws and ways to efficaciously enforce them. A true reflection on the regulation of psychoanalysis cannot adhere to this conspiratorial logic.

However, the story continues. One of these religious groups, so common in Brazil, has representatives in government. It is a relatively important group known as *Bancada Evangélica,* and has members in many parties and constitutes a significant force in the House of Representatives. Recognizing the lack of a formal designation for psychoanalysis, that it had no defined required educational format, or governmental regulation, this religious movement proposed itself as a regulatory agency for the state, governing the practice of psychoanalysis.[2] A Federal Representative, connected with these churches, composed a Bill that was discussed in a commission especially created to address this subject.

Many psychoanalysis societies and associations united following the clear consensus that we do not know what would be the best form of regulation, not even if regulation would be desirable, but that we do know that "this is not the way". The bizarre and unusual character of the Bill was able to achieve the improbable: a consensus among the disparate psychoanalytical factions in a vast country marked by much dissent in this field. The meeting of the discontents succeeded in blocking the Bill. On the day scheduled for the decisive debate, in the House of Representatives, the representatives of evangelical psychoanalysis did not appear. The project was set aside, but, importantly, we did not go back to the point of the game. Now, the game begins marked by a double problem: the shadow of real peril and the questioning of internal self-regulation by psychological associations.

Having prevented the bill that was sent to Congress from being passed into law, we all believed that the problem had been resolved. However, we were surprised to find that variations of the same bill appeared two more times, proving that what we had initially believed to be a one-time opportunistic drive was, in fact, a long-term strategy.

We could add to this real case a conjecture: what if, instead of a religious lobby, we faced a psychiatric–pharmaceutical lobby? This verifies for us that the situation appears problematic. Would the word that I chose to demonstrate the other side of the problem, concern then the establishment of a psychoanalytic lobby? This is an alternative as dangerous as the previous one, which could be seen in the case of France, where it appears to be an invitation for psychoanalytical societies to devour themselves. Even more dramatic would be verifying that this lobby is already constituted and functioning, when we consider the British scenario, emphasizing certain idiosyncrasies, such as trying to acquire a patent or control over the use of the word "psychoanalysis". In other words, I am suggesting that the demand for governmental regulation of psychoanalysis does not introduce new problems, but only exploits and accentuates the segregatory reasoning and parasitism between psychoanalysis and psychotherapy that we already currently see.

I am referring to the parasitic relationship between psychoanalysis and psychotherapy because this is a typical example for the thesis that there is no universal that cannot be negated by an inherent element. The recurring argument is as follows: take psychotherapies as a universal field definable by certain criteria of homogeneity and congruence. Introduce this universal as a subset of the professional practices regulated by the state and the legal system. Next, verify that there is a contingent case within the psychotherapies, which is the case of psychoanalysis, that contradicts, by its own existence, the universality of the universal from which it comes. In other words, it is a form of psychotherapy (and it would be difficult to argue against this historically) that is not governed by the universal of psychotherapies. It is an exception, an exception that falls in the necessary vacuum between ethics and the law.

The immediate movement is to force a reintegration of the exception, making it either a particular case of this rule or opening a new universal rule. It happens that the universal of psychotherapies is already, in itself, a false universal, in actuality only a summation of contingent variants, as my first example (the worst case scenario) hoped to demonstrate. In other words, it is enough to take a step forward to see how the exception function reappears in a displacement mode. The example shows, additionally, how the distinction between psychotherapy and psychoanalysis is a positional distinction and not an essential one.

One could counter-argue that this is irrelevant, that the regulation of psychoanalysis manifests only the progress of juridical forms and the transformation required by these modern, "market segment" times of global economics. This consideration does not apply. Psychoanalysts maintain that this exceptionality is intrinsic and a constituent of psychoanalysis, and here the arguments are many: transference relativizes the universality of the diagnostic practice; the subject relativizes the necessary objectification of "practical" scientific criteria; the demand for personal experience in psychoanalysis (for one who wants to become an analyst) relativizes the impersonality of the production technique of this "service"; finally, the disparity in criteria impedes the universalization of the criteria of efficacy and the "product guarantee". In other words, contrary to other practices, psychoanalysis appears to place itself, intentionally, within exceptionality. We should, therefore, consider a form of regulation that has the same positioning. In other words, a problematic inclusion designed to resist its own success.

A proposal

One of the objectives of this collection is to produce proposals that may contribute to the debate on regulating psychoanalysis. I will present, therefore, five points in the spirit of the premises I have previously discussed.

1. We may presume that regulation should be the duty of a council composed by direct vote by all psychoanalysts in a determined region or country. "Psychoanalyst" should be understood as meaning any and all who declare themselves as such. The council would be provisional and change periodically as well as the arrangements it would make. Its only compositional criteria would be self-declaration. I understand that the principal merit of this point is that it presumes the lack of utility of the rule that it should constitute. If the regulation must ultimately say who is and who is not a psychoanalyst, who can legitimately practise and who is excluded as a charlatan, then the criteria of self-declaration nip the problem in the bud. There is no rule that obliges anyone to declare him or herself as such, nor is there any rule preventing such a declaration. At heart, it is a kind of practical but unnecessary incorporation, following the principle that the psychoanalyst does not authorize him or herself without being one.
2. Psychoanalysis is a form of psychotherapy that does not require a specific university education and is not restricted to criteria from any particular association or institution. Regulation of psychoanalysis by the state must be understood as referring to regulation of psychoanalytical associations by the state. In this case, the psychoanalytical associations should be treated as non-governmental organizations (NGOs) and not as autarchies or agencies specifically regulated by the state. NGOs are characterized by their plurality of membership, both juridical and political, and, primarily, they are not necessarily tied to the

workings of any specific state. As such, they work to secure the diversity between the psychoanalytical associations and their educational models, or to institute as multiple that which must be a single, following the intentions of its own regulations.

3. Consider the Brazilian example of an attempted religious coup. It is clear from this that there is no strong interest or desire by psychoanalysts to regulate psychoanalysis themselves, but there is a decided consensus that it not be done by others. Then, of course, it is much easier to define what *is not psychoanalysis* than what *is psychoanalysis*. Negative definitions, in general, are segregatory in nature but, in this case, are important. Why not elevate the object to the dignity of the Thing? The proposed principle is then that the only rule with which we all agree is that no psychoanalytical association is prepared to rise to the hegemonic position of governing the regulation of the others. The primary function of a regulating agency of this type would be to designate the actual case where a psychoanalytical association is not, in fact a psychoanalytical association. We know that a psychoanalytical association is, above all, secular. As such, with this movement the question is dislocated from "what is a psychoanalyst and how should one be?" to "what is a psychoanalytical association and how should one be?", and "what does secular psychoanalysis entail?" In actuality, this question has been historically insoluble in its extension. We are thus left with the proposition of regulating an object that cannot be defined.
4. The theses in favour of regulation have insisted that the importance of regulation arises from a need to protect the lay public; in other words, the question is: who will defend the candidate for analysis from the unskilled analyst? Who will defend the general public from both the self-declarations of charlatans and the risks represented by the suggestion and by the manipulation of patients? If psychoanalysis is a healing and investigating method, then who will defend us from misuse of this method for ulterior motives? I suggest that the state employ the resource, virtually mobilized to regulate in mass clarifying campaigns for the population on the risks, indications, contraindications, limits, and restrictions relating to psychoanalytical treatment. If they address the potential for abuse in a practice

that may offend the consumer, if they address the relative question of lack of information, then, as such, they would become a psychoanalytic "decree" and amply promote it.

5. This point I would like to present as a general principle for all possible regulation of psychoanalysis, regarding the aforementioned Brazilian experience. When we speak of regulation of psychoanalytical associations, this presupposes that analysts are trained in their personal analysis, in practices and studies supervised by the associations. However, this type of direct and total oversight in the education of psychoanalysts is rare. In Brazil, as in other parts of the world, education is increasingly becoming a blending process wherein the aspiring psychoanalyst progresses through various psychoanalytical associations, joins different and differing groups, enters many specializations, and progresses in his or her clinical, university, and psychoanalytical studies, combining a wide variety of references, at times within a single theoretical orientation. For example, an aspiring analyst might undergo various analyses with different supervisors along a sinuous route among diverse psychoanalytical associations. These associations, in turn, spread out in innumerable intersections, accords, and collaborations. It is in the middle of this diversity of paths and experiences that suggest a horizontalization of analytical education that the demand for regulation gains impetus. It only becomes necessary when it is no longer possible. How can one measure and weigh this diversity of experience in a homogenous way when it is quantitatively and qualitatively so different? A solution that would respect this new configuration would correspond to a regulating model so elastic that it would, in the end, become ineffectual.

Conclusion

The object of this presentation is to demonstrate how the issues that arise from the question of regulating psychoanalysis should not be seen as foreign intrusions into psychoanalysis, but as integrals. We should recall that Lacan (1995) thought of the transmission of psychoanalysis as a paradoxical relationship between psychoanalysis in intension (the experience of treatment) and psychoanalysis in extension (psychoanalysis in culture). What would articulate these two forms would be transference, which, in this case, operates as a kind of Moebius strip. Following this structure, the exterior and interior are separate at any single point, but merge when the whole is considered.

I have demonstrated that psychoanalytical education should not be considered as a universal, able to be summed up in a regulated and unified system. The concept of a global psychoanalyst is thus a contradiction in terms, and this contradiction should be what constitutes our point of consensus. Throughout my presentation, I approached this contradiction by means of exception, and proposed, in an experimental and merely speculative way, the application of this principle to the formulation of certain rules. I think I have made it clear that, both in the analysis of the real case of the evangelical-psychoanalysis in Brazil and notes on psychoanalytical self-segregation, that our problem is not only about defending ourselves from exterior forces, presumably the state, but also finding a non-terrorist solution to psychoanalytical terrorism.

Notes

1. See, for example www.psique.org/modules.php?name=Forums.
2. The manifesto related to this Bill is available at: www.estadosgerais.org/gruposvirtuais/manifesto_conselho_federal_psicanalise_clinica_do_brasil.shtml.

References

Lacan, J. (1995). Proposition of 9 October 1967 on the psychoanalyst of the School. *Analysis*, 6: 1–13.

Rancière, J. (2007). *Hatred of Democracy*. London: Verso.

Žižek, S. (1999). *The Ticklish Subject: The Absent Centre of Political Ontology*. London: Verso.

CHAPTER NINETEEN

Unconsciously generating inevitability? Workable accountability alternatives to the statutory regulation of the psychological therapies

Richard House and Denis Postle

It is our intention in this text to have it reflect the live dialogue of our joint presentation. We begin by outlining its scope. We start by saying something about why we are here, what brought us to contribute to this book, and, following that, by cataloguing the downside, as we see it, of current proposals for statutory regulation of the psychological therapies. We then move on at greater length to introduce the Independent Practitioners Network (IPN), a substantial innovative response to the culture of institutional professionalization that has in recent years come to dominate the British psychopractice field. We end with a perspective on the likely next steps that will need to be considered if present plans for statutory regulation are to be successfully interrupted and undermined (and here, note, we refer to "statutory regulation" as an aspect of the "state regulation" which is the main concern of this book).

Why are we contributing to this book?

We are two experienced therapy practitioners who come from a broadly humanistic, human-potential background (though we are deeply influenced by a range of therapeutic approaches and perspectives), and together we share almost four decades of consistent therapy practice of diverse kinds and in a range of different settings. We have both published extensively in the literature on the professionalization of psychotherapy and counselling (see, for example, *Ipnosis*, an Internet journal for the Independent Practitioners Network [IPN] and before that g.o.r.i.l.l.a., now an Internet archive of the many cogent attempts to confront the professionalization of psychopractice in the last 15–20 years, during which time we have been at the forefront of the British challenge to the statutory regulation of the psychological therapies in this country).

The early stages of the professionalization of counselling and psychotherapy looked and felt like colonization, or turf wars between rival factions—one of which, the United Kingdom Council for Psychotherapy (UKCP), behaved variously like a trainers' club and a trade association, speaking the rhetoric of "client protection" while, seen up close, being driven by the need to capture and sustain the practitioner "training industry" (Gladstone, 1977). Denis Postle (DP) began taking the colonization seriously when the then chair of the UKCP started talking about overgrown gardens and getting rid of the "weeds", of which, according to her criteria, he was clearly one.

A second wake-up call was the bizarre episode of the Alderdice Psychotherapy Bill that sought to capture the high ground for the psychoanalytic community; a text in which everyone mentioned is male, and which did not survive first contact with the British Association for Counselling and Psychotherapy (BACP), who were understandably furious to have been ignored in the Bill's development. Richard House (RH) had a lot to say about the damage wrought by professionalization, including editing and contributing to two books, and writing a third. The corrupting effects of the drive for professionalization were soon confirmed by the extraordinary experience of a publisher turning down the RH/Totton co-edited text *Implausible Professions* (1997) on the grounds that they did not want to upset the UKCP, who also published with them.

DP's resistance took a different route, using family resources to build and maintain several web sites devoted to writing for and building archives of essential texts. (See the relevant web address at the end of this chapter.) Our experience overall has been that what there is to say about the damage that statutory regulation will cause has been said, much of it many times over. Our experience, as Nick Totton has remarked, has been of *Totsweigen*, being ignored to death. We have yet to find a substantial text that argues cogently, and with adequate evidence, in favour of statutory regulation.

Both of us were freshly energized by Richard Mowbray's eagerly-awaited and long trailed book, *The Case Against Psychotherapy Registration: A Conservation Issue for the Human Potential Movement*, which proved to be well worth the wait when it eventually appeared in 1995. The Case (as it soon became colloquially christened) very quickly became the "bible" for practitioners in the field who had severe doubts about the whole direction in which the British therapy field seemed to be headed. RH remembers with great clarity and pleasure the effect that The Case had on him when he first read it—like one of those profoundly integrating "a-ha" experiences where previously disparate ideas and feelings suddenly cohere into an integral "whole". Here, for the first time in Britain, was an immaculately documented and thoroughly compelling rationale for all the unease he and others had felt since the professionalization–accreditation issue had come to prominence some years earlier. Certainly, for anyone wishing to acquaint themselves with the history and advisability of therapy regulation, Mowbray's Case is surely the indispensable starting-point, and is as freshly relevant today as it was well over a decade ago.

For those sufficiently open to see it, there seemed to us to exist a growing undercurrent of deep unease about the form and direction of therapy professionalization in Britain; and hot on the heels of The Case, a second book and natural kind of sequel, *Implausible Professions*, which RH co-edited with Nick Totton, sought to give a coherent form to those previously disparate voices. In the succeeding years it was followed in 2003 by *Ethically Challenged Professions* (co-edited by Yvonne Bates and RH) and RH's *Therapy Beyond Modernity: Deconstructing and Transcending Profession-centred Therapy*, also in 2003. More recently, DP has published his collected writings from seventeen years of scrutiny of professionalization and statutory regulation, *Regulating the Psychological Therapies: From Taxonomy to Taxidermy* (2007).

A third element of concern for us has been the extent to which regulation proposals seem to be another instance of the UK's "surveillance culture", which sees regulation of psychotherapy and counselling in terms of targets, measurement, and "evidence-based" practice. As if this "audit culture" were not only too obviously a form of attempted (but, we maintain, futile) domestication of the unavoidable unpredictability, wildness, and uncertainties of working with the hurts, humiliations, and unhelpful happenstances with which clients come into therapy (Cooper, 2001). As with most overweening, control-fixated state interventions like this one, the unintended negative side-effects will almost certainly outweigh by far any benefits which might ensue from the regulatory regime. What is perhaps most disturbing of all is that no attempt seems to have been made either by the government or by the therapy institutions to research into such side-effects, and to make an informed decision about statutory regulation based on all the possible complex countervailing impacts—including looking in detail at the system-wide impact of introduced regulation in other countries (*cf.* Hogan, 1979). That such an investigative process has apparently not even been considered strongly suggests that the regulatory process has far more to do with ideology (modernity) and economic self-interest than it does with either client protection in particular or rational argument more generally.

The downside of statutory regulation

We have been diligent across our decade and a half of resistance to statutory regulation to point to the accumulated research and inquiry of other people who have broadly shared our concerns. Hogan (1979, 2003) and Mowbray (1995) show how statutory regulation will very probably restrict the supply of practitioners; inflate costs of services; stifle innovation in education and training; discriminate unnecessarily; and lead to defensive therapeutic practice. All the major psychopractice organizations have openly used fear of being left out, fear of not being able to work, the "trance inductions" of the "inevitability" of statutory regulation, together with the unresearched assertions of the need for "client protection", as crass instruments with which to shepherd (or scare) their generally deferential flocks in the direction of signing up to whatever might be the current form of regulation.

And as problematic in its own way is the tolerance of (or ignorance about) substantial incongruence between "power over", top-down "command and control" in the accountability structures that administer statutory regulation, on the one hand, and "power with" behaviour in the working alliance with clients, on the other. Does no one else see this as damaging to clients interests? After all, as David Smail and others have argued (e.g., Smail, 2001), do not many, or even most, clients bring issues to therapy that in some sense centre on questions of authority, deference, exploitation, and victimization?

We have also become aware of the widely shared sense that statutory regulation rides on several fallacies that have been vigorously contradicted by a variety of critics. One of these is that advanced/extended training and further (often quasi-academic) education necessarily lead to (increased) therapeutic effectiveness. There are also compelling arguments and associated research evidence suggesting that newly qualified or lightly trained paraprofessionals in the field can do therapy work that is at least as effective as highly trained practitioners (RH has set out some plausible reasons to account for such an important counter-intuitive finding—see House, 2001).

An equally important fallacy is the taken-for-granted assumption that the advent of statutory regulation will necessarily have a beneficial effect on the level of client safety. One way of viewing training schools' embracing of statutory regulation is to see it as a tacit admission that their trainings are, in practice, unable to provide adequate ongoing quality control protocols in trainees. Curiously, this level of educational inadequacy is somehow regarded as acceptable, even inevitable.

The overriding rationale offered by both government and therapy institutions alike for the introduction of statutory regulation is that of providing a means of protecting the public from practitioners who are deemed unfit to practise and who could cause harm to those who seek their services. Given that this is indeed the central *raison d'être* underpinning the drive to regulation, the first and most obvious question is: what is the evidence that statutory regulation, compared with a "no regulation" counterfactual comparison or scenario, would actually succeed in protecting the public by reducing the net level of abuse in the system?

We take it, first, that those arguing for statutory regulation would need to demonstrate that there currently exists, in the unregulated field, a level of abuse that is greater than the level that would plausibly obtain under a statutorily regulated therapy field. In turn, this requires detailed information about the level of abuse that currently exists within the therapy field. Now, of course, no one would seriously deny that abuse exists—after all, it exists everywhere in life; the crucial issue here concerns the scale of existing levels of abuse. We estimate that there are at least 20 million contact hours annually in UK psychopractice, not counting supervision or continuing professional development (CPD), yet nowhere have we or our colleagues seen any empirical evidence about the current level of abuse within the British occupational field. Has any serious systematic research been carried out into this issue, and if so, why have its findings not been made public? After all, we presume that if such evidence did indeed exist, then it would be in the interest of both government and therapy institutions to shout it from the rooftops, in order to legitimate their position. But our repeated attempts to elicit empirical evidence on this key question from the British Department of Health have consistently met with vague anecdotal assertions that "we know substantial abuse exists"—but nothing more.

Of course there are pressure groups representing "users" and clients (some possibly with axes to grind) who are calling for regulation; but this of itself does not make anything approaching a sufficient case for the appropriateness of statutory regulation, without the accompanying research on the current scale of abuse and dissatisfaction having been carried out (and the scale of unintended negative side-effects mentioned earlier). In short, we maintain that in any rational world it is not justifiable that dramatic and wide-ranging changes be made to our occupational field (and potentially harmful ones at that—see below) simply on the basis of a comparatively small number of high-profile, emotionally charged, and anecdotal complaints or representations by user-groups, without comprehensive independent research first having been carried out.

In the literature referred to earlier, there is lengthy "chapter and verse" on just why the "public protection" argument does not hold water—or is, at the very least, highly questionable. As the American authority on psychotherapy regulation, Professor Daniel Hogan, has written, "... a similar array of horror stories could easily be assembled about highly credentialed psychiatrists and psychologists, all of them licensed" (Mowbray, 1995, p. 105). In other words, client and patient abuse occurs in professions that are already licensed and have specific sanctions against abuse and malpractice; and there is no clear empirical evidence in the literature to suggest that its incidence differs significantly between licensed and unlicensed settings.

Moreover, and as Richard Mowbray has pointed out, the various cases of abuse discussed by Jeffrey Masson in his well-known book *Against Therapy* were mainly perpetrated by involved practitioners who were already licensed professionals (i.e., medical doctors, clinical psychologists, etc.), and their registered professional status within the community if anything made it harder to challenge their abusive behaviour. Mowbray:

> If protection of the public from harm has not been a proven consequence of [licensing] systems in general, there is little prospect that such a system would protect the public in a field as indefinite as this one. [Mowbray, 1995, p. 114]

Another compelling challenge to the "public protection" rationale is that, as we all know, potentially abusive practitioners who are determined to abuse will simply find another way of doing it: e.g., either by calling themselves something else that is not regulated, or else by finding another arena/forum in which they can perpetrate abuse relatively unhindered. So, on this view, perhaps the most one can say is that the statutory regulation of psychotherapy and counselling might merely redistribute abuse within society as a whole rather than removing it—thus invalidating the "abuse reduction" argument for statutorily regulating the occupational field.

It might be countered that it is public perception that matters most, and that it is important for the government to be seen to be responding to concerns about abuse, whether those concerns have wide-ranging substance or not. In our view this would amount to expediency of the worst kind, where appearance ("spin") matters more than substance and authenticity. Many cultural critics (including ourselves) maintain that the increasingly routine triumph of appearance over substance constitutes one of the most harmful trends in modern cultural and political life, and one which it would be potentially disastrous for the therapy field uncritically and incongruously to embrace and collude with. It would also surely constitute dishonesty of the most damaging kind for either our occupational institutions, or for government itself, wittingly to generate substantially exaggerated fears and anxieties about the dangers of abuse in our field in order to create a pretext for legislation, when in reality the empirical evidence that would be needed to substantiate a rational case for regulation simply does not exist.

What is to be done?

We believe, first, that there is an urgent necessity for the personal/institutional naturalization of dominance that lies at the centre of institutional professionalization to be challenged and transformed, and a more enlightened "power with" approach to accountability be adopted that is more congruent with the widely accepted therapeutic aim of clients' responsible empowerment. Specifically, we envisage the building of accountability institutions at macro and micro levels that embody "power with" rather than "power over" principles of organizational and human relationship.

The Independent Practitioners Network (IPN), in which we have both been full participants for nearly fifteen years, offers one approach to addressing these important questions of the building of mature and congruent accountability structures (*Self and Society*, 2004). What might be plausible criteria for adequate client/service user accountability? Rather than regulation, accountability is a better and more widely acceptable way of framing ethically sound client–practitioner working alliances.

Well over a decade of IPN theory and practice has helped to identify several key elements of effective accountability:

1. Ongoing, long-term, face-to-face contact with a settled group of peers that demonstrates a practitioner's capacity to form working alliances based on respect, negotiation, mutuality, and rapport.
2. Declaration by each participant to the peer group of their training, competencies, special area of expertise, if any, the client

population for whom they are competent, their client workload, their continuing personal–professional development commitment, and their supervision arrangements.

3. Mutual disclosure in the peer group of challenges, deficits, difficulties, achievements, and significant developments in their practitioner work, coupled with disclosure of any developments in their personal life that might affect their fitness to practise.
4. Agreement between the practitioner group members about how disputes with clients should be handled.
5. Self and peer accreditation in such a group institutionalizes practitioner–client accountability in a way that greatly increases the likelihood of client satisfaction, and, we maintain, reduces closer to zero than any conceivable alternative the chances of abusive or exploitative practitioner behaviour.

Some people have objected that the close personal contact of this process invites collusion. In the IPN model, when such a group has formed, they contract with other similar groups to establish external validation of their accreditation/dispute resolution process and possible collusive agendas. There is also a vested interest carried by every group member that their group colleagues' practice is sound and ethical (not least because if it is not, then that will reflect unfavourably upon their own judgement and practice). Moreover, this approach to accountability also draws fully upon what is commonly a very well developed intuitive and perceptive sense in therapists and counsellors, such that our "peers-in-relationship" are best placed by far to "pick up" concerns about any given practitioner's fitness to do this demanding work (Heron, 1997; House, 1997).

As IPN demonstrates, such a framing of psychopractice accountability can be orchestrated in innumerably different ways (House, 2007).

If a regulation process lacks this mix of autonomy and external validation, how can it avoid being perceived by practitioners as coercive and stressful, and an unwarranted imposition? Will it not prove to be lacking in credibility, resulting in low compliance, and ineffectiveness in protecting clients, should the latter indeed prove to be a significant, evidence-based requirement?

Incorporating the key elements of a self and peer accreditation approach into Department of Health policy recommendations (to be implemented in a variety of ways by all the diverse organizations presently in the field) could ensure that quality assurance of practitioner–client relationships would be intrinsic, i.e., eliminating abuse through continuous monitoring, not as the threatened Health Professions Council route seems to indicate, extrinsic, via the detection, investigation, and adjudication of complaints. In so far as quality assurance is intrinsic, state regulation of the psychological therapies would be redundant.

Next, we advocate the building of political alliances that bridge cultural divides—on the assumption that in the broad field of "therapy" (i.e., psychoanalysis, psychotherapy, counselling, counselling psychology . . .), what unites us in regard to statutory regulation is greater than what divides us (House, 2005). This very collection has, to our knowledge, been the first time outside of the humanistic and human potential movement that major concerns about the state regulation of psychopractice have been raised in a systematic and concerted way. We are delighted that, within the field of psychoanalysis, at least some practitioners are at last waking up to the realities of state regulation and the deleterious effects it could well have on the freedom to practise in way that is driven by the singularity and particularity of each unique helping relationship, rather than by power-infused institutional and bureaucratic imperatives.

A related, if apparently paradoxical, strategic imperative is, wherever possible, to contradict the desire on the part of organizations that favour statutory regulation to present UK psychopractice as united and homogeneous when this is manifestly not so. This suggests one plausible perspective on the unconscious drift of the organizations that seems to be towards the formation of a spurious psychological monoculture that seeks to hide their shaky foundations behind endorsement by the power of the state.

Finally, there is the exciting possibility of developing a non-credentialed registration approach to accountability (Mowbray, 1995; Hogan, 1979, 2003; Postle, 2007), an attempt to think "out of the box" around accountability, to create a way of institutionalizing accountability that would be congruent with clients' needs and practitioner values. DP has drawn up a carefully specified alternative approach to regulation based on this approach: his Practitioner Full Disclosure

List proposal (Postle, 2003), which is a variant on the so-called "Non-Credentialed Registration" (or NCR) approach to regulation expounded by Professor Dan Hogan and others, and successfully implemented in several states in the USA (e.g., in Vermont).

This model avoids many of the worst features of conventional statutory regulation, with practitioners opting into a national practitioner database in which their listing is endorsed and dependent on the support of identified practitioners who are publicly prepared to stand by their fitness to practise, competence, and ethical stance, and an outline of how they will resolve disputes. On the basis of such practitioner self-description, made available via the Internet with local printed supplements, clients would be able to make a much better informed choice of whom to select to form a working alliance than are offered by current listings or registers of names and modalities. Such a public commitment to practitioner openness might, of course, be difficult for psychoanalytic practitioners for whom personal disclosure might be anathema because of the very nature of psychoanalytic practice; but leaving that aspect of the non-credentialed approach aside, assembling a group of colleagues who know you and your work well enough personally to publicly endorse it on an ongoing basis seems only reasonable. If, we would provocatively ask, a practitioner was not able or prepared, with effort, to do this, should they be working in this field at all?

The Full Disclosure List, while not an instrument of state control, would ideally be state administered, in the sense that the financing and resourcing of the database, and management of the IT structure, would be contracted out from the Department of Health. Two examples of this non-credentialed approach to accountability have been in place for several years in the USA, in the states of Vermont and Colorado.

In conclusion

What has become clear as a result of the College of Psychoanalysts—UK conference and this book is that there exists an unexpected common interest and shared understanding between the position of the College of Psychoanalysts and that of the IPN; and our strong hunch is that this commonality of purpose and perception in relation to regulation is shared by a large (but unknown) number of other therapy practitioners in the many other organizations and modalities. Evidence of this emerged through an initiative some months after the conference, which gathered support for a "statement of opposition" to statutory regulation, that collected over 600 signatures; and there are several petitions to the Prime Minister in the same vein. There is surely ample scope for expanding the informal links between like minds that have already begun to be forged through this important initiative.

Along with a number of other committed colleagues, we continue to do all in our power to challenge and derail the regulatory juggernaut, and we welcome approaches from like minds interested in coalition-building or other approaches to protecting the integrity of the psychological therapies from what we believe both personal experience and research evidence show to be an unnecessary and harmful intrusion into the very heart of therapy work.

References

Bates, Y., & House, R. (Eds.) (2003). *Ethically Challenged Professions: Enabling Innovation and Diversity in Psychotherapy and Counselling*. Ross-on-Wye: PCCS.

Cooper, A. (2001). The state of mind we're in: social anxiety, governance and the audit society. *Psychoanalytic Studies, 3*(3–4): 349–362.

Gladstone, G. (1997). The making of a therapist and the corruption of the training market. In: R. House & N. Totton (Eds.), *Implausible Professions: Arguments for Pluralism and Autonomy in Psychotherapy and Counselling* (pp. 171–185). Ross-on-Wye: PCCS.

Heron, J. (1997). A self-generating practitioner community. In: R. House & N. Totton (Eds.), *Implausible Professions: Arguments for Pluralism and Autonomy in Psychotherapy and Counselling* (pp. 241–254). Ross-on-Wye: PCCS.

Hogan, D. B. (1979). *The Regulation of Psychotherapists*, 4 volumes. Cambridge, MA: Ballinger.

Hogan, D. B. (2003). Professional regulation as facilitation, not control: implications for an open system of registration versus restrictive licensure. In: Y. Bates & R. House (Eds.), *Ethically Challenged Professions: Enabling Innovation and Diversity in Psychotherapy and Counselling* (pp. 160–171). Ross-on-Wye: PCCS.

House, R. (1997). Participatory ethics in a self-generating practitioner community. In: R. House & N. Totton (Eds.), *Implausible Professions: Arguments for Pluralism and Autonomy in Psychotherapy and Counselling* (pp. 321–334). Ross-on-Wye: PCCS.

House, R. (2001). The statutory regulation of psychotherapy: still time to think again. *The Psychotherapist, 17*: 12–17 [reprinted in Y. Bates & R. House (Eds.), *Ethically Challenged Professions: Enabling Innovation and Diversity in Psychotherapy and Counselling* (pp. 142–147). Ross-on-Wye: PCCS; see website http://www.uea.ac.uk/~wp276/article.htm].

House, R. (2003). *Therapy Beyond Modernity: Deconstructing and Transcending Profession-centred Therapy*. London: Karnac.

House, R. (2005). The state regulation of counselling and psychotherapy: sometime, never . . .? *Journal of Critical Psychology, Counselling and Psychotherapy, 5*(4): 176–189.

House, R. (2007). The be-coming of a therapist: experiential learning, self-education and the personal/professional nexus. *British Journal of Guidance and Counselling, 35*(4): 427–440.

House, R., & Totton, N. (Eds.) (1997). *Implausible Professions: Arguments for Pluralism and Autonomy in Psychotherapy and Counselling*. Ross-on-Wye: PCCS.

Mowbray, R. (1995). *The Case Against Psychotherapy Registration: A Conservation Issue for the Human Potential Movement*. London: Trans Marginal Press.

Mowbray, R. (1997). Too vulnerable to choose? In: R. House & N. Totton (Eds.), *Implausible Professions* (pp.34–44). Ross-on-Wye: PCCS.

Postle, D. (2003). Psychopractice accountability: a practitioner "full disclosure" list. In: Y. Bates & R. House (Eds.), *Ethically Challenged Professions: Enabling Innovation and Diversity in Psychotherapy and Counselling* (pp. 172–178). Ross-on-Wye: PCCS.

Postle, D. *Ipnosis*. www.ipnosis.org.

Postle, D. g.o.r.i.l.l.a. Internet archive of statutory regulation texts www.g.o.r.i.l.l.a.postle.net.

Postle, D. (2007). *Regulating the Psychological Therapies: From Taxonomy to Taxidermy*. Ross-on-Wye: PCCS.

Self and Society (2004). Special theme issue on the Independent Practitioners Network. 32(4).

Smail, D. (2001). *The Nature of Unhappiness*. London: Robinson.

CHAPTER TWENTY

Psychoanalysis and regulation

Darian Leader

Despite its many vicissitudes since the early 1980s, the project to regulate the talking therapies in Britain has been gathering momentum and many now believe it is set to happen in 2010. The Department of Health has commissioned a certain amount of survey work, and with little heed of both the misgivings and plain contestation of most of the institutions consulted, the Health Professions Council has been chosen as regulator. Although there has been an assortment of groups, individuals, and orientations that favour regulation by the state, it has been a crucial question for many others whether the state should play any role at all the field of psychotherapeutic practice, and, in particular, in that of psychoanalysis.

As in many of the other European countries, psychoanalysis in Britain finds itself under an ever-increasing pressure from the ideology of market society. The values of accountability and transparency are vaunted as the new ethical framework for all professional and personal relations. Psychoanalysis and the psychotherapies are expected to replace their antiquated speculative systems and outdated therapeutic aims with new standardized evidence-based models. Regulation aims to ensure that these new professional standards are upheld and, crucially, that talking therapies conform to criteria imported from the field of service provision. Why? The answer falls under three rubrics: protection of the public, good practice, and the scientific development of the field.

Why regulate?

Any discussion of state regulation should begin with a differentiation. Forms of regulation have been present in the field of the talking therapies for decades, and the training organizations currently operative in Britain have codes of practice, requirements, and usually quite stringent criteria for admission, training standards, and qualification. Umbrella organizations such as UKCP exist that monitor these forms of regulation and that require participant groups to match their requirements to those agreed by the umbrella organization. This is regulation across the professional field, to be differentiated from state regulation. State regulation opposes statutory regulation, and proposes to override it for the purposes of the protection of the public. Statutory regulation, it is claimed, is inherently biased towards the profession, since the regulator is the group or the organization to which the group belongs. State regulation, on the other hand, would introduce clarity, transparency, and new standards of safe practice.

Underlying this claim is the general tendency noted by social theorists of changes in the investiture of power. Just as the 1980s saw the crippling of the trade unions, so the 1990s and the 2000s bear witness to a concerted effort to weaken the so-called "professions". Bodies traditionally assumed to wield a certain autonomy and power now become weak and defensive, organized primarily along legalistic and managerial lines to protect themselves against the threat of legal action. Protection of the public becomes synonymous with protection of the profession, but in this specific sense of legal position: in all other senses, the profession loses out. As for the public, this category now subsumes what the traditional notion of "minor" once described, with ever-lengthening chains of responsibility to distance the causes of human action from the individual.

Philosophers and political theorists with no knowledge of or interest in the talking therapies have long urged detailed scrutiny of rationalizations for social initiatives that claim protection of the public as their grounding. This has been used for such a disparate range of projects that its context and meaning must be unpacked in each case. When we speak of protecting the public, for example, what aspect of the public do we mean? A basic feature of psychoanalysis is the assumption that the human subject is a divided one. No longer an autonomous, freely-choosing individual or agentive self, the subject posited by psychoanalysis is split between conscious wishes and demands and unconscious desires, phantasies, and forces that might, in fact, be quite opposed to conscious volition.

When a patient asks for help with a specific problem, the analysis may uncover the fact that the unconscious desire is to leave the problem unresolved. Or, that the problem is actually a vital factor in that person's survival and is thus best left undisturbed. Or, that remaining true to a desire may cause pain and turbulence in that person's relation to others. More generally, psychoanalysis posits that conscious demands and unconscious desires rarely coincide. Analysis reveals that many of our unconscious ideals and phantasies deliver a yield of pleasure which we are loath to give up, despite the fact that this pleasure is often experienced consciously as pain and suffering.

This paradoxical aspect of mental life was emphasized by all the major psychoanalysts, from Freud to Klein and Lacan. As Ernest Jones, one of the founders of British psychoanalysis, put it,

> the patient comes for help to sustain the disease and resists all the efforts to cure it. To give up a neurosis would signify . . . to surrender certain cherished wishes and to dispense with the only protection [the patient] knows against the accompanying anxiety and misery. When a person is disturbed by neurotic symptoms his distress is only in part due to the painful effects of the symptoms themselves. What disturbs him far more is the inner feeling that his defensive systems are beginning to break down, which is indeed what the presence of manifest symptoms mean. What brings him for help is his need to strengthen and reinforce these defences—that is, the neurosis itself. [Jones, 1977, p. 360]

This basic assumption divides psychoanalytic approaches from many other psychological therapies. It means that where the patient will seek analysis in order to restore their neurosis, the analyst will aim, on the contrary, to challenge and alleviate the neurosis itself. This signals an irresolvable tension at the level of any model that sees psychoanalytic therapy as a service provision: what the patient hopes for and what the therapist offers are radically incompatible. It is this very tension that provides the motor for the therapy itself. Should the analyst, then, act in the best interests of the patient's unconscious or conscious sources of pleasure? To what extent should the neurosis, as it were, be honoured? The further these questions are pursued, the more we see how the notion of the protection of the public is hardly transparent.

This is complicated further by the facts of resistance, defined by Freud as a central feature of any analytic approach. According to this view, people not only wish to ignore the unconscious dynamics of mental life, but they actively pursue a passion for ignorance: they desperately do not want to know. Massive amounts of energy are channelled into the area of resistance, and one of the main vehicles of such resistance is rationalization. If resistance is so important, it is surely a question whether it should be protected in itself. This is hardly an abstract issue, as any extensive analytic process will interfere with the patient's view of both their own well-being and their best interests.

The obvious solution to these complexities is simply to define symptoms and health in terms of independently observable symptoms. Dysfunction is made to exist independently of the person's experience of it, a bias that merely reinforces social, non-subjective criteria of normality. Symptoms are no longer subjectively experienced questions or sources of satisfaction, but independent, autonomous entities, the result of developmental dysfunctions. An external observer will be able to tell what is a dysfunction and what is not, and, hence, what should be cured and what should not, thus ensuring optimum protection of the patient.

We see this tendency already in contemporary references to "psychiatric disorder", often mentioned in the regulatory literature as a variable separate from any other human trait, yet usually not defined beyond the implication that it is an independently existing entity. This is antithetical not just to an analytic approach, but to any perspective that privileges a patient's experience of their life. A symptom is not an observable feature of behaviour, but what a human being experiences as symptomatic. This is a fundamental fact of all demands for therapy: people see some aspects of their lives as problematic and others as less so. But it is for them and not an external agent to determine what is felt to be symptomatic. Here is a significant difference with the medical discourse, where symptoms can be externally classified. It is the key difference between the talking therapies and mental hygiene.

This brings us to another well-known problem. Medical approaches, and many therapeutic ones, set a premium on removal of symptoms. Yet psychoanalysis has never been aimed at symptom-removal. Rather, it aims at accessing unconscious structures, generally via an analysis of symptoms. In many cases, this accessing will have therapeutic effects, but the removal of the symptom is never considered a primary goal. In some cases, it may be quite dangerous (such as the attempt to "remove" a phobia in a monosymptomatic adult patient). This sets psychoanalysis aside from other health-related endeavours, and suggests that it cannot be construed in any sense as a health profession, focusing instead on individual exploration, with the very uncertain results that this will produce, rather than the neat goals of symptom-removal favoured by cognitive styles of therapy.

Good practice

To speak of good practice automatically introduces the technology of inspection and evaluation. Although talking therapies should never be shy about scrutinizing their results and suppositions, today's popular evaluative apparatuses always set norms against which individual paths and practices can be measured. Measurement otherwise has little sense in these frameworks. Yet psychoanalysis, as an exploration of unconscious structure, has results that vary from one individual to another. Each subject is deemed unique, and no standardized result of analytic treatment is sought, a point emphasized by Freud, Lacan, and Winnicott.

The most common misconception here is to see psychoanalysis as a technique that can be applied. Yet psychoanalysis cannot be separated from, is embedded in, context, and resembles less a plaster that can be applied to a wound than a property of a relationship between two people. Unlike a pill or an injection, it cannot be given by one person to another. Psychoanalysis involves a long-term exploration of an individual's history through a process of dialogue and through an analysis of the relationship between analysand and analyst. It is not a technique that can be learnt and then applied to every patient, since it must emerge in the encounter between the two parties. It is primarily the patient who does the work here and not the therapist: the therapist's role is to encourage the eliciting of unconscious material and, in a careful and unpredictable way, to respond to this material.

Psychoanalysis thus involves input from both parties, and without this dual input cannot properly be said to exist. Analysands are, as it were, put to the test, and it often takes a considerable number of meetings with an analyst to determine whether analysis will actually start to get going. Visits to a psychoanalyst and psychoanalysis are not always the same thing. Psychoanalysis involves a questioning of one's history, and this may take a long time to become established, if at all. Analysts cannot make this happen, or even claim to "offer" it. This situation is made more complex by the tension between conscious and unconscious processes that lies at the heart of the analytic approach.

Formulations of the work of analysis vary from one analytic orientation to another, but all recognize the existence of transference, the mobilization of unconscious forces that forge the details of our lived, affective experience of other people and processes. These transferences are a central motor of analytic treatments, and are learnt from, analysed, interpreted, and worked with. But, in themselves, they cannot be regulated. They generate a dangerous chemistry, which a skilled clinician will not aim to "manage" but to work with in the most fruitful way possible. Since transferences shape our experience of reality, according to all the major analytic theories, standard evaluations and ratings become useless. There is no neutral observation language with which to distance oneself from a situation that one is actually immersed in.

This is not to say that psychoanalysis should not and cannot be tested for good practice. This involves a making explicit of clinical aims in the context of an individual case, and giving accounts of one's practice. These may be subjected to comment and criticism, just as different schools of analysis regularly engage in critiques of each other's theories and practices. Good practice must be evaluated from within the context of particular modalities, rather than via a norm imposed from the outside that relies on measurable, observable features that are not those germane to analytic treatment. Crucial, however, to any serious evaluative approach is a recognition of the facts of transference and resistance.

The central place of transference to analytic work poses another question here. Some efforts at state regulation have urged that the selection of the clinician should not be the choice of the analysand, or, at least, should be determined by the possibilities of a sanctioned list of competent practitioners. This well-meaning idea is sadly antithetical to the very logic of any talking therapy. We choose the clinician due to transferences: links and associations that will be unique to our own histories and that often select features that society may deem unsavoury. The clinician will be chosen because he is a womanizer, corrupt, feeble, a secret drinker, a tyrant, etc. It is nothing less than the exploration of these associations and details that will allow change and true analytic work, and so it makes no sense to try to sanitize the image of the clinician.

Without transference, there is no analysis. The choice of analyst should be made according to the direction of one's transference, and this is an individual matter that can never be externally directed. Trying to do so breaches a basic human right: the right to have false beliefs. If transference is a belief system, regulation implies that the state can tell someone what to believe and what not to believe. The next logical step would be to determine which are the good and which are the bad religions, and then to instruct the public. In fact, it is not unlikely that this will happen in the not-too-distant future, as recent outbursts, particularly against Islam, by politicians have shown.

Scientific development

The third aim of regulation is described as the scientific development of the discipline. This is linked to what is surely one of the greatest success stories in the history of public relations: evidence-based practice. We are told that we have to move away from authority and group pressures to base our judgement on real evidence. Yet a century of history and philosophy of science and sociology is simply ignored here. The lesson of that century is that the distinction between authority and evidence is hardly a simple one: to see something we have to be inclined to both look at it and then see it *as* the something we have been told to observe.

After Cochrane, evidence-based medicine derived largely from the theories of David Sackett and his associates at McMaster University in Ontario. It aimed to undo irrational appeals to authority in medicine in favour of a judged consideration of evidence, which came largely in the form of epidemiological and statistical studies. Since psychoanalysis treats individuals and their unique histories, epidemiology is automatically ruled out. Where epidemiology can learn from the presence of the same groups of symptoms in a population, psychoanalysis posits that the same symptoms can have radically different causes from one person to another, and even at different moments in the life of the same person.

Evidence-based research has now become a rhetorical feature of the landscape of professional practice. It had been successfully manipulated by attachment theorists, who have claimed to adhere to an unproblematized concept of evidence in their research. Psychoanalysis, on the other hand, questions the idea of a neutral observation language that is uncontaminated by the effects of transference and unconscious phantasy. It also rejects normative views of human development. These views, in fact, have become increasingly popular today among practitioners of talking therapies. Clinical intervention is justified simply to patch up bad periods in the developmental process. The evidence appealed to stems from simplistic accounts of development and brain chemistry, as if the goal of therapy becomes to affect changes in the brain. Naïve and poorly informed references to neurotransmitters and brain structure jostle with the more traditional concepts of psychoanalysis. This recent trend indicates less the richness of the biological hypotheses than the poverty of the theories of talking therapies: outside help has to be sought in the form of "science" to confer legitimacy.

This view that psychological "disorders" are correlated with specific brain dysfunctions is now quite widespread in the British and American psy-environment. The function of analysis or psychotherapy is to provide a set of techniques that the mind can use to overcome a biological deficit. Neuroscience will help patients use "mental strategies to cope with weaknesses in their brain function" (Fonagy, 2004, p. 358). This new pseudo-science of subjectivity is encroaching further and further into the psychoanalytic groups. Conference interventions in both analysis and psychotherapy meetings are filled with references to the fight-or-flight response, to brain function, to catecholamines, and especially to the demon cortisol, which is described in ways very similar to the "bad mother" of the 1950s and 1960s. Analysis and therapy work by affecting brain chemistry, and it is a tragic and comic spectacle to see clinicians who know very little about either biology or chemistry start to use this new language as if it conferred a respectability and scientific dignity on their work. Rather than think through their own conceptual vocabularies, there is an appeal to the supposedly neutral vocabulary of "observational" science. No one seems to notice that embracing brain chemistry to explain aims and results will render therapy itself obsolete, since the same changes can clearly be made more swiftly by chemical intervention.

The other flagship of evidence-based research is the clinical trial. But how could a clinical trial operate in a psychoanalytic framework? There is no such thing as a control subject, since each case is a unique one. To reply that someone may be found who has the same symptoms is to miss the point, since the symptom for psychoanalysis is defined by the analysand's experience of the symptom and not by any objective measure. Psychoanalysis does conduct its own clinical trials, but these involve just one subject. In a well-established procedure used in Europe, known as "the pass", for example, an analysand will talk about their case in detail to a number of designated listeners, who then discuss what they have heard with a small group of other analysts. The aim is to enable research into how changes have taken place in an individual case, and there is now a substantial literature on this question.

Conclusion

What effects will the pressures we have discussed above have on psychoanalysis? We can already point to certain trends in contemporary psychoanalytic discourse that indicate that a new "adapted" version of analysis is emerging. In a recent book by two well-known analysts, the self is defined as "a rational agent with understandable desires and predictable beliefs who will act to further his goals in the light of these beliefs" (Bateman & Fonagy, 2004, p. 302). This extraordinary definition is, in fact, identical to that found at the start of textbooks on rational economics. What has happened to the Freudian unconscious? What has happened to the split between conscious demands and unconscious desires? And what has happened to the Freudian thesis that a large part of human activity is not directed to instrumental goals such as the pursuit of wealth, power, and happiness?

This sanitized definition of the self leads inevitably to a sanitized version of psychoanalysis, one with no unconscious or transference to speak of unless they are construed as errors in learning that can be undone by cognitive methods. This effort to remove the dimension of the subject seems to be moving closer and closer to what resembles a dated picture of medicine, construed as a sum of external procedures to be applied to the organism to act against ill-health. This version of analysis, emptied out of subjectivity, is, of course, perfect for regulation. With no real subjectivity, it becomes simply a process involving the transfer of knowledge and skills: to unlearn symptomatic behaviour, to learn how to analyse from one's analyst, and to enlarge the field of self-knowledge. These new aims are completely antithetical to Freudian psychoanalysis, which privileges instead the encounter with what we do not know. Analysis is not about acquiring knowledge, but about putting knowledge and its effects in question. If anything, the subject's very relation to knowledge will change during the course of analysis.

Conceiving analysis in terms of the transmission of knowledge and skills will also have significant effects on how supervision is regulated. It seems likely that the less personal analysis shows suitability to regulatory intervention, the more this will shift to the field of supervision. Already, most recent discussions of supervision take it to be a process of management of the supervised case. The more that poorly trained mental health workers are drafted in to deal with waiting lists, the more supervision will function to extend the chain of clinical responsibility. Supposedly better trained clinicians will provide management classes to the lesser trained. Supervision is now seen almost exclusively as a practice serving only the interests of the case "under supervision". One of the effects of this shift has been to find analysts and therapists reformulating their theories so as to adhere to this model: analysis becomes a knowledge-based procedure, with the aim of transmitting skills. This contrasts, of course, with the spirit of any Freudian approach, which aims at a point where the analysand realizes that the analyst knows precious little about him or herself, and that knowledge as such has decisive limits.

With the government intent on regulating the talking therapies, there is every danger that these changes, together with the emphasis on sanitation, will produce a new "adapted" psychoanalysis. The three issues we have discussed all move psychoanalysis in the direction of mental hygiene, and this, after all, is the only thing that the state can really regulate. Personal anguish and pain become desubjectivized and transformed into variables that can be externally verified and measured: that is, sets of observable behaviours. These will then be classified and linked to developmental problems that the analysand must be taught to unlearn, reducing the gap between observed behaviour and desired behaviour. Lost is the subjective truth articulated in the symptom, and the formative powers of the transference. Analysts must decide which of the two paths they wish to follow: psychoanalysis or mental hygiene.

If they choose psychoanalysis, they must have the courage not only to transcend their factional discords to work together against the forces of prejudice and unreason, but also to give up the lures of respectability and recognition that seem to hold out the promise of safety and security. A register of psychoanalysts? Why not, but one that stipulates, beyond the facts of their training and the details of the organization to which they belong, that they are unlicensed and non-credentialed. It is then up to the analysand to make his or her choice, knowing that no external institution can guarantee the work that takes place in the consulting room.

References

Bateman, A., & Fonagy, P. (2004). *Psychotherapy for Borderline Personality Disorder*. Oxford: Oxford University Press.

Fonagy, P. (2004). Psychotherapy meets neuroscience: a more focused future for psychotherapy research. *Psychiatric Bulletin, 28*: 357–359.

Jones, E. (1977). *Papers on Psychoanalysis* (5th edn). London: Karnac.

INDEX

For Product Safety Concerns and Information please contact our EU representative GPSR@taylorandfrancis.com Taylor & Francis Verlag GmbH, Kaufingerstraße 24, 80331 München, Germany

Batch number: 10725973

Printed by Printforce, the Netherlands